P9-DDU-560

Also by Brando Skyhorse

The Madonnas of Echo Park

Take This Man

A Memoir

Brando Skyhorse

SIMON & SCHUSTER

New York   London   Toronto   Sydney   New Delhi

Simon & Schuster
1230 Avenue of the Americas
New York, NY 10020

First Simon & Schuster hardcover edition June 2014

SIMON & SCHUSTER and colophon are registered trademarks of Simon & Schuster, Inc.

For information about special discounts for bulk purchases,
please contact Simon & Schuster Special Sales at 1-866-506-1949
or business@simonandschuster.com.

The Simon & Schuster Speakers Bureau can bring authors to your live event.
For more information or to book an event, contact the Simon & Schuster Speakers Bureau
at 1-866-248-3049 or visit our website at www.simonspeakers.com.

Interior design by Erich Hobbing
Jacket design Rodrigo Corral
Jacket photograph Danielle Donders–Mothership Photography/Flickr/Getty Images

Manufactured in the United States of America

1   3   5   7   9   10   8   6   4   2

Library of Congress Cataloging-in-Publication Data

Skyhorse, Brando.
Take this man : a memoir / Brando Skyhorse.—First Simon & Schuster hardcover edition.
pages cm
1. Skyhorse, Brando—Childhood and youth. 2. Skyhorse, Brando—Family. 3. Authors,
American—21st century—Biography. 4. Authors, American—21st century—Family relationships.
5. Mothers and sons—United States. 6. Fathers and sons—United States. 7. Identity
(Psychology)—United States. 8. Mexican Americans—California—Los Angeles—Biography.
9. Echo Park (Los Angeles, Calif.)—Biography. 10. Los Angeles (Calif.)—Biography. I. Title.
PS3619.K947Z468 2014
818'.603—dc23
[B]
2013047740

ISBN 978-1-4391-7087-8
ISBN 978-1-4391-7090-8 (ebook)

Mom & Grandma

I wish I had a better memory

"We only love just once, you know."
—SERGEI ESENIN

Take This Man

I was three years old when my father abandoned me and my mother in my grandmother's house atop a crooked hill on Portia Street in a Los Angeles neighborhood called Echo Park. My mother, Maria Teresa, a Mexican who wanted to be an American Indian, transformed me into Brando Skyhorse, a full-blooded American Indian brave. I became the son of Paul Skyhorse Johnson, an American Indian activist incarcerated for armed robbery who my mother met through the mail. She became Running Deer Skyhorse, a full-blooded "squaw" who traded in her most common of Mexican names for the most stereotypical of Indian ones.

My mother was mesmerizing and could make crazy schemes and lies sound electric and honest. Her deception was so good, or so obvious, she fooled each of her five husbands, our neighbors, her friends, my elementary school vice principal, even me. I lived most of my childhood without knowing who I really was. All I knew was the power in my own name: *"Brando Skyhorse? That's beautiful."*

My biological father, Candido Ulloa (*oooh-YO-ahh*), was replaced by a chain of boyfriends and five fathers—one new dad about every three years. Along with Paul, whom I first met while he was in prison, there was Robert, a restless, habitual Aleutian Indian thief; Pat, a restaurant chef with a penchant for disappearing; Rudy, a man who answered a singles ad from a homeless shelter; and Frank, a Mexican-American office "straight" (what Maria called men who worked actual jobs) who wanted a son but could not marry my mother. The only

1

way to keep them straight was to imagine what actors would play them in a movie made from my life:

Paul Skyhorse Johnson: Will Sampson, the American Indian "Chief" from *One Flew Over the Cuckoo's Nest*.

Robert: Esai Morales. A "hot" Esai Morales. *La Bamba* Esai Morales.

Pat: *Roseanne*-era John Goodman.

Rudy: Present day Robin Williams. Plus thirty pounds.

Frank: I've known him the longest so I can't imagine him in caricature. If he were asked, he'd say Chris Noth from *Law & Order* or Michael Nouri from the movie *Flashdance*. In that order.

These men were never simply my mother's "boyfriends" or "partners." They weren't "surrogate dads" or "stepfathers." I couldn't call them by their first names, nor was I allowed to speak about any past father in the presence of a new one. My mother made it clear that these men, trying to *be* men, were my *fathers*, absorbed instantly into our tiny clan of mother, grandmother, and me, so we could be, or pose as, a family. Life with each of these fathers followed a similar path. First I was forced to accept them, then slowly I trusted them, then I grew to love them.

Then they left.

"Some boys don't have *any* father in their life," my mother would say, bucking me up. "You've had *five*. Plenty for one boy."

I was father rich but family poor. Our house shook as if it were filled with people—brothers, sisters, a chorus of screaming children—but really belonged to just two angry women who were five foot and change tall. We shopped at the Smart & Final warehouse for commissary-sized Shake 'N Bake and restaurant-style cartons of frozen burgers, purchasing family-size packs in gross for a family that could fit in a hatchback.

We were a triangle trying to fill a circle.

When I grew out of that circle, I tried searching for the true ends of my mother's stories; ends I thought explained who my father was. Who *I* was. Each father took a piece of me when he left, leaving a hole that got bigger as I got older. I wanted those pieces back. I wanted that hole filled.

My mother would say, "I can't tell you what *really* happened," as if she were protecting someone else's truth and not her own exaggerated version of it. Her stories had ominous detours and switchbacks, contradicting prior layers of her own facts. When cornered, my mother hissed, sizzled, and exploded like fireworks, and then offered, by way of explanation or apology, five words I'd come to know by heart.

I found out I was Mexican when I was around twelve or thirteen. My mother forbade me from telling anyone our story. I kept our secret long after I needed to because my mother's lie had become my whole truth.

It would be thirty-three years from the time he left before I tried to find my biological father, Candido Ulloa, in earnest. By then I'd had so many fathers that even the idea of a father—the very word *father*— seemed absurd, like a joke whose punch line had to be explained to me. I'd grown proud of my wounded independence—*I stand here as my own man*—because I'd built it myself from the wreckage each father left behind, shred by abandoned shred. I didn't believe that understanding my biological father's abandonment and vanishing could offer me anything except explanations I claimed I no longer needed or a reconciliation I bragged I wasn't interested in. Daddies were for children, not grown men. All I had of Candido were some pictures and the Mexican surname he'd left behind. (My mother had much less from her own Mexican biological father; she was raised by her Filipino stepfather, Emilio.) Years of speculation and misdirection led me to imagine every sort of fantastical reason for Candido's disappearance: amnesia, murder, abduction back to Mexico. I knew he'd stay lost if I didn't search for him, and I suspected already how little of my father there'd be left for me if I *did* find him. I'd been prepped by books and movies for how long and impossible a search for an estranged father was.

It took Google about ten minutes to find my father. There he was one winter night in 2010 on WhitePages.com. His home was a half-hour drive from the neighborhood where I was born and raised.

I'd found him. What now?

I'm a writer. I write to understand what I don't know. So I wrote my father a letter. And I started to write this book.

My letter was unremarkable and efficient, accompanied with a Spanish translation, and signed with my current legally changed name. (The name my father gave me was in a parenthetical.) Attached were five scanned photographs from my childhood that had miraculously survived my mother's habitual purging of the past; the idea of that, I think, was to make it easier for her to carry only the truths she wanted into the future. I also included a recent photograph of me as an adult. I imagined this picture might have resembled the kind of man my father was at my age, though I had no photos of him after 1976. He had been twenty-six years old when he left our family for good. I was thirty-six when I sent him my letter.

I chose these pictures to rend heartstrings and appeal to a conscience that my mother, and thirty-three years of silence, had led me to expect didn't exist. There'd been no letters, birthday phone calls, Christmas cards, or a penny in child support. How could my father be anything but a coward and a monster? Yet there he is in a photograph spoon-feeding me in an outdoor café on Olvera Street, cradling my infant head. Or carting me like a chubby pillow to a sleepover while my mother, in a goofy wool cap, vine-clings to his arm with a flirtatious daddy's girl smile. Another photo is from my third birthday party, and it's the last picture my father and I took together. My cake has Indians and a teepee on it, which I'm sure my mother picked out. The camera cuts off most of my father. He leans in from the side, holding me at arm's length so I won't follow him out of the frame. Later my mother would caption this picture on its back, "Brando Skyhorse Johnson and Uncle Candy."

I'd spent my whole life trying to follow Candido out of that photograph, through lies, misdirections, and detours in other men. I was scarching for a father and for who I was. When you're a child, you think your family works in a straight line. Then you get older and find out where the curves are. What I found was a lesson about how a broken home can make a whole family but not until I was willing to listen to the *whole* story. Patience helps you put the pieces together. Sifting through my mother's lies, I discovered she'd told me one real thing over and over again—five true words—if only I'd paid attention:

"At least it's never boring."

1

My grandmother's breath. Racing across my baby shoulders like western clouds. I'm propped against the sofa between my grandmother's thick varicose calves dressed just in toddler shorts, like an oversized stuffed bear. A phalanx of whirring plastic fans don't cool the soupy air as much as shuffle it in a circle around us.

"Shhh," Grandma says, and blows on my hot neck, rustling the pouty tips of my shoulder-length hair off my back. Some days my grandmother's breath blots out the violent heat. Some days it blows the storms ashore.

My mother's voice forms over our mountain range of a couch. It could shower a loving rain, tickle me with a sing-along for the summer ants crawling up my legs, or change the air above into a "run home to Mama" sky like a russet storm.

"Where's my *Pappas*?" Mom asks, shoveling me into her arms and blowing a raspberry on my tummy. *Pappas* means "potatoes" in Spanish.

"Shhh, be *quiet*," my grandmother says. "And hold him like *a mother*."

My grandmother's breath. My mother's voice. My whole world. My every happiness.

I was born and raised in Echo Park, California, with my mother, grandmother June, and my Filipino step-grandfather Emilio. I can see my old neighborhood like an iris-in movie shot, a pinprick of Southern California light so bright it'd crease your corneas, opening up into a fragile tapestry of shaggy green lawns and sunbaked terracotta roof tiles. White flight transformed Echo Park by the 1970s into a Latino oasis with sizable Vietnamese and Filipino enclaves, but its history was awash in silver nitrate. Mack Sennett built Keystone Pictures Studios here in 1912, and many of its early Keystone Cops comedy shorts were shot in Echo Park's loping emerald green hills and valleys. Its silent era stars migrated west (wealth always moves west in California, to the ocean), but the land stayed behind, its colors bleeding into a grainy seventies movie patina of tall, open fields of weeds bleached to a white wine finish and palm trees, their fronds beckoning with a campfire sizzle in the strong Santa Ana winds. In a documentary about the legendary Sunset Boulevard, the beginnings of which run through the neighborhood, Echo Park was pronounced "the most beautiful ghetto in America."

We lived midway up Portia Street, mispronounced to rhyme with *tortilla* by neighbors and impatient bus drivers. Like its Shakespearian counterpart, our Portia offered a choice of three distinct directions, connecting at one end with Sunset Boulevard, which snaked into Hollywood and Beverly Hills and ended at the coast in Pacific Palisades, a town as wealthy as it sounds; Scott Avenue at the other end, a short cut-slash-escape route from Dodger Stadium to the freeways that led to the season ticket holders' suburban homes in the San Fernando Valley; and Galveston, a slug of a street that jutted up at a 30-degree angle toward the hills and oozed its way through gang territory, where each street seemed to be its own treacherous canyon. Two or three times a week, shots rang out and police helicopters rumbled overhead, slicing the night open with powerful search beams, scouring the area my grandmother called "the Steps," an outdoor staircase by Laveta Terrace that, when the cops came, *cholos* used as a getaway slide down to Sunset.

I'd be tempted to call this God's country except that my grandmother didn't rent out to God. We lived in *her* house. It squatted atop a steep, exhausting hill accessible by a crooked winding staircase: slabs of uneven concrete blocks spiraling down to the street like a row of dominoes. Emilio bought June the single-family house in 1952 for twelve thousand dollars. Built in 1921, it was a one-story, 1,200-square-foot, three-bedroom, one-bath Mediterranean-style home. When my grandparents moved in, a neighbor asked June to sign a petition to remove a black mailman from their route. My grandmother, a lightish mix of Mexican, Spanish, and Swiss, refused. In retaliation, the neighbor set a crank-style Victrola record player in a side window abutting our shared fence and put on at a high volume, "The Band Played On," a waltz she played again and again, on, and on, and on.

"If I hear about that 'strawberry blonde' bitch once more," my grandmother said, "I'm gonna smash that record to pieces. I don't want her 'white' music in *my* house."

Out front a virile jacaranda tree made a lifelong enemy of my grandmother, shedding pulpy blossoms that stained the staircase black. Armed with a push broom, a transistor radio, and a Dodgers cap, she'd sweep through thick lavender rainstorms twice a week. There was also a lemon tree in back, honey-colored kitchen cabinets, and exterior stucco walls painted cornbread yellow.

"All this damn yellow," my grandmother said. "Looks like cowards live here."

My grandmother was "the man of the house." She was overseer of chores, washer and clothesline hanger of garments, food shopper (with a personal two-wheeled basket trolley she pulled up the stairs), head chef and dishwasher, payer of utilities, trimmer of hedges, sweeper of our front staircase, and controller of the single television in the living room complete with a cable hookup and an oversized recliner that Emilio had originally bought for him and June to share. Well into his midsixties, Emilio dressed for work in a suit jacket, tie, and fedora. He rode the bus almost an hour to and from his job as a line cook in a Glendale delicatessen and came home exhausted. After feeding our dogs fermented chicken and liver dinner leftovers from a greasy paper bag, he wanted nothing more than to watch television in a comfortable chair. Instead, Emilio floated like a ghost across my grandmother's line of television sight without a kiss or a greeting to his own separate bedroom. (My mother, grandmother, and grandfather each took the three small bedrooms in our house; I shared my grandmother's bed until I was sixteen because my mother wanted to save her bed for husbands.) No matter how late he came home or tired he was, out of respect, Emilio never sat in that recliner. That was his *wife's* chair.

June's beat started with a predawn coffee. On Sundays before church at La Placita on Olvera Street, she'd splash in some Kahlúa. "I know God is bullshit, but it makes me feel better for an hour," she'd say, sipping from an oversized mug.

A pink, smog-tinged sunrise melted atop an endless field of marzipan streetlight while she readied me like a mother for school. My mother, Maria, was elsewhere, getting herself ready for work. She *hated* mothering me.

"Don't run too fast on the playground," Grandma said while tying my shoes, "because you still can't tie your laces. Make sure you have your lunch tickets with the right date on them," she said, and patted down my pockets, "or else you won't eat." I "blech"-ed out my tongue, imagining my government-sponsored school lunch choices: sloppy joe paste on spongy hamburger buns, shellacked pizza toast, and fruit that tasted like old toothpaste.

"Don't be spoiled," my grandmother said. "And don't untuck your shirt like a cholo," she said, slipping a Le Tigre shirt over me. "Make friends with them. *They* know how to fight. Now take my hand," she said, "and walk on the outside, near the street. So men won't think I'm a whore."

I pulled my hand away from hers in fourth grade and then at her escort to the bus stop in seventh grade; after that, she settled on her crow's nest of a front porch. The vantage point was wide enough that she could watch me walk down the entire length of Portia Street to the corner, where I'd wave good-bye from the front of Little Joy Jr.

"It's a gay bar," my grandmother said. "Go inside if any pervert follows you. It's the safest place in the neighborhood."

When I was off to school, it was time to start *her* day.

If every ghetto has a hierarchy, my grandmother June was the unofficial mayor of Echo Park. She collected our neighborhood stories and bartered them with everyone, whatever their language. She could float with uncommon ease among Echo Park's different worlds and ethnicities, telling dirty jokes to the blood-cloaked Mexican butchers at Roy's Market who'd pull me *chicharrones* (fried pork rinds) from heaven; the beautiful azure-smocked Latina cashiers at Pioneer Market (my first crush was a black-haired Pioneer cashier named Felicia); the Korean-run video stores in the 1980s that smelled of boiled cabbage whose owners called her Grandma; the Italians at Capra's Deli who made the mistake of putting an underwhelming Snoopy fondant on my birthday cake: "I don't know what the hell that *thing* on my grandson's cake is, but that ain't Snoopy!"; and the Jewish owners of Gerry's Department Store, one of several local businesses that extended our family in-store credit for years of loyal patronage despite, sometimes, periods of absence punctuated by a grotesque fight, like the one with the store's matriarch, Shauna, over ten dollars.

"Now I knew why Hitler shoved all the Jews into ovens," my grandmother said, clutching my hand tight, "and it's a shame he missed you, too!"

"Grandma!" I said outside the store. "I don't think you should have said that."

"Oh, I was just making her day interesting," my grandmother said. "Stop taking everything I say so goddamn seriously." No apologies later, in a month or two we were back there shopping like nothing had happened.

When the "politicians downtown" refused to put up a stoplight on Sunset after a child died crossing the boulevard, June rounded up my mother and a friend in a three-woman protest and began randomly stepping out into traffic disruptively until a light was installed.

This was how the mayor did business.

My grandmother loved the movies. She'd switch on cable in the morning like she was checking with a good friend on the day's gossip. If nothing good was playing, she'd take the bus downtown to dilapidated one-dollar-a-ticket movie palaces that'd become makeshift homeless hotels, staving off bums with her house keys in the bathrooms. Her favorite memories were of watching movies in those same theaters with her mother, Lucille. She died in 1941, but my grandmother spoke of her daily, as if she'd just gotten off the phone with her. Lucille often needed "time away" from being a mother, and she'd send June, whom she nicknamed Eek for her inability to speak in a clear voice, to a series of convents and reform schools, including the Ventura School for Girls. They'd celebrate June's releases by going to the movies. When she was eleven, Lucille took June to the premiere of *City Lights*, standing outside the Los Angeles theater downtown as part of a teeming mass of twenty-five thousand fans lining Broadway, tiptoeing and flamingo-necking for a glimpse of Charlie Chaplin. When the churning crowd almost crushed June, her mother beat her with a belt for being clumsy. Once, June was released to the custody of a family friend who accompanied her to Long Beach, where her mother was living. She arrived on the day of the 1933 Long Beach earthquake that killed over one hundred people. Lucille said, "You brought the damn earthquake with you, Eek!"

Gone With the Wind was the last film she and her mother saw together. When Clark Gable said, "Frankly, my dear, I don't give a damn!" there was a collective audience gasp.

Lucille stood up and shouted, "You tell her, Rhett!"

My grandmother valued the dead. On her always-on TV, June cat-alogued the opening credits of black-and-whites with a *Hollywood Babylon* encyclopedic knowledge of every deceased actor's sordid backstory: "Gable, he's dead. Womanizer. Monroe, she OD'd; beau-tiful but no talent. Montgomery Clift, he died a drunk. My God, they're *all* dead! Clift was such a gorgeous man but liked to swing both ways." (Confused look from a six-year-old me.) "You know, he liked women *and* men!"

Like many of the women in my family, my grandmother rooted for the bad girls in movies. Every month, cable played the same twelve movies multiple times a week; an endless loop of my grandmother's favorite roles. Shirley MacLaine tearing up her "ungrateful" daugh-ter Debra Winger in *Terms of Endearment.* Faye Dunaway as Joan Crawford in *Mommie Dearest,* my grandmother shouting in unison with Joan from her oversized recliner, "Don't *fuck* with me, *fellas!*" Susan Hayward played Barbara Graham in one of my grandmother's favorites, the "based on a true story" potboiler *I Want to Live!* My grandmother told me again and again that Graham lived behind our property for a few months before she was arrested in 1953 for pistol whipping an elderly woman to death in a botched robbery and sent to die in San Quentin State Prison's gas chamber.

"What a woman!" my grandmother said.

I'd walk up to the thicket of trees and bushes that separated our backyard from Graham's former house to see what ghosts this pretty murderess had left behind. What I found were swarms of cats the house's current owner hosted, fed, and watered. When he died, the cats mewed for days as they succumbed to malnutrition. By the time the stragglers crawled through the chain-link fence to our yard look-ing for food and water, most of the cats had died. Solemn, I rattled kibble in pie tins for the survivors but my grandmother said it was hopeless.

"It's the Graham curse," she said. (John Waters would have loved my grandmother.)

Floating above them all in my grandmother's canon was Saint Bette Davis. When Davis's daughter wrote *My Mother's Keeper* in 1985, a *Mommie Dearest*–style memoir, my grandmother was as indignant as if the book had been written about her.

"What a disgraceful, ungrateful child, telling all her family's secrets for money," she said (writing this sentence, I nod uncomfortably) and was moved enough to write Davis a fan letter pledging her support through this difficult time.

You could also find my grandmother burrowing into a stack of murder mysteries from her Book-of-the-Month Club along with *True Crime* or *Official Detective* magazines she purchased at the local news stand. The magazines, printed on a ground stock paper with a buxom woman falling out of her tube top on the cover, were anthologies of murders or burglaries committed across the country, most of which involved rapes or bludgeonings from jealous lovers. When the Night Stalker serial killer crimes gripped Los Angeles in the mid-1980s, my grandmother ordered a small pistol that shot mini tear gas cartridges from one of the companies that advertised in the magazine. She kept it under her pillow next to a crucifix.

Years later, when it came time to sort through my grandmother's possessions, in her "valuables" drawer was the gun (never fired), a tub of talcum dusting powder calcified into a brittle chalk, and a crisp thank-you note with the letters *BD* in a royal blue art deco font, a handwritten expression of gratitude from Bette Davis for my grandmother's fan letter. To me now, these things *are* my grandmother.

If my Grandma June was a factory steam whistle calling me to work and my grandfather Emilio a whisper to be ignored, my mother was a siren whose songs were her stories.

"You almost weren't born," my mother says. I'm watching her, wide-eyed, expectant, an eight-year-old perched on her bed mouthing words I know by heart.

"You were on a date?" I ask.

"Yes," she says.

"And then you got in a fight with the guy who brought you to a park in his car?"

"It was a lovers' lane," she says.

"What's that?"

"It's where men take women to talk them into something. I didn't want to talk that night."

"And then you left the car and another guy showed up?"

"He was very handsome," my mother says. "He pulled alongside me and asked if I was okay. 'Let me drive you home,' he said. He seemed like a gentleman."

"You got in?" I ask.

"He was a real fox," my mother says. "Really hot for a white guy."

"Then what happened?"

"He drove further into the woods. Deeper and deeper, like he was looking for something. All he told me was his name. 'I'm Ted,' he said."

"And then?" I ask.

"Ted found some kind of clearing, stopped the car, turned off the headlights, got out, and opened the trunk. I looked behind me and saw he was holding something. Silver, like a pipe. I didn't know what to do."

"Then what happened?"

"These bikers—Hells Angels—roared up and shouted, 'What's going on?' He ran off into the woods, and one of the bikers gave me a ride back home. They saved my life."

"And then?" I ask, edging up on my mother's bed like a puppy. She smiles, cocking her eyebrows as if she'd forgotten we were talking at all.

"And *then*?" I ask, about to explode.

"Then I saw his face on TV. His name was Ted Bundy."

"Wow!" I'd say. "Ted Bundy!"

"They won't execute him until he loses his looks," she says. "Bundy's

15

adaptable; he's a Sagittarius. Not a strong Aries, like me. Or Hitler. But if Ted Bundy had killed me that night," my mother says, "I'd have never been able to meet your father and have you."

What a story! Delusion requires charity, which I, like many people who loved her, was more than happy to offer. There was something about my mother that made you not only want to follow her off a cliff but also to cushion her blow when you both hit the ground. She didn't perform chores or cook any meals; when my mother made dinner— and I *loved* her dishes—it was a tub of cottage cheese sprinkled with Lawry's seasoned salt, or a pound of ground beef mashed into tiny pebbles and either fried to crispy burnt scabs or snacked on raw. My mother nourished me with words.

She started me off young, teaching me to read at two, when, she said, I plopped a book in her lap.

"Teach me," I said. (The book, in her later retellings, morphed into a dictionary.) My mother enrolled me briefly at a Montessori pre-school. I spoke out of turn and was punished with an hour of sitting on a green felt mat in the center of the classroom.

"If that's how you punish talking, my son's already smarter than you," she told my teacher. I didn't finish out the week. Later there was a Christian school with a no-hair-below-the-collar policy. My "Indian" hair was to my shoulders.

"Jesus had long hair," I said, and was gone the same day.

My mother bought me phonics workbooks by the stack and checked my answers each night after work. If I did well, as a reward she'd let me brush her long, cherished hair, guiding my hands with a heavy brush across her scalp and down to her waist in a slow, languorous rhythm that was like sipping hot tea.

I graduated to learning, and participating in, my mother's narratives. I couldn't hear the lies in her stories. Their frequency was too low for my young ears. Much the way certain singers perform a song a different way each time they sing it, my mother told her stories a different way every time she spoke them. Every one of her stories had at their core one seedling of truth that allowed her, like a jazz musician, to improvise its telling depending on her audience. I loved being her "rhythm section"—sharing our secret language of winks, nods, smiles, and interjections that corroborated her stories as they evolved on the spot in their multiple retellings. In some versions, her embellishments ran over her cup's edges like hot foam; in others, she'd carve out the bottoms of her multiple truths to fit whatever awkward conversational moment she'd stumbled into, like when she met someone eager to hear more about her Indian knowledge and ways. Her history and her experiences were mercury in a barometer, fluctuating based on what she felt you wanted to believe. My mother didn't enjoy movies like my grandmother; those were *other* people's stories. She wanted to *be* the story and live her life through these stories. In her stories, though, death, like angry smoke, always found a way in.

"I won't see you grow old," my mother said. "I'm going to die young."

"No!" I said. "You can't die!" Every day, she told me I was wrong.

"I won't live past forty," she said.

Forty came and went. Then: "I won't see you graduate from high school." That passed, too. Finally, bored with years of death scares, I said, "You're not going to die, Mom."

"You're wrong, Brando," she said. "When I was little, I lied to Death. Death doesn't forget."

When my mother was four, my grandmother moved to Lompoc, California, for a brief time to get away from Los Angeles and Emilio. June and Emilio had dated off and on for several years before June had my mother. "Learn how to take money from men you don't want to marry," June's mother, Lucille, told her. "He's a *chango*, a monkey man with a tail between his legs, like all Filipinos." June took Emilio's gifts and rejected his marriage proposals. Then June met my biological grandfather, Tomás, at a bar in the Grand Central Market downtown. He taught her how to drink beer the right way, *cerveza mexicana*, he said, with a lemon wedge she sucked on and a dash of salt she licked off the rim of his glass. She shared many *cervezas mexicanas* with Tomás until he learned she was pregnant.

"I can't be tied down to a woman," Tomás said, and left. My grandmother wasn't surprised. Her own biological father, Steven Scolari, had long since vanished, sending her every couple years from Europe treasured penny postcards with sailboats on them. The women that raised me were themselves raised by stepfathers. They believed men left simply because that's what men did. To expect more from a man meant you'd better find yourself a woman.

While in Lompoc, little Maria stepped on a splinter that infected her foot and led to blood poisoning that almost ended her life. Death appeared at the foot of her bed and beckoned her to a tree outside her window. She agreed to go but changed her mind and hid under the covers. My mother didn't follow Death that long night and survived. The scare brought June and Maria back to Los Angeles. Only then did June agree to be Emilio's wife, bearing him his own son, Oscar, who moved away as a young man and was never close to his mother or half sister.

A pudgy, well-behaved child with pigtails, Maria won good citizenship awards in school seven years running. She was a good girl at home, too, and couldn't understand why her mother would sometimes, while combing Maria's long, tangled hair, lose her patience and strike her back with a wooden brush. Maria turned to her collection of ceramic statues of Catholic saints for answers, but they kept quiet. When June threatened to kick my teenage mother out of the house, Maria smashed her saints to pieces and tossed them into a garbage bag. It would not be the last time my mother cleaned up her past this way and erased any trace of something to which she'd been so devoted.

Maria stopped being a good girl at Belmont High School. She had either on a dare or through intimidation joined a street gang and became a *chola*.

"They're a teenybopper gang," June scoffed. "They don't even use knives!"

The experience was scary enough, though, to get June and Emilio to transfer my mother to Hollywood Professional, an all-grades private school on Hollywood Boulevard that, in 1963, cost three hundred dollars a semester. A half-hour bus ride from Echo Park, the school was for kids who needed classes arranged around a budding musician's or actor's schedule. At Hollywood Professional, Maria was free to wear her long, dyed, blood red hair beehive high. She showed off her dark skin in tight black dresses and spoke what little Spanish June had taught her to attract the white boys. She wanted to be new, dangerous, and sexy, everything she had never been and could never be in Echo Park. Here my mother would come to understand the power of being exotic; the power of being "the other."

She refused a small role in *Spartacus* offered by a casting agent who hung out at the school. She met Dennis Wilson of the Beach Boys, high on coke and drunk all the time, doing his best to transform his drug-addled palsy into charm as he played with her hair during study period, called her "Baby," and said he'd ask his brother Brian to write a song for her. She hung out with James Mason's daughter, Portland, and earned a bevy of female admirers and friends by throwing a young, bratty Charlene Tilton (future jezebel of TV's prime-time soap opera *Dallas*) down a flight of stairs. She was voted Duchess of the Harvest Ball, 1963, and made rich friends who encouraged her to live with the kind of reckless, self-destructive abandon only money and privilege can afford. Her best friend was a spoiled Bel Air Jewish princess named Betty. They drank, drugged, and partied together until the early nineteen seventies, when Betty married an Asian man, moved to Florida, had a child, and in a fit of depression and rage bashed her baby girl's head in with a hammer and was sent to death row.

After Hollywood Professional, my mother had fallen in love with a sandy-haired blond named Mike and gave birth to two children before me, both of whom had befallen their own separate inconceivable tragedies. A son named Shane, who in his black-and-white photograph looked like a porcelain doll with onyx marbles for eyes, had a congenital heart defect. A hole in his heart, which my mother instinctively knew was there but that an unsympathetic hospital staff ignored, claimed his life at three. My mother's snow-white, blue-eyed, blonde daughter, Janaine Deborah Patterson, had been kidnapped, also at three, by a jealous babysitter and disappeared. The police scoffed at my mother's claims to the Caucasian baby, letting crucial time lapse after Janaine's abduction. In a grainy color photograph taken in our house's backyard in the 1970s, my mother holds Janaine, dressed in a pink jumper, high in her arms—the one piece of evidence that my mother had given birth to a beautiful girl that nobody believed was hers.

What else didn't people believe? I mean, how much of this was true?

Spartacus had been in theaters for three years when my mother transferred to Hollywood Professional. Dennis Wilson never went there, though his younger, shyer brother, Carl Wilson did, to escape ravenous fans at Hawthorne High. Portland Mason and Charlene Tilton, who went to Hollywood High School several years later, aren't noted among Hollywood Professional's illustrious alumni. There were no women on Florida's death row at the time my mother claimed that Betty was there.

Shane and Janaine both exist in photographs, Shane's in my memory, Janaine's in my possession. While I *maybe* saw a trace of my mother in Shane's face, I realize now there's no possible way a woman with my mother's features and skin color gave birth to a blonde, blue-eyed, fair-skinned girl. Years later, I noticed a tiny time stamp on the trim of Janaine's photo that says August 1977, which meant that Janaine would have been my younger, and not older, fake sister. Yet for years these children were resurrected whenever I misbehaved, a make-believe sister and brother to go with my make-believe father and ethnicity, who met horrible make-believe ends. My mother had so much pain to share that she had to *invent* people to hurt.

Yet in every lie she told, she always made sure to give something back to *you*. It could be a Weight Watchers meeting where she claimed a ribbon for losing fifty pounds after submitting a falsified weight loss card. Then she'd hit another meeting at another Weight Watchers branch later in the week, claiming the same weight loss ribbon twice.

"She lost all that weight in six weeks?" someone whispered. "She looks great!"

"If I can do it," she told a rapt group of hopeful women, "you can do it too."

It could be the Overeaters Anonymous group where she ran into John DeLorean, the disgraced auto executive who had beaten government drug trafficking charges and was at OA because he'd "started eating lots of junk food during his trial" and needed to find "a self-empowering Christian way to lose weight." He told his fellow OA'ers not to lose faith and gave my mother his business card.

"Come work for me," he said. (My mother never found his card, no matter how often I asked.)

It could be leading a group of wide-eyed "Pilgrims"—my mother's term for whites—around a jewelry store rubbing "southwestern" squash blossom necklaces and sterling silver bracelets between her fingers. Using a just-for-white-people "Indian" voice—a taffy pull on her slight Latina accent—she'd pronounce whether a piece of turquoise had been crafted by a real "on the rez Skin."

Of course, my mother had no idea which pieces were authentic, but if her details didn't line up—or connect at all—you still *wanted* to believe her. Why? You felt privileged that someone with such an extraordinary story would choose to confide in, of all people, *you*. You'd forget meeting a hundred people, but you'd remember meeting my mother. Her story became *your* story.

"I can't wait to tell my friends I met an Indian!" one of my mother's Pilgrims told her in a sincere embrace. She rattled with the jewelry my mother helped her buy. "Thank you."

Hey, she'd say, at least it's never boring.

• • •

Maria met Candido Ulloa when she was twenty-five at a Mexican LA nightclub in the summer of 1972. He drove a big American car with a velvet burgundy interior and wore checkerboard polyester shirts with flashy jewelry—all those tempting accessories that make you forget you're poor. His mustache and wavy shoulder-length hair made him a ringer for the soon-to-be-famous *Chico and the Man* star Freddie Prinze. My mother's blood red hair from high school was now an inky Morticia Addams black that didn't drape so much as slide down her body, accentuating the svelte curves she would later spend years and thousands of dollars on worthless exercise videos and equipment trying to get back.

My mother did most of the talking with Candido. Though she had been born to Mexican parents, she spoke—and would learn—nothing beyond fast-food Spanish. It's not my language, Maria told Candido. Her mother, June, was, in fact, a Plains Indian from Oklahoma, making Maria half Indian.

"And your father, Emilio," Candido asked, "is Filipino?"

"He's my papa," she said. "But he's not my real father."

"What was *he*?" Candido asked.

"He doesn't count," my mother said, "like most men."

Born in Yahualica, Mexico, to a family of five brothers and three sisters, Candido spoke just a handful of English words. He had left school in the fourth grade to work picking onions in Ensenada. When he came to Los Angeles, his first job was at a car wash working for a black man who called him amigo because he never learned his name. Then he went to work at a Love's Bar-B-Que, where, as someone without a car, he was popular both with the waitresses eager to give him lifts home and the gay cruisers driving on the boulevard. He took English classes at night and, eventually, so he could have weekends free for partying and the clubs, left the restaurant to work at a furniture factory.

When Maria got pregnant a few months later with what she told Candido was her first child, he became her husband and a temporary legal resident. They posed for a grim picture outside the city courthouse, a fresh marriage license in my father's hand. He wrote to June, "We dedicate this photo to you with all affection from your daughter and son so that you can keep it as a souvenir." Young, pretty, and stone faced, they both embrace like two precarious towers forced together by a high wind.

Watching American Indian Sacheen Littlefeather (who, like my mother, was born with a stereotypical Mexican name, Marie Cruz) refuse Marlon Brando's Oscar to protest Hollywood's depiction of American Indians convinced Maria that, if their baby was a boy, Brando would be a great name to honor her own nonexistent Indian heritage.

"If you don't like that," my mother said, "how about Pacino?"

(*Pacino* Ulloa? Pacino *Skyhorse*? As it was, my first name was misspelled Brandon on my birth certificate, and, in a weird precursor to a life filled with shifting identities, a change-of-name form was filed when I was three months old.)

Their marriage was a Napoleon complex, short and furious. Candido worked six days a week and took English classes at night. That was his life. Maria was angry that *her* life as Candido's wife was so fucking boring and always ended a fight by kicking him out of June's house, where they lived.

"I don't want a deadbeat around my son!" she screamed when Candido came home late from work.

"Why haven't you learned English already?" she said when Candido came home late from school.

He didn't know the English *or* Spanish words to calm down Maria. One time they took the bus to Disneyland, parking their car in a lot downtown. They had a wonderful time, but when they returned, the car battery was dead. Maria cursed out Candido, took the bus home, and told my grandmother to change the locks.

He was kicked out, moved back in, kicked out again—over and over during the next three years. Once, when they were separated, she told Candido she'd been raped by a black man.

"Did you go to the police?" he asked.

"Why would I go to the pigs?" she shouted "Don't you fucking care about what happens to me? What kind of husband are you? I'm seeing a real man now."

"Who is he?"

"His name is Paul Skyhorse," she said. "He's an Indian. He's in jail," she said proudly.

"How do you see a man that is in jail?"

"Have you always been this dumb?" my mother asked.

I don't remember the day my father left. I was three years old. What I'd be told, long after I found out that Candido was my father, came in slivers, the last of which I'd collect when I was in my midthirties.

It was pouring rain. My mother and Candido went shopping for toddler furniture. When Candido opened the trunk to put the furniture inside, it filled with water. Their boxes soaked in puddles. Maria was angry that their shopping was ruined and wouldn't calm down at home.

"I want you out of this house!" she screamed.

This time Candido said, "If you want me out, I will go, but I will not come back. Is that what you want?"

"Yes! You're a good-for-nothing wetback! I want you out for good!"

He packed quickly while Maria complained to my grandmother, "What kind of man leaves his wife and son?" My mother went to the kitchen and found a knife. Then she blocked the front door.

"You aren't going anywhere," my mother said. "If you leave, I'll call *la migra* on you!" Then she came at Candido with the knife.

My grandmother stood in front of him and faced my mother. "If you want to hurt this good man who goes to work every day and tries

24

to make you happy, you'll have to get through me. You'll have to kill me first."

"You've always been on his side!" my mother screamed. She put the knife on a table and then grabbed me. She picked me up and shook me, hard.

"Don't do that to Brando!" Candido said "You're going to hurt him!"

My mother said, "I'll kill Brando if I want to! He's my child!" Then she threw me onto the couch and reached for the knife again.

"Go! Go!" my grandmother told Candido.

My father ran out of the house to a friend's apartment, stayed there for a few months, and then found a place of his own in East Los Angeles. That's where he'd forget who he and his family were and start his life again.

A parent who disappears, if he's spoken of at all, is at the mercy of the one who stays behind and of a child's wishy-washy memory. Birthday parties, trips to the park, walks to the grocery store, hugs, kisses—nothing with Candido in it stuck.

My father's forgetting was more specific, more deliberate. Candido hadn't been married to my mother long enough to earn a green card. He was terrified of the power she had to potentially destroy his life. His fear was so great it made a Mexican illegal risk deportation and convinced a proud man to abandon his only son.

My mother wanted to forget Candido. There was a massive photo purge, but she kept a handful of documents and pictures she could have easily thrown away. She doctored the backs of these surviving pictures poorly with false captions, such as "My friend Candy" or "Uncle Candy," and then waited for the day when her lies wouldn't satisfy my questions anymore. I was twelve or thirteen when she told me at last who he was—who *I* was—and concocted fantastical stories of his disappearance and whereabouts aimed at definitively killing him off. He'd returned to Mexico, joined the Mexican Mafia, or had permanent amnesia triggered by a brick my mother landed on his head during his "getaway."

My imagination tried making him a flesh-and-blood person with a feel, a scent, a voice, a laugh. (In my imagination, my father's laugh is generous and honeyed.) That man never rose from my animating table. Candido dissolved into blank, empty space, like a desert sky drained of its intense blues and pinks, or an ocean horizon stripped of water. My father was like God: an unseen life-giving entity whose existence I had to accept on faith.

My mother wasn't interested in believing in things you couldn't see, but that didn't mean she wasn't eager to see if others would believe in what *they* couldn't see. A manufactured identity is nothing new in Los Angeles. For every starlet who changes her name or her breast size, there are a hundred undocumented workers who assimilate their way into the city, unnoticed, to construct their own versions of the American Dream. In my mother's dream, she saw no reason that just because we were born Mexican we'd need to live as Mexicans.

I was three years old when my life as Brando Kelly Ulloa, the son of a "good-for-nothing wetback," ended. My life as Brando Skyhorse, the American Indian son of an incarcerated political activist, had just begun.

2

"That is your father," my mother said, pointing at Paul "Sky-horse" Durant through a thick pane of glass.

Inside a heavy-security courtroom in downtown Los Angeles, my mother introduced me to a rowdy group of Paul Skyhorse's supporters as his four-year-old son. My "father," a giant with a long mane of hair, looked at us in the gallery and, with a confused grin, waved a shackled hand.

Who *was* this man? Had my mother conjured him out of her imagination? I didn't understand why he was in cuffs or behind a sheet of glass like a mannequin. I didn't want to hold his hand, climb up in his arms, or have him come home with us. What I liked was his pale blue fringed shirt with tassels like those on the end of a bicycle's handlebars. Would his fringes blow in the wind, I wondered, if he ran until he was free?

In the mid-1970s, there were a number of disenfranchised groups in every darker shade of the rainbow that trafficked in rage, looking for power and justice. In 1974 Durant, a twenty-nine-year-old Chippewa Indian, along with Richard "Mohawk" Billings, were accused of the brutal robbery and murder of a taxi driver in Ventura County. In the wake of the 1973 Wounded Knee uprising, in which armed members of the American Indian Movement (AIM) seized control of the area near Wounded Knee, South Dakota, for over two months,

Skyhorse and Mohawk, both AIM members, took on the aura of political prisoners. There were celebrity advocates, bright red Free Mohawk & Skyhorse bumper stickers, and extensive media coverage. The trial, which began in June 1977 and at the time was the longest in California history, ended with Skyhorse's and Mohawk's acquittals almost a year later.

My mother followed the trial closely and ingratiated herself to Durant by writing him "fan girl" letters that included pictures of herself: a lean, fierce, beautiful woman with flowing waist-length hair. She was as easy a sale to Durant as she was to others. Later, at a Skyhorse-Mohawk Legal Defense Fund meeting held in a damp wood-paneled community center that smelled of burning Styrofoam, my mother introduced herself to AIM cofounder Dennis Banks as one of Paul Skyhorse's wives and me as his child.

"Glad you're here, Sister Skyhorse," he said. "Your son's going to be a proud chief someday with that name."

There was, of course, the matter of Durant's actual family: his second wife and his children. Convict groupies aren't uncommon, but my mother must have known that posing us as Durant's wife and child could lead others to ask questions. So she found—or created—in another prison two thousand miles away a second Paul Skyhorse. *That* man was the Paul Skyhorse that became my father.

Two different men.

Two different incarcerated American Indians.

Two different Paul Skyhorses.

If this sounds confusing, I believed these two Paul Skyhorses were the same man until I began writing this book.

At least it's never boring.

My *own* Paul Skyhorse's history begins with a prison record.

Five days before my birth in 1973, Paul Martin Henry Johnson, a six-foot-four-inch twenty-nine-year-old Indian with dark saddle-leather skin and waist-length hair, was indicted for armed robbery, along with two others, by a grand jury in the county of McLean, Illinois. They were after a Stevens 16-gauge pump shotgun, a Browning 12-gauge automatic shotgun, a Greenfield .22 caliber automatic rifle, a .357 Security Six revolver, and nine hundred dollars in cash. The guns were, in the different stories my mother told, for robbing banks to fund the American Indian Movement or to be used in the commission of an AIM-related "political statement." Paul Johnson's robbery occurred on May 8, 1973, the same day the headline-grabbing seventy-one-day AIM-controlled siege of Wounded Knee ended. Johnson said he'd spent some time at Wounded Knee during the standoff and claimed he had the shrapnel in his brain to prove it.

Paul Johnson was sentenced on April 10, 1974, to serve seven and a half years to twenty-two and a half years in an Illinois state penitentiary. Sometime during his incarceration, he came into contact with my mother, probably though a classified ad in the back-to-the-land magazine *The Mother Earth News*. When I was older, I'd help write my mother's personal ads and sorted through the slush pile of polite, randy, and desperate replies, but as a four-year–old, I was still too young to ghost her classifieds. What caught Paul's eye might have been simple: "Young single Indian mother searching for a good Indian father and devoted husband." To weed out any playboys she would have listed *father* first.

Paul Johnson's letters came once or twice a week on canary yellow legal-size paper, written in a doctor's scrawl pulled tight at both ends and snapped back into prose. The pages had a ridged, tactile feel, the words branded into the paper. A thick, many-paged letter was filled with questions or promises. A thin, single-sheet letter came with sticky, blood-smeared twenty-dollar bills "earned" by shaking down or beating up fellow convicts.

Each letter was signed, "May the Great Spirit Guide You."

Here in these pages were most likely outlines for the transformation of both father and son Skyhorse. Paul "adopted" me as his own child, though what that legally entailed, with him behind bars, was unclear. There was no conversation in which my mother declared Paul Skyhorse my new, official father, because—a fact she was probably counting on—I didn't remember the old one. So thorough was my brain wipe of Candido that I still have no memory of being called by any name other than Brando Skyhorse Johnson.

Neither did anyone else. When my mother, now a full-blood Indian named Running Deer, enrolled me in kindergarten at Logan Street Elementary School in the fall of 1978 (the same school she'd attended as a girl twenty years earlier), I was presented as Brando Skyhorse, "Paul Skyhorse's" son. Because the Los Angeles Skyhorse Durant–Mohawk Billings trial had ended three months earlier and was fresh in the city's consciousness, there was a legitimate concern voiced that the media might swarm upon the school. So my mother offered a compromise: Johnson would be added to protect my identity from both teachers and the outside world.

Her story was accepted at its word. Why wouldn't it be? Even I had no idea that "Johnson" had been Paul Martin Henry's surname in prison.

My mother then encouraged Logan's vice principal, Judith Newman, to lobby the federal government for funds due public schools that have Native American students enrolled. Mrs. Newman sent away the paperwork and by the end of the year had received special funds for the education of Brando Skyhorse Johnson, American Indian.

(Mrs. Newman told me the above in 2010. "I had no idea all of you were Mexican," she admitted. "Your mother was very convincing.")

Perhaps adopting a new name for Paul was just as simple as adopting an abandoned child. *Thundercloud Indian Affairs*, a Union, New Jersey, newsletter "dedicated to communication with all Indian people and others of like mind," published a poem written by "Paul Sky Horse Johnson" from PO Box 100 in Vienna, Illinois. (Durant was in Los Angeles, on trial for murder.) Was Sky Horse (also spelled Skyhorse), as he said later, a family name he'd been stripped of, replaced with Johnson when he entered the "white" educational system because it was forbidden for Indian children to enroll with their original names? Or had my mother written about her activism on Paul Skyhorse Durant's behalf and encouraged Johnson to adopt Skyhorse's name in jail, blending together two different people to create the new identities that she wanted for herself, her son, and her future husband? The newsletter was sent to "Maria B. Johnson"—my mother now a "wife" to an Indian but not yet a Skyhorse.

That Christmas, I sat for a picture on the lap of a boozy theme park Santa and emerged on the back of that photo as Brando Skyhorse. Photos of me already in our albums were "revised," with my mother's hand crossing out *Ulloa* in pen or with Wite-Out, making my father Candido my "uncle Candy," and then inking my Indian name in its place. Even my first name wavered between Brandan and Brando until I was three. These white Kodak print backgrounds were my mother's first draft of me, working out my story and who I was. One black-and-white photo of me at age three had written in Paul's hand, "Our son and little chief Sky Horse." Had my mother sent him this photo, asked him to sign the back without dating it, and then return it to her for me to discover it when I was old enough? What other explanation makes sense?

On her photo backs, Maria Teresa was becoming Running Deer Skyhorse, a name she said Paul bestowed on her. No formal applications for an official name change necessary, just a new signature and a deck of fake mail-ordered ID cards. She alternated between Maria and Running Deer, but for a woman who dreamed of being an Indian somebody instead of a Mexican nobody, how she introduced herself was an easy choice.

My grandmother liked being a Mexican but loved telling a good story more. So when she found herself in a boring conversation, she'd christen herself an Indian too, calling herself "Big Bear," a name she borrowed from the local TV weather reports that covered Big Bear Lake, a mountainside community two hours from Los Angeles. To go along with her name, she created her own Indian greeting.

"*Haita hay!*" she would say, accompanied by a horizontal sweep of her arm out from her chest like some military salute in an army of very short men. "It means 'hello' and 'good-bye,' just like 'aloha.'"

It was a bastardization of the Navajo "*Ya' ah' tee*" (often mispronounced as "ya ta hay") that my grandmother and I learned from Running Deer. June taught her new Indian greeting to countless unsuspecting Mexican and Chinese women in Echo Park; people who had only a threadbare grasp of the English language learning a fake welcome in a nonexistent one.

"Running Deer" now had created two fathers for me: one incarcerated Paul Skyhorse (Johnson) in Illinois writing me letters, and another incarcerated Paul Skyhorse (Durant) in Los Angeles whom I had seen from behind a courtroom screen. What good were two fathers, though, when neither could help my mother actually "father" me every day? About as good as what my mom called "a long-distance dick." Then she met Frank, and both our problems were, for a while, about to be solved.

My mother needed work, so she joined the California Employment Development Department as a temporary claims assistant in late 1977. She hated being tethered to a desk. Her hair, back to red, blazed through the office like a wildfire, dangling alphabetic hints of her story: she was F-B-I (Full-Blooded Indian), A-I-M, and F-R-E-E (romantically available) because her husband, Paul Skyhorse, was on trial for murder.

Frank Zamora, an employment and claims assistant at "the State," wanted to know more. Sensing my mother wouldn't become a permanent hire, he invited her out for lunch. They ate together a couple times a week, meals that my mother often paid for. Frank took this as a sign that she wasn't interested in him—though he did the best he could.

"I can't believe you're thirty," he said. "You look great for your age."

"Sure, I'm not a Pilgrim. Pilgrims crack," my mother said.

"Come again?" he asked.

"Whites. 'Pilgrims.' Their looks disappear when they hit forty. White women don't last."

In my mother's dictionary, whites were Pilgrims, cops were "pigs," Indians, like her, were "skins," men were "braves," and women, "squaws."

What a sexy squaw, Frank thought.

He followed the ongoing Skyhorse-Mohawk trial but wasn't deterred from pursuing a woman whose husband was an accused murderer. Over their shared lunches, she confirmed the rumors (that she herself had started) and as proof gave Frank the *Thundercloud* newsletter with Skyhorse Johnson's poem. She presented these two different Pauls as one singular Paul Skyhorse who, she believed, would be found guilty at trial and never get out of jail. My mother also gave Frank, an avid souvenir collector, a poster drawn by incarcerated AIM activist Leonard Peltier, which she received because she was in AIM, too, and glossy black-and-white Marlon Brando photographs that she insisted weren't publicity stills (though they could be nothing else).

"Marlon Brando gave me those pictures. He's my son's godfather. Because of everything Paul did for 'the movement,'" my mother said. "Would you like to meet my son?"

Frank came to the house and chatted with my grandmother in the living room while she watched television. Emilio was at work; when he was home, he was asleep. Any intersection with the rest of the family was an accident.

"Do you like the Beatles?" Frank asked my grandmother.

"They're a bunch of pretend goody-goodies. Give me the Stones any day," she said.

"Oh, you like their music?"

"Hell, no," my grandmother said, "I just like the way they move."

Frank liked her on the spot. She reminded him of his own lively and opinionated grandmother, who had recently passed away. Frank had been sent to live with his nana at the age of three or four, when his parents divorced and neither was in a position to take care of him. His father, Frank Sr., drove trucks at night, called Frank "Junior," and was generous with everything except affection and time, since exhaustion stole his hours for parenting. On days when his father was supposed to visit, Frank spent long, hazy Los Angeles afternoons "father fishing" on his nana's porch, dressed in the Dodgers uniform his father had given him for his eighth birthday. Sometimes Frank got a bite, but most of the time he didn't.

Frank played football, basketball, and baseball in high school, and his father would keep track of his son's accomplishments by checking the box scores in the newspaper. Drafted by the army in 1971, Frank had poor marksmanship that kept him out of Vietnam. He served out his nineteen-month, twenty-two-day hitch at Fort Ord in Northern California, smoking dope and forging a lifelong passion for the Beatles and his favorite songwriter, Paul Williams, a 1970s version of Pharrell Williams with better lyrics.

When he was discharged, Frank lived briefly with his father, whose idea of demonstrative love hadn't changed, and then moved back in with his grandmother, shuffling between colleges before landing at the University of Southern California. One day on campus he saw on a bulletin board an ad posted by the California Employment Development Department seeking fluent Spanish speakers to work part-time as claims examiners.

"Must be Mexican," the ad said. (Because, its writers assumed, *who else in Los Angeles would know how to speak Spanish?*)

Worried that he'd face competition for the job, Frank ripped down the ad even though the only Hispanics he saw on campus were athletes on scholarship who didn't need jobs.

The state job offered a salary higher than minimum wage and a promise for job security, but that wasn't what interested Frank. He had *plans*, focusing at any one time on: the police academy, the comedy club circuit, the theater, and, ranking above them all, the recording studio.

He couldn't play an instrument and knew he had no voice, but he took songwriting classes and workshops, entering songwriting contests and festivals with knockoffs of popular songs. He wrote a variation of Paul Simon's "Kodachrome" with the lyrics changed around and an original tune called "Little Miss Emotion": "You have my love, you have my devotion / C'mon, c'mon, c'mon, Little Miss Emotion." Working for the state turned out to be a good temporary job—he'd met his "babe" Maria there, and the mother sitting across from him was so much like the *abuelita* he'd lost—but he needed to remind himself that he was destined for big things.

Frank felt a small tug at his side. I'd approached him, holding a book. At that age, books held my hand everywhere.

"Look it," I said. "My grandmother is reading this."

"Really?" Frank asked. "What is it?"

"The Lincoln Conspiwacy," I lisped.

Frank looked at the book jacket. "That's right," he said and smiled.

He'd tell his friends, his stepmother, anyone who would listen, about the Kid That Reads Adult Books, but nobody was as impressed as he was. What was wrong with them? *C'mon*, he thought, *this kid is really something else*. What they couldn't see was how a little boy could remind Frank of himself just by holding a book.

"That's my tiger!" Frank said, and held me aloft in his arms.

If you asked what my first "father" memory is, there is just Frank. Six foot, more than 225 pounds. "Tall and big for a Mexican," he liked to say.

He spoke in a warm, un-Latino-accented declarative voice full of confidence that could make asinine pronouncements sound like jazzy traffic reports: "The Beatles didn't make history, they *are* history."

He fire-rubbed his palms together and schoolboy *"Woo-hoo!"*-ed before a drive anywhere. He revved up his 1970s avocado green Dodge van, with its wood paneling, shag carpeting, leather bench seat in the back, and Beatles-fan license plate reading LENNMAC, and played "Macca's" *Band on the Run* or Jackson Browne's *Running on Empty*. If it was cold, Frank wore a custom-made nylon silver jacket with the title of his favorite Jackson Browne song, "The Pretender," stitched across the back.

If Candido is a blank space, memories of Frank are like flashcards. Pictures of a young man, madly in love and maybe in a little over his head, becoming an actual father a piece at a time. There he is, driving us down I-5 to suburban Buena Park on Halloween, where the houses had glowing orange jewel doorbells, there were no security gates on the windows and doors, and the candies handed out weren't loose single pieces but packed in actual *bags*.

There he is again, dropping me off at an overnight summer camp in the afternoon and then driving back that night to take me home when I wouldn't stop crying in my cabin.

He's got an ice pack on my head in the next one. A spunky tomboy named Carrie invited me to her birthday party, and, when I laughed and told her I didn't want to go to a "girl party," she creamed me on the head with her metal *Land of the Lost* lunch pail. Later Frank drove me to her house bearing apology Hostess Ding Dongs.

I'm at a Paul Williams concert with him and my mother. She's brought pajamas and a bathrobe for me to change into in his van if I get sleepy on the ride home. Williams is hours late, so my mother changes me in the concert hall's ladies' room. Frank's holding my hand while we return to our seats amid chuckles and applause, when somebody shouts out, "Enjoy the show, Hef!" Frank thinks he's making fun of me and snaps back, "Hey, *thanks*, pal!"

Then he's running, panicked, carrying me to hard asphalt. I had dived into a backyard pool, unaware I needed swimming lessons first.

Each day with Frank was our own parade where I marched in his footsteps, shooing my mother's hands from his belt loops. I idolized his manner of being a man. He called my mother—and tall, skinny blondes—"Babe" and ordered Heinekens, "No glass," in restaurants, which for years afterward I considered the classy, sophisticated way to order beer. There were warm, milky baths in his ancient oversized tub after hard days of sweaty horseplay, sleepovers on the couch in Frank's drafty childhood home, and backyard barbecues of frugal cuts of steak on a grocery-store-bought hibachi.

"He loves you two," my grandmother said. Then she shook her head and laughed. "Too bad he's so cheap."

They'd been dating for a year when my mother told Frank she was taking me on a trip to meet my father: Paul Skyhorse.

Frank felt like he'd grown into some kind of father to me, but he didn't want to come between me and my "real" dad. Paul Skyhorse, my mother said, had moved to Chicago after his acquittal in Los Angeles, and while things were over between her and Paul, she wanted her son to know his father. (This, of course, was Skyhorse Johnson. Skyhorse Durant stayed on the West Coast, first in Seattle and then San Francisco.) How could Frank refuse that?

There's a white-bordered photo taken at Los Angeles's Union Station that has, written in my grandmother's hand, the date, September 8, 1978, and three names: Frank Zamora, Maria Banaga Johnson, and Brando Skyhorse. We're packed for a trip on the Southwest Limited, headed east. My mother still enjoyed posing for photos then.

She sits in a throne-like leather armchair while I'm astride her lap. By her feet are two large suitcases, one of which has bulging sides, packed in what would become my mother's characteristic "rush and stuff" style when visits to my father became manhunts to *find* a father.

I had just turned five. I'm dressed in white overalls, a checkerboard shirt, and am holding a kids' Amtrak travel pack, a cross between a doctor's bag and a purse. I keep trying to brush the itchy long hair that I hate off my shoulders.

"All American Indians wear their hair long," my mother explained. Perched on the armrest behind us is Frank. He couldn't stop thinking about how I was going to see my father and that this might be the last time he ever saw me. One of his hands grips my mother's arm as if he's trying to keep her from leaving. His other hand braces him up so that he doesn't fold over like a pocketknife. Frank stares at the ground, visibly mourning our loss and already fatigued from the long journeys that he seems to understand lay ahead for us all.

I remember that two-day train trip in filmstrip bursts: a desert at sunset; creaking through mountainous passes; filling out the phonics workbooks my mother bought by the stack; my first kiss, with an older African-American girl (she must have been seven or eight) who told me if we kissed under a blanket, nobody would see us. In full view of everyone in the coach car, she threw a blanket over our heads and brushed her dry lips against mine.

We changed trains in Kansas City, Missouri, and then connected to Saint Louis. There we met Paul's friend Nakome, who'd let us stay at his trailer and then drive us to Paul's prison, the Vienna Correctional Center in southern Illinois. His affectionate behemoth German shepherd nuzzled my hand.

"That's Botchi," he said. "Trained him to attack FBI agents." Botchi, the World's Friendliest Dog, jumped up and licked my face.

Nakome, I was told, was an Indian medicine man. The night before we visited Paul, Nakome sat us in a circle on an upholstered bench in his trailer and passed around a peace pipe filled with peyote. I sucked long puffs and told Nakome what I saw: the trailer disappeared around my body while I flew into the clouds. A large bird circled over my head three times.

"You're having a vision," Nakome said. "That bird must have been an eagle. Only the son of a chief like your father would see an eagle."

My father, a chief? And me, the son of a chief? Why hadn't my mother told me? I looked at her, dragging on the pipe, with wide, expectant eyes. She looked back at me, giggled uncontrollably, and then passed out.

• • •

The morning we drove to Vienna was cloudless, the way all mornings on eventful days are in memory. That name, "Vienna," had an exotic, magical lilt to it, something that made me think we were visiting some kind of castle. In the back of a pickup truck, I was spread out on top of the vicious FBI-hunting Botchi, who patiently cushioned the rocky ride.

Paul was brought into a large fluorescent-lit waiting area with long metallic benches and tables. He jangled like loose change, wearing wrist and ankle cuffs, and his hair, which drooped to his waist, reached the top of my head when we stood side by side. Vienna was a level-six minimum-security prison, meaning we were allowed one greeting hug and kiss. There was no divider between Paul and us.

"My little big chief," he said, and picked me off the ground.

I felt I was soaring at the top of a flagpole. His voice was a low rumble from the mountaintop of his head. I could see him in our now tiny seeming Echo Park house, bending down like an ancient oak while he rustled between rooms, and, with his massive arm span, wrapping our entire family in a protective turtle shell embrace.

I had found my father.

Frank, waving us off in Union Station less than a week ago, wasn't even a memory while we packed for our trip home. I couldn't think about anything except Paul. When would I see him again? How long before he got out of jail? Would he come home to Los Angeles to live with us? On this trip, my mother had already gotten in the habit of giving me responsibility for safekeeping important documents, checks, and tickets, which became routine as I got older. "You're already five years old," she said. "You're not a child anymore."

Kellogg's Frosted Flakes had a special promotion that allowed kids to travel free on Amtrak if they had a pair of box tops from specially marked boxes of the cereal. My mother thought she'd given me the box tops for safekeeping. She hadn't.

"What do you mean you can't find them?" she screamed. Calming her down was impossible. Nakome and I were trying to decelerate a moving train. I was filling with a drowning panic, triple-checking under cushions and in my pockets for what I knew wasn't there. I had jeopardized our trip, and now neither of us could go home, ever.

"We can't leave now! I don't have any money to buy your ticket!" (Once we were back home, I'd see her pull from between her breasts an egg-shaped clump of blood-stained twenty-dollar bills Paul had slipped her during our visit.)

"I'll just leave you here!" she shouted. "You've taken enough of my life from me!"

My mother grabbed my throat. Then she pulled me across the trailer the way a girl would drag a lifeless doll up a flight of stairs. She threw me shivering onto the bathroom floor and then snatched one of Nakome's leather knife holsters and stabbed at my neck with it. It was empty; the holster tip didn't cut, simply folding inward. She tossed it aside and yanked me over to the toilet like a mop.

My mother wrapped her hands around my neck again and pushed my face in the toilet water while I flailed my short arms trying to reach the flush handle. My resistance frustrated my mother; her grip tightened, and her nails pierced my skin. I was drowning and choking, and it would be seconds before I lost consciousness.

Nakome wedged himself in the bathroom doorway, grabbed my mother's shoulders, and uncorked her off me. My head slapped in a wet puddle on the ground. There was a synchronous sound of shallow breathing from us all, our chests rising and falling at different rates, our breathing a relay game.

When the box tops were found, an apology was grumbled, but my mother explained to me that being strangled had been a natural consequence of my "carelessness." Not being given the box tops wasn't an excuse; I should have *asked* for them. Later, as I got older, whenever my mother got unwelcome mail from the welfare office or the IRS, when I couldn't unjam a tape from her VCR or "fix" her wonky phone line, when I was the closest male at hand on whom to take out her frustrations with men, or, above all, whenever she was afraid, she'd bellow for me from her bedroom.

"Brrrrraannndo!"

It was a chain-saw howl, a concussion blast, that to this day makes me jump at loud noises. When she called my name, I stopped being her son and turned into a hunchback lab assistant scurrying through our horror B-movie castle, searching for the one essential ingredient she needed to complete her experiment. Of course, I'd *always* lack this one crucial piece of her puzzle. It was, like those box tops, something she'd already forgotten she'd never given to me.

Paul was paroled in November 1978, two months after our visit, but instead of moving to Los Angeles to be with us, he went to the Saint Louis area to live with his wife. A wife my mother hadn't known existed.

While he was incarcerated, Paul began a correspondence—interestingly, under the name that my mother might have helped him create, Paul Sky Horse Johnson—with a high school girl named Frances. They'd been married in prison several months after my mother received Paul's first letter, in the fall of 1977. Paul told his bride he had a son named Brando in Los Angeles and proudly hung a picture of me as a toddler—taken back when Candido was living with us—on his wife's apartment wall.

My mother now had to share a second Paul Skyhorse with his own legitimate wife. First, she was stunned, then angry, and then . . .

"That's what Frank is for," she said.

In my memory, the transition between fathers happened that fast.

Paul's holding me one week, and Frank's back to holding me the next, loading me into his van's prized shotgun seat for a ride to the drive-in.

"Babe, he's five," Frank said. "I don't think a child his age should watch a horror movie."

"Brando's not *like* children his age," my mother insisted "He'll be the first to tell you that. And don't talk about him like he's not here. I hate when people do that. Brando, do you want to see *Halloween*?"

"Halloween! Halloween!" I said. I didn't know what the movie was about. I just wanted to go everywhere my mother went. (My unintentional love of horror films and the macabre comes from her.)

"He won't remember a thing," my mother said.

My mother and Frank "watched the movie" from the van's rear couch bench seat while I sat stupefied as a forty-foot Michael Myers stabbed his way through, and then disappeared into, an ethereal fog that steamed up the inside of the windshield.

We drove to a supermarket to get chips for the ride home. Frank said I could keep my seat up front so that I wouldn't have to sit in the back of his darkened van. I hadn't moved, spoken, or (it felt like) breathed since the credits. My mother dozed off in the rear while we idled in the blackness of an empty parking lot. Off in the distance, I thought I saw a shadowy figure. There was the boogeyman by that light pole! Or pushing that row of shopping carts!

Suddenly a huge pumpkin shot up from the passenger window inches from my face as the tall figure holding it screamed, "Boo!"

I shot out of my seat, knocked my head against the roof of the van, and started screaming, loud gasping whoops of terror. I couldn't breathe. My mother rushed me to the van's couch bench and cradled my head in her lap.

"What the fuck is the matter with you, Frank?" she shouted. Being a pal instead of a parent had its limits.

Frank understood my mother's temper protecting me, but her explosiveness defending *herself* made him afraid. He stumbled into it face-first when, in a silly fight over whether Warren Beatty was "Mr.

Hollywood" or a hack womanizer, my mother, a foot shorter than Frank, leapt up at him with her nails out and tried to dig into his cheeks. Frank had his hand out to protect himself.

She screamed to June, "Call the pigs, momma, this motherfucker tried to hit me!"

At first Frank laughed it off, thinking this was a weird, twisted play on my mother's unusual sense of humor. Then he realized she was serious. Figuring the best way to defuse her anger was to leave fast, Frank got into his van, revved the gas, and sped off.

Their relationship disintegrated over the next year, with a series of breakups and hasty reconciliations. The sound of Frank's loud, gunned engine would sometimes be my only good-bye. I chose the front bedroom window when it was my turn to "father fish" the same way Frank had as a boy, exhaling disappointment on its glass, tracing endless circles in my breath with my finger. I sometimes knelt there looking for Frank's van even on days I knew he wouldn't come. Even when he did, he could stay the night or leave in an hour. His shortest visit was six minutes—enough time to plop on my mother's bed, exchange words with her, threaten to leave if they continued to argue, and then take off.

In early 1979 Paul sent us train tickets to come visit him. My mother knew already about Frances, but Paul made no mention of her in an accompanying letter. With Frank around less, my heart ping-ponged back to the man I believed was my "real" father. Our train was waylaid in Kansas City because of a massive blizzard that piled snow as tall as the engine. When we arrived in Saint Louis, Paul had a pregnant Frances drop him off at the station and asked that she not accompany him inside. Instead, he sent her to "go buy my son a coat."

She returned with an oversized gray wool overcoat, its sleeve ends covering my hands like gloves. My mother called it my "Mafia coat" because wrapped inside it I looked like a tiny "don," a perfect little "Brando." It was much too warm for Los Angeles, but when we got back home, I'd wear it on windy days, let my sleeves flap in the breeze, and imagine my coat filling with enough air to carry me aloft like a kite. Flying in the air, "a real Skyhorse" in my mind.

Paul's wife gave birth to a real "Sky Horse"—a son, Dustin—in September 1979. Abusive and alcoholic, Paul left Frances and their son a few months later, headed to Minnesota, maybe, but still not to Echo Park. His letters from parole—invariably thin ones without money—promised some kind of reunion, but between that Saint Louis visit and my early adolescence, I'd see Paul just once, possibly, in a horror film called *Wolfen*.

"Your father's in this," my mother said, playing a tape she had recorded off of cable. In the credits, "Paul Skyhorse" is listed in a group of "Native Americans" that appear, true to stereotypical Hollywood form, in a bar called the Wigwam. Was this, in fact, Paul Skyhorse Johnson? Or was it Paul Skyhorse Durant? Perhaps *another* Paul Skyhorse entirely? The credits list neither surname, but that didn't stop me from rewinding and replaying the barroom sequence, squinting close into a nine-inch television set, trying to steal a one-second glimpse of Paul—whichever one it might have been—in a Hollywood movie about murderous superwolves.

He continued sending me gifts (one year a set of Lincoln Logs) and letters admonishing his "little chief" to do well in school. Paul "Skyhorse" had abandoned his biological son but still found a few minutes here and there to be a father to his fake one.

My mother had already left her state job in 1980 when Frank tapered off their relationship He figured that as long as he didn't move the relationship to the next stage by moving in together or proposing marriage, he could indulge their fights because he could leave whenever he wanted. His greatest fear was being trapped in our house with her and my grandparents and having nowhere to go if my mother tried to attack him again. How would he explain to anyone at work why his face was covered with scratches?

Frank hid his drifting away to another woman because he felt it would have cost him any opportunity to stay in my life. In this little boy he'd practically adopted, Frank saw both an echo of who he was at my age and a way for him to pass along a part of himself. Here was a chance to mend his brokenheartedness over his beloved nana. The price would be wrestling with my mother's rabid heart and ignoring the feelings he still had for her in his own.

They tried an uneasy friendship. On the day that John Lennon was killed, Frank called my mom in tears. She cried on the phone with him. The next time they spoke, an argument flared up like a rash. "What kind of man cries about a man—a musician—he never met?" my mother said. "You have fucked-up priorities."

My mother thought these were box steps in a breakup waltz where Frank would lead them right back to reconciliation. It took her a while to realize that Frank's dance would continue on just with me, not her. She'd plead for them to reconcile, and then, when he rejected her proposals, unleash an indiscriminate wrath that was as cruel as it was boundless. She tried to ignore him, but she never learned how to *stop* loving him.

"I'll never stand between you and Brando," she declared. Over the coming years, this would prove true enough when she was married to someone—there were four husbands ahead—but less so when she was single. Those times, she'd invite Frank over to "spend some time with Brando." If he accepted, he'd drift to my mother's room instead and close her door. Sometimes he'd emerge with cheeks flushed, sometimes with eyes glazed from smoking a jay out of the stash he brought. Then he'd pat my head, and we'd launch into our day together, adventures in which Frank was more careful about his time and money than I remembered. When I was a tween, he'd introduce me ambiguously as his "friend, Brando Johnson," never using Skyhorse unlike every other adult so eager to latch onto that name. When we talked, he asked superficial questions, like a prospective college student visiting a campus. Frank acted like an ex-husband who, I noted angrily, hadn't even bothered to marry my mother. I was turning into a child of "divorce," learning to resent Frank as an absentee father rather than my "real" father Paul or the father I didn't know about, Candido.

When Frank left, I learned that in each broken heart lies what we know we should do to heal and move on. Then there is what our hearts are capable of doing instead. This is what both my mother and I called love.

3

I was watching *Psycho* with my grandmother—I was her reliable nine-year-old movie-on-TV date companion—when I heard a gurgling from my grandfather's Emilio's room. We rushed in and found him choking on rancid foam bubbling out of his mouth. My grandmother called an ambulance.

"I'll have to go to the hospital," she said. "You're old enough to stay here on your own." My mother was out with a man I'd never meet, like every man she saw right after Frank.

The paramedics came and maneuvered Emilio's gurney down our uneven flight of stairs. Neighbors fluttered to their front porches like moths.

"Mind your own goddamn business!" my grandmother shouted as she followed him down the hill.

Months before he was due his pension, Emilio had been fired from his line cook job because of chronic incontinence and forgetfulness. Before he was let go, he'd been robbed on the city bus twice, once by a cross-dressing prostitute who jabbed him with a sharpened wire coat hanger that gouged a cut deep into his suit jacket and ended up sticking out the back like a broken wind-up key. Gout, from a lifetime of his beloved pigs' feet dinners, left Emilio bedridden. He regularly soiled his mattress, which my grandmother often chose not to clean—she'd tend to the sheets three times a week if he was lucky. In the kitchen, my grandmother and mother laughed at Emilio's messes while I crept into his bedroom and asked him to play. Emilio's rough,

47

putrid-smelling hands wrapped around my neck in a game I'd created when I returned from Illinois called "I choke you!" I'd ask Grandpa to choke me for doing something wrong, but he never wrung my neck with conviction, breaking down into laughter as his arms folded me into a warm flannel-bathrobe hug. I loved my grandfather Emilio, but I never counted him as a father figure. He was already a ghost to me, living in the bridge from the 1970s to the 1980s, caught between senility and death.

I opened his bedroom window to air out the smell of shit and bile. When my grandmother returned from the hospital, she said, "Grandpa's had a stroke. He won't be coming back. This is your room now."

I stared into that empty blackness of space where Emilio had lived much of his life, alone, as June's husband. A vacuum of air from the opened window caught the door and snapped it shut.

The difference between a leap of faith and a leap of madness depends on where you land. Where my family landed at the end of the 1970s was in a halfway house: that is, halfway between the routines of my grandmother's normalish life and the freedom waiting in my mother's "at least it's never boring" one.

We were a lower-middle-class trio subsisting on money from temporary office jobs, and welfare and food stamps in an intolerant Reagan-era environment that packed our Sears Kenmore fridge with government cheese (sawed off in peanut brittle–like chunks), briny rectangles of government butter (wrapped tight in cardboard, drug-style kilo packages), and plastic gallon pitchers of tooth-tinglingly sweet cherry Kool-Aid. These were the staples of a diet that left you ricocheting off the ceiling with an empty stomach.

My mother hated cooking. "Takeout" was how she said, "I'm sorry." Her actual apologies came with a meek knock at my door and the greasy nepenthean scent of pepperoni pizza. She collected delivery menus like trading cards and was the first to order from any new restaurant in the neighborhood. My mother couldn't be trusted with supermarket trips. Instead of buying ingredients to cook, she opted for finished meals themselves. Once, when my grandmother sent her on an errand to buy bread and sandwich meat, my mother went to the deli counter and ordered eight sliced-to-order sandwiches for three people. A man at the checkout line said, "Looks like someone's afraid of the stove."

Of course, this set off a huge fight between my grandmother and mother. In one corner, my mother, who'd saved us crucial sandwich-making time because I'd said I was hungry. In the other corner, my grandmother, who would have actually *made* the sandwiches because my mother didn't "cook," and done so for less money. I had to take a side—but which one? It was a familiar problem. Every day, I was caught in a dangerous elastic-magnetic field. Move too close to my grandmother, and my mother's rage siphoned the air like a backdraft. Drift too far toward my mother, and my grandmother froze over the shipping lanes that fed affection and love. Their alliances formed and dissolved like waves crashing ashore, often in the same conversation if I could somehow be made the object of their anger. ("Brando said he was hungry! That's why I bought so many sandwiches! Then he didn't defend me when this asshole insulted me at the checkout line!") When the fights were over, both the loser and the winner retreated to their rooms with thunderous footsteps that shook the whole house. Their bedroom doors were deadbolt equipped, which left me stationed postargument in the living room in front of a muted and always running television.

At night, I shared a room and a bed with my grandmother, where I'd slept since I graduated from my crib in my mother's room. When my grandfather's bed was replaced with a small couch and a desk for schoolwork, my grandmother said there wasn't enough space for a new bed of my own. She was right, kind of, though the couch had been her idea. My mother said I should stop asking questions and keep my grandmother company.

While I waited for her to finish reading for the night, I performed a list of security checks in the house before bedtime.

"Did you lock all the doors?" she'd ask me.

"Yes, Grandma."

"Did you fit the security pipes into the sliding door tracks?"

"Yes, Grandma."

"Did you turn on the back porch lights and see if you saw anyone out there?"

"Yes, Grandma."

Asleep, I was wedged between a faux-wood-paneled wall and my grandmother's hilly sand dune range of a body. Awake, I was sandwiched between my mother's mania for Indians and the Mexican culture in which I was immersed, oblivious that I was anything more than an observer of the people and places around me every day. I felt like an alien, an "Indian" boy with only the vaguest sense of what being an Indian meant, and unable to connect with other Indians like me, living in a Mexican neighborhood filled with boys and girls *exactly* like me whose language I couldn't speak and whose large families I didn't understand because they didn't look like mine.

Although she never confronted my mother directly, my Spanish-speaking grandmother tried to tease out clues for me—some small, some *very large*—about my identity. When we were alone, she taught me Spanish words like a call-and-response song:

"Napkin? *Servilleta. Servilleta*, napkin. See? Easy. *Facil. Facil*, easy."

When my mother caught me practicing, she said, "I don't want to hear you speaking that language. *Ever.*" The Spanish words never stuck.

On weekends, when my grandmother wasn't hand flipping tortillas on the gas range burners and singing along with *ranchera* music on her tinny AM kitchen radio, we'd go out for *huevos rancheros con chorizo* at El Rodeo restaurant. She'd play Lucha Reyes and Chayito Valdez on the jukebox and drink an ice cold Bohemia. She watched Raúl Velasco on the popular in Mexican households Sunday-night musical variety

TV show *Siempre en Domingo* and took me to Mexican vaudeville shows at the Million Dollar on Broadway with full mariachi bands, or Vincente Fernández, the ranchera music king, riding onto the stage on a horse with blinding silver accoutrements. She rooted for Latina heroines in the movies, a scarce commodity in 1980s Hollywood, and was heartbroken when she discovered that the badass *Chicana* marine alien killer Private Vasquez in *Aliens* had a Jewish surname.

Together we saw a live performance of *Zoot Suit*, a landmark fictionalized play about the Sleepy Lagoon murder trial, in which a group of twenty-one Latino males received one of the most lopsided racist show trials in Los Angeles's history, and the subsequent zoot suit riots, the flashpoint of which centered around a group of thuggish sailors attacking and stripping random Mexican zoot suiters.

For the show, she bought and dressed me in a sailor's outfit, complete with a Dixie cup hat and a whistle. The path to our seats was a sea of hostile looks and double takes. Seeing *Zoot Suit* dressed as a sailor is like wearing a Nazi uniform to *Schindler's List*. The sailors are the bad guys.

"I was a *pachuca*," my grandmother said when we sat down. She had joined a loose street gang that preyed on white girls leaving war factories, jumping women coming from jobs that *pachucas* couldn't get. On her bicep was a gang tattoo she got in her early twenties of two intertwined hearts with a banner wrapped around them. I mistook her hearts for two train engines colliding in an explosion of barbed wire.

The lights dimmed in the theater. "This is my history," she said. "Pay attention."

The sailor suit helped me remember the moment but not concentrate on what I was watching. I think that was my grandmother's plan. I was just too young to know it then. Frightened, confused, I quietly puffed on my whistle and scratched at the shaggy Prince Valiant haircut that always got me mistaken for a girl and not the stoic little Hiawatha my mother was trying to make me into instead.

51

• • •

I was an unconvincing Indian brave from the start. In first grade, when my teacher asked me to rise with my Mexican and Vietnamese classmates for the Pledge of Allegiance, I stood and recited from memory the words my mother had drilled into me the night before:

"Because of this country's treatment of my race and my people, I cannot pledge allegiance to this flag or this country." Then I sat down.

Unsure what to do, Mrs. O picked a child to lead the pledge. He fumbled with the words as the rest of the children craned their heads back at me, staring and mumbling through their recitation, unsure of whose lead to follow. Sensing she was losing control of the room, Mrs. O ran to my desk, yanked me out of my chair, and grabbed my hand, placing it over my heart in time for the pledge's final words: "with liberty and justice for all." (My mother savored this detail.) Mrs. O had me stand outside our squat bungalow classroom until recess, where I listened through a closed door to my classmates sing counting songs we were learning in English, Spanish, and Chinese.

I'd never been reprimanded, let alone touched, by a teacher before. What had my mother made me say? I started to cry. What kind of Indian brave was I?

"Did she really put her hands on you?" my mother asked that night, incredulous that I'd been punished, as well as overjoyed with possessing, at last, her own personal story of nonviolent resistance and accompanying Indian persecution. She asked me many times to replay what had happened, as if I were a favorite song. I loved it. No matter how old I got, I'd cherish the extra attention I earned for telling stories that weren't boring.

"It's time," my mother said, "to call your father and tell him what happened."

"Paul?" I asked. "I don't want to get my teacher in trouble."

My mother rustled a few papers in her filing cabinet and, like a magician, conjured Paul's voice on the phone. She knew how to get in touch with him whenever she wanted but kept her distance because of Frances. His voice was just as I remembered it: robust, deep, and slow, like a coffee drip; his words had the tautness of crisp linen.

"You did nothing wrong," he reassured me. "Your teacher is to blame. This too will pass," he said.

My mother arrived after class the next day with a tall Indian man wearing denim jeans, a black cowboy hat, and long hair that unfurled to his waist like a ball of sable yarn. Was it Paul? Could she make him appear at her will, too?

Like most of my mother's men during this time, he came and left without a name. I was ushered to stand outside the bungalow classroom again, but this time I knew I wasn't the one in trouble.

Raised voices soon flowed like a river into a warm ocean of laughter, that calming sound that always overtook my mother's public conversations. Outside the house, my mother's anger never crested the dam of appearances. She never lost her temper in public; she'd just misplace it and find it at home later. What had been conceived as a lunch counter act of civil disobedience became, in my mother's hands, a simple cultural misunderstanding. She'd charmed my teacher into the belief that an American Indian radical's son was a student in her classroom. Now here was her chance to teach the teacher, a well-intentioned white liberal woman teaching in an ethnic neighborhood, what it meant to be a "skin."

The next morning before class, Mrs. O said I could read, color, or rest my head during the pledge—whatever I wanted, as long as I was quiet.

Flush from her victory, my mother prepped me with fantastic tales of Indian rituals I'd eventually participate in as the son of a chief, such as periodic fasting and a chief-making ceremony in which I'd be tied to a pole by my hair and swung around like a tetherball. (I'd learn much later, when I saw the ceremony in person from a safe distance, that my mother's misappropriation of reality was tamer than real life. The "hair-swinging" ritual was her interpretation of a sacred sun dance ceremony in which men's chests are pierced with wooden pegs attached to ropes that are pulled over a high tree branch, hoisting the man into the air until the skin breaks.)

She took me when I was nine to a sweat lodge in the San Bernardino Mountains. The site was guarded by an "AIM Checkpoint"—a wooden sign and a log stretched across two sawhorses—which, when we arrived, was moved out of the way by two young ponytailed whites in their twenties in T-shirts and jeans. After stripping down to towels because "nothing white," my mother said, could come into the sweat lodge (the actual rule was nothing metallic, to prevent burns), participants were divided by gender into two wooden structures shaped like inverted bowls. Young children, like me, went with their mothers. Hot coals were pitchforked into a hole in the center of the lodge. Then water was splashed onto the rocks, and the lodge's entrance flap flipped shut. In the darkness, a librarians' army of *shhhhing* exhalations rose from the smoldering hole.

My eyes started burning, and I gulped the remaining air as if wringing it from a sponge. The other kids, all girls under ten, watched silent while I cried and screamed to get out. The lodge leader tried to soothe our circle (me) with a calming prayer, but nobody could hear her over my shouting. My mother restrained me from leaving, so I poked a small breathing hole in the lodge's deerskin wall. How clever I was! Then we crawled out into the sun, where none of the baby squaws with long, dark knotted braids would look at a coward like me.

Just as I was learning how to be an Indian, my kidnapped, white-as-snow sister reappeared, another of my mother's magician tricks. I was nine when my mother and I flew across the country to meet Helen, a woman my mother said was my long-lost abducted sister, Janaine.

"She's family," my mother said. "You'll be 'Uncle' Brando to her kids."

"Why does she have a different name?" I asked.

"That's what the kidnappers named her," my mother said.

I mailed off a signed school photo, "Love, from your little brother" as if *brother* were a new pen name. I thought family members were like trading cards. You collected names, and maybe you'd stumble onto one you cherished, but otherwise they'd just sit there crammed away somewhere, to be brought out simply as something to make other people envious. I was a full-blooded Indian boy in a Mexican neighborhood who now had a white older sister that lived on another coast. It made perfect sense to me. There was no bar for admittance into our circle. Those who wanted to be a part of our family could just attach themselves to us as if they were Lego bricks.

When Helen picked us up from the airport, she was ten years older than Janaine would have been and had two young children. We stayed at a large two-story house down a long dirt road deep in the woods. I slept in a room with my very own bed, opened the window at night to air out that strange "new house" smell, and soaked in the roar of grasshoppers and silence. I grew homesick for noise and my grandmother.

It was fun at first. I played backyard games and drank apple juice with Helen's daughter and son, my "niece" and "nephew," played a family round of Clue in the heat of a summer afternoon, visited a lawyer's office with lots of books to distract me, oblivious to the "giving Brando a better home" discussion shuttlecocking over my head, and won a stuffed dog in a German lederhosen costume at an amusement park for the trip home.

Then I noticed Helen acting more like a mother than my big sister. She assigned me chores, giving me specific instructions on how to set the table, fold my bath towel, and take out the trash. Why was she telling me what to do? Was I going to collect mothers now the way I'd been collecting fathers? I already had a mother, and she didn't act like a mother at all. She was my best friend. Why did I need a new mother when I already had my grandmother? Were all mothers so distant and formal? Helen was like some kind of . . . authority figure.

Our stay ended with a fight over an innocent comment Helen

made about American Indian history. My mother locked herself in a bedroom and told me to pack while Helen crouched on the floor by a closed door and pleaded apologies for "offending your people."

I'd get occasional letters and Christmas cards from Helen throughout the years but didn't learn until my twenties that she'd answered an ad my mother placed in a magazine dangling me out for adoption—the same venue my mother frequently used in her efforts to find me a father and an identity. Perhaps my mother thought her life would be easier without me—"No one else feels any obligation to stay!" my mother would scream—but when she looked into the abyss of letting her child go, unlike Candido, she flinched. When as an adult I confronted my mother with Helen's truth, she dug into her Janaine story, not deviating one detail from the narrative she'd been living with for years.

"She told me she was my daughter," my mother said. "I don't know what else to tell you." She paused. "At least it's never boring."

But my mother was bored. She'd been single for almost a year after Frank left her, so we hit the road, with prepaid Amtrak, Greyhound, and airline tickets, looking for dads for me, and men for her, but not really in that order. When you're a child, you go where you're pulled and trust whoever's doing the pulling. What started as a couple trips to visit Paul was now a full-scale cross-country manhunt.

"We'll always stay safe as long as we're together," she said. "Nobody's fucked up enough to hurt a mother *and* her child."

My mother dated three-dimensionally, keeping track of the men she met through her evolving singles ads like a chess master in the park playing five games at once. She chose prospective suitors based on what parts of the country she wanted to visit. New men meant new adventures on buses, trains, and planes, with phonics workbooks and "early readers" to cover my short "vacations" from school. Staring out the large airport windows, my mother, always a nervous flyer, would watch a plane take off and whisper, "Come on, Big Bird. You're gonna make it."

Our visits were measured in days or hours, accommodated some-times—but not always—with our own beds, and garnished with healthy dollops of charity and good luck. We traveled to Oakland, where Larry, a kind, wheelchair-bound Vietnam veteran, introduced me to Pong. There was an Amtrak trip on the Coast Starlight to Klam-ath Falls, Oregon. Karl, a man in his early sixties, loaded us into his pickup truck and drove to a literal shack with a tin roof and newspa-per insulation where he and his three children slept in one common bed. In Oxnard, California, we stayed with Stan, an obese man whose bratty tween daughters hissed at me through their retainers and kept their sunglasses on indoors. A man in Albuquerque, New Mexico, tried to teach me the harmonica. A scary redneck named Rick, who lived in a San Antonio trailer park, served me milk in glasses with topless Playboy models on them. I named a stuffed rabbit bought at a Greyhound bus station Redding, in honor of the California town we fled at four in the morning. By my tenth birthday, my stuffed animal collection—one toy per man—had grown into a Versailles menagerie of felt ears, cotton bellies, and button eyes.

A disabled man in Atlanta never got us home from the airport. My mother spotted him from the Jetway and, thanks to her habit of never sending photographs of herself, walked right by him, made a U-turn, and headed to a ticket gate saying that we needed to return to Los Angeles because she'd forgotten my insulin.

"Look sick," my mother said. I frowned and sucked in my cheeks.

We had our pick of seats on a boomerang flight back to LA, during which a crew of concerned flight attendants checked up on us throughout, complimenting my mother on how "calm and strong" I seemed.

Whenever a prospective man didn't work out, I nurtured a small, flickering hope that my mother would abandon her cause and choose to remain single; that she would remain mine alone but that we could continue our fantastic journeys together. I loved them. I had elaborate fantasies of a life spent with my mother rail tripping to far-flung American destinations. In my dreams, instead of searching for men, we were stars of our own television show: a mother-and-son detective duo out for adventure, new people to meet, and new stories to collect. Each "manhunt" included a cast of warm ancillary characters: relatives, shopkeepers, waiters and waitresses, bus and cab drivers, Amtrak dining car companions—all of them with intoxicating accents and strange-sounding American hometowns and festive backstories so unique and memorable in our moments together. Then, after a flurry of information exchanged on loose napkins and floating sheets of scrap paper, they were lost and forgotten, like names scrubbed clean from a headstone.

Impermanence was both my mother's ally—"Don't make friends with anyone," she said—and my own fiercest foe. For me, if any man was nice for more than a day, he was a potential father. If a woman smiled and rubbed my head, she could be my mother's new best friend. I couldn't help it. Sometimes neither could my mother. Her compassion and tenderness toward total strangers were a constant surprise. Something about the road, being away from the claustrophobic house and a codependent June, revealed her deeper generosity and stripped away her characteristic fear and disappointment. I'd love to tell you all these strangers' names and stories here, how each one of them was crucial in helping us make a connecting flight or a just-about-to-depart train, or covering a meal in a diner when we were short of cash, or buying me a chocolate bar "for the road," but they're all a jumble of receding faces and closing doors to me now. (Whoever you were, and wherever you all are, I thank you.)

The children were, for me, harder to forget. We met men who'd been set adrift by their younger wives and who were simply too old to keep up with their kids. I saw the loneliness in these children's eyes and imagined them kindred brothers and sisters, siblings that could come home with me and replace my stuffed animal forest. We'd hide away together from my mother when she was angry, and laugh, play, and clutch one another tight in my closet when her thunderous footsteps got too close. These kids, forced to be adults before they were ready, weren't authority figures like Helen. They were just like me, searching in their own fathers for the same thing I had traveled halfway across the country to find. Little kids also ask brave questions: Why was my hair long like a girl's? Did I live in a teepee? How come I didn't wear feathers? My mother ignored these questions or sometimes invented her own answers, but she always left town with the same encouraging words: "We'll be back." Sometimes the men followed up with notes from their kids, who told us in large capital letters that floated like balloons across three-hole-punched paper how much they missed us, asking when they'd see us again. My mother never answered them. She was writing her own letters, too busy singing to me the virtues of a new and coming father to listen to the dreams of children.

4

"You wanna play catch, Son?" Robert asked.

My first live-in stepfather, Robert, took me into the backyard with a baseball and a pair of gloves one smog-crusted afternoon when I was ten years old. Bored with the repetitive play, he roughhoused me atop his shoulders and then hoisted me over the neighbor's fence, dangling me by my ankles above a gully filled with broken glass.

"Say 'Catch'!" he said.

"Catch!" I said.

"I can't hear you!" he said and dropped me down a couple inches. I swayed aloft in midair like a pendulum, the tips of my hair grazing shards of cracked windows, and howled with equal doses of giddy joy and shrieking terror.

"My arm's feeling tired, Son! Say 'Catch'!"

"Catch!" I screamed. "Catch! Catch! Catch!"

I was lifted back over the wall. He handed me my baseball. "Boring game," he said and ran in the house. Robert was a lightning flash: hot, blinding, and gone before the thunder came.

Robert was serving his fifth year of a five-year sentence at Arizona State Prison at Florence when he met my mother through one of her personal ads. He was born on St. George Island, Alaska—his Aleutian name was "Tall Fox"—and sent to the Chilocco Indian School in northern Oklahoma, a boarding school created by an act of Congress aimed at "educating" Indians with a useful trade. When he was sixteen, Robert was expelled from Chilocco for driving over a cop's foot. He graduated to a series of youth authority camps and second-string county jails before arriving at "Arizona State," which is what he called the prison in conversation, as if he were discussing his alma mater.

He appeared late one night in a taxi at our front steps with a canvas duffel bag and the musk of an all-day Greyhound trip. His was a weaselly physique, with cords of stringy shoulder-length hair and a splotchy complexion set off by hollow-point-bullet cheekbones. Sitting at the bottom of our staircase, Robert lit up a tracer fire of Camel cigarettes, tripping into a dry-heave stutter but full of a stand-up comic's confidence.

"I brought something for you, Son," Robert said.

Who is *this man?* I thought. I'd never heard of him before. He made *Son* sound like a punch line. From his tight jeans pockets, he scooped out moist dollops of dollar bills. Money like this, I'd learn, was meant to befriend.

The next morning, Robert moved into our house as my mother's fiancé, having proposed marriage in a letter from prison. They'd known each other maybe two or three months.

"Why not marry?" my mother said. Frank had never asked. Paul had done nothing more than give her his "name." (She was never formally divorced from Candido.)

"We don't have to move anywhere," she said. "Your grandmother doesn't want to be alone."

My grandmother said, "Your mother doesn't want to pay rent somewhere."

I was ten years old when I "gave" my mother away as acting father of the bride in a Baha'i faith marriage ceremony—a religious flirtation that would end as soon as my mother had redeemed her member's discount for the wedding space. Robert wrote several pages of vows, which took him almost a half hour to read.

"O Mighty Grandfather to the North," he said, and gave thanks to the wind that protected his ancestors.

"O Mighty Grandfather to the South," he said, and blessed the clouds that the Great Spirit gave us to nourish Mother Earth. His filial piety extended gratitude to sixteen different grandfathers.

"Oh, mighty grandfather," my grandmother intoned at the wedding dinner, "was that a lot of Indian bullshit." Our celebratory feast was at the Love's Bar-B-Que down the road, the same branch of the restaurant chain where Candido first worked as a busboy.

Robert wasn't a worker. He had a "Let's Spend the Night Together" swagger that young, lean, and confident men use to get away with murder, though he didn't indulge my mother's high bar of outlawness by pretending to be a killer. He was a lover. As in, he loved himself and loved others to love him. He ingratiated himself to strangers with a stutter and a smile and traveled shirt unbuttoned to his waist, flaunting his muscular, jaundiced smoker's skin as a healthy "beachcomber's tan." His maxillary dentures became, in his hands, half of a clown's set of chattering false teeth. "If I forget these at home," he'd say, "I'll just gum my dinner to death!"

Every day, Robert invented his itinerary from scratch. He didn't work a full-time job. Life with us filled his schedule. Before I met him, I thought that men worked reliable hours, being neither seen nor heard, like my grandfather Emilio, or they jealously guarded their "private" time like Frank, who'd show up at our house cranky and tired, close my mother's bedroom door, and then leave fast in the morning. When I needed a father, Robert was there. He was *always* there—at first. It took some getting used to.

I was seduced again and again by watching a man doing "man" things around our house. On a rotating monthly basis, Robert negotiated money from my grandmother for odd job house repairs. I wanted "in." He'd do a two-thousand-dollar roof retarring for five hundred dollars, including essential supplies: cartons of Camels and tall-boy Buds. Off went his plaid western shirt, and up he went on top of the house while I eagerly ferried large purple buckets of roofing tar up a rickety broken ladder. Then I kept his supplies "clean" of insects with endless hours of spraying layers of Raid ant poison that congealed into cold, thick foam that clotted on the ground like fine snow, breathing in the sweet pine-scented clouds of nozzled death until I was dizzy.

In his jeans, with a cigarette dangling from his mouth, swabbing his mop in sloppy athletic circles, he resembled some kind of construction-site cowboy or desert-camp-honed outlaw. He painted our house with haphazard bursts of attention and cheap paint. Robert "repaired" our crumbling gazebo by dismantling it and repurposing the boards into a makeshift fence to hold back mounds of dirt he'd excavated from underneath the house's concrete and wood support pylons in the basement. Who cared if the leaks in the roof got worse or if his plans for a "rec room" were literally undermining the house's very foundation with each shovelful of dirt that I obediently wheelbarrowed into the backyard? This was what a man at work looked like.

There were long "errand" drives into cinder block neighborhoods by the airport to meet "friends" he'd made chatting on his new CB radio. Or beach trips—boardwalk "trick" hustling—where our feet never touched the sand or the ocean. Danger never looks as sexy as when it's young; when it has the blush of not recognizing its own recklessness. Each trip somewhere with Robert—outfitted in ass-tight blue jeans and seventies porn-star frames that covered a third of his ruddy, angular face—had the potential to spiral out of control, but the tensile pulse of a chase scene throbbing underneath lured me out with him anyway.

A good report card once earned me a promise to visit to Golf N' Stuff, a miniature golf complex in Norwalk with go-karts, bumper boats, and a water slide. Instead, we took a long detour to a housing project by the airport with shirtless tattooed men hanging out on street corners. There were security bars and gates on every window and door. (My grandmother added similar ones to our house right around when Robert moved in, which later came to seem like a deeply ironic gesture.)

"Stay in the car," he said. "You'll be safer here."

I locked the car doors behind him, slid down the shotgun seat, and pretended to myself that being motionless made me invisible. He emerged from the house many minutes later with a twitchy, juiced energy—Robert in double time—and a couple large, taped-up boxes that went in the trunk.

We drove home. I stared out the window at the gray expanse of Los Angeles freeway. On a road like this, you were moving somewhere, yet everything appeared identical no matter how far you drove. In the mirrored reflection, I saw Robert and me dueling in tiny Indy style go-karts to see who was the fastest, ramming each other on life preserver–shaped boats on a chlorinated blue lagoon, and knocking Day-Glo-colored golf balls into an oversized windmill. It looked like a great day. There'd be a hundred more days like this, perfect father-and-son moments reflected in a car window I stared out of while I sat in a parking lot in a bleak part of town. I was learning, though, that imagination could always give me the father I wanted when my own imaginary father couldn't.

My mother loved to laugh. She'd forgive anyone of anything if she was laughing. And there were just two men on the planet that could make my mother laugh: Richard Pryor, and Robert. He wasn't a comedian, but it's funny to watch someone try to talk his way out of a lie even when he's caught red-handed. Robert could joke his way out of anything with her. When our beloved German shepherd, Punky, died, Robert said he'd remove the dog himself to bury him "the Indian way" and disappeared for several hours. He returned with a moving story about how he'd put Punky to rest "underneath a spreading cherry blossom tree" and had uttered an ancient Aleutian Indian prayer to Mother Earth.

"Where in the hell is there a cherry blossom tree around here?" my grandmother asked.

The next day, animal control removed Punky's bloated corpse from where it had been dumped in our neighbor's glass-strewn side yard, the same spot Robert had dangled me over the fence a year before. Our street's resident drunk, Mike, cried in the street as a cherry picker crane moved Punky's corpse to a truck.

"I was praying for the Great Spirit to come and soften the truth," Robert said. My mother laughed.

Once, after an all-night drunk, Robert took a long wake-up piss in my mother's garbage can. Robert said, "I didn't want go out there last night and face your grandma's eh-eh-evil eye!" My mother laughed, so I laughed. Then it was my job to empty out the bucket in the toilet, pick his beer cans off the front lawn, and bring him a plate of my grandmother's breakfast. There wasn't time to resent or hate Robert. I was just trying to get through every day without getting yelled at. Anger was a luxury for those without chores. Messes were made, my mother said. Somebody had to clean them up.

"I don't cook, clean, or do windows," she said. "I'm my own woman."

With Robert around, my mother and I were no longer the tight traveling unit we'd been. On a Vegas getaway with Robert, we stayed at the Stardust in a ten-dollar-a-day 1950s "atomic era" bungalow at the rear of the hotel's property, next to the trash dumpsters. My mother said things like, "Not now, Brando," and "I'm talking to Robert." I'd been demoted from being her "little big man" ("a brave Lakota Sioux warrior, like you") to the child I actually *was* but never had to act like before.

Our first day, Robert hit the blackjack tables and by suppertime was up over a couple thousand dollars and climbing. He checked us into a suite as large as the front half of our house, on a high floor with a glittering night view. I stared out into the Vegas night and knew how the hotel got its name. This view, I thought, was what stardust was.

Robert asked my mother to hold on to his money in case his luck changed. Instead of handing it to me for safekeeping, she ordered us several rounds of room service and made reservations for all-day spa and hair salon treatments. The next day, the losing streak hit like a storm front. My mother had spent the money as fast as she could, but what Robert didn't ask for back, he lifted from her purse. Two nights later, we were back in the bungalows with twenty dollars in cash and nonrefundable return bus tickets (bought specifically so they couldn't be exchanged for cash) that wouldn't get us home for another two days.

Robert treated for breakfast at the Westward Ho casino next door with a coupon book offering free donuts and orange juice for break-fast and "hot dogs anytime." He played nickel and penny slots with what money was left, and then disappeared for the day. My mother and I gorged on hot dogs and, when the coupons ran out, salivated over casino prime rib buffet TV commercials.

Robert reappeared an hour before our bus trip. We fed him the cold hot dogs we'd stashed in the dresser drawers to lure him back to LA. When Robert walked back to the bus bathroom deep into our drive through the saltine desert, my mother said conspiratorially, "Look what I have." She reached into her bra and extracted an egg roll of money, hidden the same way she'd done with Paul's.

"Why didn't you buy us some food?" I asked. I hadn't eaten in over twenty-four hours.

My mother was confused. "Because he would have known I had money and taken it from me," she said. "Did you want *that*?"

Once we were home, she and Robert locked themselves behind her bedroom door. The empty fridge glowed a delicate Kool-Aid cherry red from the pitcher inside; my grandmother said Robert had stolen her grocery money.

"He took all the goddamn double coupons too," she added. From then on, she kept her checkbook wallet tethered securely around her neck during the day with an elastic band.

The next morning, Robert rushed outdoors and down the stairs, too fast for me to hitch a ride with him. My mother offered to order a pizza and reached for a small silver buff cloth polishing bag where she kept her money stash—bills with the scent of polish on them. The bag was empty.

"Robert, fucking come here!" my mother shouted to the empty space he'd left behind.

I asked, "What happened? What did Robert do?"

"He's Dad, Brando," my mother said. "*You* call Robert 'Dad.'"

In the meantime, my other in-state "dad," Frank, had vanished. He had reason to stay away. A few months earlier, my mother had asked Robert to break into Frank's house while he was at work. Robert stole a circus-cart-shaped popcorn maker, a Leonard Peltier poster, a "Free Paul Skyhorse–Richard Mohawk" button, a silver Gemini pinky ring, and a cheap watch. These were, in their entirety, every item my mother had given Frank in the course of their three-year relationship. If Frank knew what had happened—and how could he not?—he never pressed charges. But he also didn't come around to see me. My mother offered me up for day trips, but, claiming to respect her marriage, Frank's visits were few and brief. We did go out together once, though, waiting several hours in a parking lot to buy Billy Joel tickets.

"How old are you?" a guy assigning randomly numbered cards asked me. The cards guaranteed your space in line. Frank and I answered together.

"Ten," I said.

"Twelve," Frank said.

I glared at Frank. The guy shrugged his shoulders and gave me a card.

"Why'd you lie?" I asked Frank.

"You have to be twelve to get one of these," Frank said by way of apology. "It's okay to lie if you're not hurting anybody or if you don't want to hurt somebody's feelings."

I hated the thought of him lying, though I didn't mind helping my mother lie or (unknowingly) lying about who I was. I had different standards for Frank. I knew parents lied, but he was more than just a parent. He wasn't the father my mother had chosen for me. Frank was the father *I* was rooting for.

Later I told my mother what happened.

"See, he lies to you the same way he lied to me. You don't need him anyway. You have someone in this house right now ready to be your dad," she said. "Give Robert that chance." Robert, I realized, was a fresh "father" who seemed eager to work and try harder than Frank. After some resistance, I gave Robert his chance. With enough time, I'd give that chance to every man that asked for it. I was a willing son.

Robert soon found out that his new "son" wasn't like most ten-year-old boys. I passed my hours in three solitary places: the backyard, where I chased stray cats; sitting under a rain of jacaranda blossoms on the front stairs with a library book; or playacting inside parts of my cubicle-sized bedless room. In a skinny closet behind a wood-grain vinyl folding door was my recording studio—a Fisher-Price tape recorder—where I replayed *Fraggle Rock* episodes I taped off TV to "watch" later, along with movie excerpts that I interspersed with my own fake commercials and "play-by-play" commentaries of Stomper toy truck races.

On bad days, when my mother veered from playful to angry, that closet became a makeshift bomb shelter. On good days, I'd wait for the all-clear siren of my mother's coyote-yelp laugh and corral a pair of mismatched, peeling dining room chairs to role-play lives different from the ones we lived. It was my mother's game—"make pretend," I called it—for just the two of us, which started after Robert moved in. It was a chance for me to act out stories that kept my mother from being bored, because I knew that her boredom led to arguments. There were roving-reporter monologues outside famous murder trials throughout history; courtroom lawyering scenarios with me in the role of the good-guy prosecutor; and frolics in an enchanted forest where she played a skunk named Sheree, who had the misfortune of falling in love with me, a human. (She killed off Sheree in a forest fire when I tired of the storyline.) I created an anonymous orphan who, in a baby falsetto, answered every question she asked with the word *unknown*.

"Your name?"

"Unknown."

"Your race?"

"Unknown."

"Your father's name?"

"Unknown." (I'd tire of this game too when I realized how close to home I was cutting.)

I took this love of role playing to school, where I had to be cautioned by my teacher for reenacting the Kennedy assassination during charades.

On a long wooden toy bench was the plush zoo that spilled into forests of stuffed animals—my father-hunting trophies—throughout the room. As an extension of our game, my mother gathered teddy bears, sweet-faced tigers, and *Sesame Street* refugees onto her bed, where, in helium-soaked voices, we said the things to each other that we didn't say in our real ones. She told me through a blue-eyed teddy bear named Sunny that she was pregnant with Robert's child and was going to have an abortion.

I squeaked through Redding, my bunny rabbit, "Murderer."

My mother stopped the game. That night, she wrapped up all of my stuffed animals in airtight plastic bags and placed them away on a high shelf. "I'm not playing with you anymore," she said.

"Stop playing faggot games with your mother," Robert said and pushed me outdoors with the neighborhood bullies for street football, rock fort wars, and box sled racing. "Dirt and blood's good for a boy," he said later, examining a deep gash earned on my left ankle, which healed into a patch of permanently hairless scar tissue.

"I need to study," I said. The school had identified me as gifted/talented in early second grade. Math was my weak subject. As a gifted student in an Echo Park elementary school, I had the privilege to leave my classroom in the mornings twice a week to sit around a large set of tables in the school's auditorium with six or seven Asian kids, talk about commercials we saw on television ("Honey Smacks, dig 'em!"), and play board games with missing pieces.

Robert said, "I'm good with numbers."

He helped me tackle four-digit multiplication and long division. When he went out nights alone on "business," I'd wait for him to come back to check my work. If I was lucky, he'd return between midnight to two in the morning. If I wasn't, he'd be gone for two to three days without a phone call, and then reappear without house keys and tell jokes through the security gate until my mother opened the front door with a slap and a kiss.

"You can't keep staying up for me," Robert said before going out one night. "A boy needs his sleep."

"You're the only one here who can do math," I insisted.

"Know why?" Robert asked. "I'm a jailbird. Counting's your life in jail. Gimme the book."

He penciled the solutions in my textbook before he left. I checked my work against his and realized I'd gotten most of the problems wrong. In a delirious late-night panic, I copied Robert's answers and scrubbed them out of my textbook, their faint shadows popping sweat beads on my forehead when I opened the book in class. What would happen if such a big rise in my grades gave me away?

I got a D on my homework. Robert had completed every fourth or fifth problem correctly and made up random answers for the rest.

Never ask a con to help you con someone else. And always learn your lesson. Next time I "checked" my work with a friend over the phone by asking him what he put down for each problem and wrote down all his answers.

I didn't get caught. This was easy! Robert taught me well.

When a kid dared me to break my LCD digital watch, which he'd (accurately) sneered was "cheap and plastic," I smashed it in anger on a tree planter in the school's concrete playground and pinned it on him. The watch had been an honorable-mention prize from a candy drive, earned for "selling" four cases of hard-as-calcium World's Finest Almond Chocolate bars. My mother and grandmother, disappointed with "stingy" local shop owners buying just one or two candy bars and afraid of my traveling in the neighborhood alone, bought over one hundred dollars of candy themselves and stored it Armageddon-style in our freezer. Money was tight enough already from both bimonthly welfare checks and colorful coupon booklets of food stamps, but my grandmother had a perverse sense of pride at being able to "game" the system to try to win the drive. What she hadn't counted on was the mega-choco-capitalists in the upper grades whose parents worked in factories and could sell three hundred chocolate bars in an afternoon.

"Someone just took that watch off your wrist and broke it?" my grandmother asked. "You know how much damn chocolate we still have in the freezer?"

I knew. But I was convinced that, like Robert, I'd get away with it. Then my grandmother burst into my classroom before recess and interrupted my teacher midlecture.

"Why'd you let a kid take my grandson's watch and not punish him?" she shouted. Kids froze in terror, like someone had set off a discipline bomb. "If you won't do anything, hand the boy over to me so I can spank him right here out in the hall!" Mrs. Perkins fire-blanketed my grandmother and then spoke with her quietly for a minute. They looked over at me and laughed. Whenever adults laugh together, a kid knows trouble's coming.

"Can you talk with me and your grandmother a moment?" Mrs. Perkins asked. Then she left me alone with my grandmother.

"Are you a bum like Robert?" she asked. "Don't *ever* lie to me again." Just before she left, she said, "I thought you were a man."

• • •

"Let's skip your grandma's breakfast and get corn dogs at Venice Beach," Robert said. I'd already learned not to go anywhere with Robert without (a) a bus pass, (b) emergency cash, and (c) spare change to call home. I didn't have emergency cash that morning—Robert knew every one of my piggy bank hiding places and had cleaned them out—but I didn't want to stay behind and listen to my mother and grandmother argue. I could be out exploring uncharted worlds with "my" father. Or, at least, a father *figure*.

"Okay," I said.

Robert pied-piper strutted up and down the Venice boardwalk in oversized sunglasses that covered his face, scoping out "bikini babes" and disappearing into men's rooms for minutes at a time.

"When are we getting corn dogs?" I asked.

"I didn't come here to eat!" he said. "All I got is this," he said, and showed me a dime.

"I'm starving," I said, and pocketed the coin.

He picked a clear spot on the boardwalk and approached a stranger. "Can you help me get sha-sha-something to eat for my shun?" he asked. Robert was skilled at conversations when he had time to gauge the gullibility of his mark, but in a cold approach where he needed directness, he was sometimes out of sync. I stood mute by his side like a mangy German shepherd nestled at the feet of a homeless person. In a half hour, he collected four cents. Stuttering panhandlers don't make much money.

On the ride back, two transit cops pulled our bus over a couple miles from home. They stepped hard into the stairwell like they were boarding a boat with contraband. Robert sat at attention. I heard a cop say "sunglasses." Robert threw his shades to the floor and kicked them under the seats.

One cop took the lead, patting his hand upon each seat rest back as he walked up the bus, while the other stood by the front exit doors.

He walked right to our aisle, and then asked Robert to stand up and walk off the bus. I followed. This was my father now, right? You stick by your father.

"Look, I just wanna go home," I said in a cracked voice that made the cop laugh.

We got off the bus, and I sat on the grimy curb as Robert was cuffed against the transit police car. The passengers stared at us from behind the scratched tinted windows, and then grew bored and were driven away. The cops ran his name and found an outstanding warrant. An LAPD car arrived and Robert was handcuffed. He made a futile gesture to ask one of the cops to "give his sha-sha-shun" a ride home, but cops ignore men in handcuffs. Nobody spoke to me, so I walked down the street to find a pay phone. The cops drove Robert off.

With Robert's dime, I called my house from a pay phone a block away.

"I think I can walk home," I said. "But it's really far." Two miles on Sunset Boulevard was about an hour's walk, which could have been Mount Everest to a Los Angeles boy, even one raised without a car.

"I'll come get you," my grandmother said.

When my grandmother arrived, she found me crouched in a ball near a parking lot dumpster. I was curled up trying to stop myself from going to the bathroom in my pants, but my grandmother thought I was cowering in fear and I didn't correct her. We got into Mike's car, the drunk from across the street. He had a beer in a brown bag between his legs and drove us home with a surprisingly steady hand.

"You doing okay?" Mike asked, and took a swig.

"Forget okay," my grandmother answered for me. "Brando, why in the hell did you get off the goddamn bus?"

"You won't believe what they pulled me in for," Robert said when my mother bailed him out.

"What did they—" I asked.

"Uh-uh-uhn-believable," he stammered, cutting me off. Robert never talked about what got him in trouble. He'd only talk about what he'd do *after* he got in trouble.

"Let me make it up to you," Robert told me. "Disneyland?"

Somehow Robert acquired a car—there's not enough evidence in my memory to use the word *bought*—and he, my mother, and I headed to Disneyland. I'd gone over a dozen times with my grandmother, though she hated the place. "I like roller coasters, not baby rides," she said. My grandmother couldn't drive and hated cars but could plot out a bus route from Echo Park to anywhere in the Southland. She and I would catch the Disneyland special on skid row, a block away from the Greyhound bus station on Sixth and Los Angeles Streets. We waded through bum fights, ignoring harassers or harassing them back. "What kind of man begs an old woman for spare change?" she'd shout. Later, as the park was closing, she'd get us to the last bus out, parked outside the tall hedge walls, and then ask the bus drivers to inch up the curb until we had a good view of the closing fireworks.

At Disneyland with Robert and my mother, I felt I was part of a real American family, like one of the dozens of grumpy, nagging trios slogging around the park. How happy they must be elsewhere when they're not at the Happiest Place on Earth! I led Robert to the Tinker Bell Toy Shop underneath Sleeping Beauty Castle so he could "make it up" to me by adding to my stuffed animal collection. The shop was a maze of Eeyores, Tiggers, and Winnie the Poohs that frolicked throughout in soft mounds. Atop an open, dramatically lit platform sat a monstrous five-foot-tall Mickey Mouse. Robert picked up a doll here, a Donald Duck there, weighing them in his hands as if they were loaves of fresh bread. He bought me nothing. I went outside with my mother to sulk.

Imagine that first burst of delight, then, when Robert emerged carrying the enormous Mickey Mouse itself, a stuffed animal that weighed as much as I did. Was this really mine? For a stuffed animal menagerie, here was the Hemingway trophy kill of a lifetime!

Tourists gawked, pointed, smiled. I had a minute of happiness before a knotting fear plunked in my stomach. *Where did he get the money to buy this?* On the other side of Sleeping Beauty's Castle, a Japanese couple asked if they could take their picture with Mickey. They posed with him on the guardrail next to the castle moat. Robert charged them five dollars and then carried Mickey up to the railing that surrounded the grotty moat surrounding the castle and pushed him in. I was heartbroken as Mickey—snout up, arms spread— drifted under the drawbridge upriver, like a gangland corpse.

"Quit standing around," he said, and took my hand. "We're leaving."

Robert quickened his pace as we pushed our way through the oncoming crowds on Main Street, U.S.A. to the exits. Why were we walking so fast?

We were almost at the railroad bridge where you cross back into "the real world" when three men in ties, business suits, and dark sun-glasses—*Men in Black* ringers—materialized and shoved the three of us down a side pathway to a bungalow office with the words *Disn-eyland Police* stenciled on a window. My mother and Robert were brought into the office, and a door was closed in front of me. I was left alone, outside, again.

Where, I wondered, was the kindly Disneyland police officer with a coloring book or a piece of candy? Weren't we at the Happiest Place on Earth? Of course, I realize now what I didn't as a child: we were "backstage." Backstage didn't have to be happy.

Robert signed statements agreeing that in exchange for never returning to Disneyland, no charges would be pressed. My mother was already crafting how the tale could be less "boring" in its retell-ing. In her version, someone in a Goofy costume busted us by doing a somersault to entertain a group of children and pushed us into the suits.

Years later, on the night of my high school graduation, I returned to the Tinker Bell Toy Shop. Seated on the same platform was an identical oversized stuffed Mickey Mouse, now ensconced in a Plexiglas cube and tethered by his neck and belly to a post. I rapped on the glass and, filled with a bizarre storyteller's pride, wanted to tell someone, "One of my dads did this." But how could anyone with just one father have understood?

First, the Christmas tree flew through the air. Not much of a tree, more of a long upright branch on a cross of wood, really, with bits of puffed tin for decoration. Then the decorations followed, one at a time: shiny Charlie Brown and Snoopy orbs, plastic Jesus-in-manger scenes, and, on a string from my kindergarten art class, a brittle clay handprint that cracked into large clumps.

"He's not coming back!" my mother screamed. "Are you satisfied? *Are you satisfied?!?*"

Of course, my grandmother wasn't satisfied, because he *was* coming back. My mother always let him back in the house. In the year and a half he'd been with us as a father and husband, Robert had been arrested six or seven times, for everything from drunk-and-disorderly, to petty fraud, to driving on the highway wearing an oversized pair of radio headphones, and had slept with a handful of women in Echo Park, including the ex-wife of a neighbor. He bought himself a pinky ring and a watch on my mother's in-store account at a jewelry store, and then hocked them. He shoplifted from the neighborhood supermarket and racked up hundreds of dollars of Levi's on my grandmother's script account with a local clothing store, and then sold the jeans on the street.

He stole several thousand dollars in rare gold Krugerrand coins from my grandmother's bedroom. "*Brando's college education!*" she screamed, but didn't report the crime. In a weird defense, Robert insisted that, by his count, what he stole was worth closer to several hundred dollars, not thousands.

"I wouldn't rob you out of your school," he said. "If there had been that much there, you think I'd have come back?"

At one point, two burly muscle men with long hair from the Indian center on skid row came to "talk" with Robert about the van he borrowed to drive his "dead mother" back to the reservation. The stripped and burned-out van was found a few days later abandoned on I-5. Robert was lucky that Indians didn't talk to cops and luckier still they never returned.

Robert joined Alcoholics Anonymous, winning people over with his mostly true tales of inebriation, sobriety, and redemption. On receiving his white six-months-sober chip, he gave a thrilling keynote "hitting rock bottom" qualification/testimony to a large assembly of San Fernando Valley AA groups. He spoke with compassion and energy, without stuttering, and got a standing ovation. Robert let me bang the gavel that brought people back from the midsession break. Later someone discovered a significant short count in the collection plates. Robert wasn't arrested because his sponsor Mitch believed in second chances. Robert repaid him by cleaning out his wallet too.

There were at least three active warrants for his arrest. Police detectives brandishing good manners and crisp business cards were regulars on our front porch, asking for Robert and for his aliases too: my absent uncle Oscar, my poor dead grandfather Emilio, Frank.

None of this mattered to my mother. No one ever turned him in.

"I'm not a snitch," my grandmother said. "I hate Robert. But I hate pigs more."

If Robert's sloppiness with the law meant he was getting restless, I was growing bored with my "father" too. I'd visited him three times so far in his stints at the "Glass House." Located in the junkyard sheet metal badlands of downtown LA, the local metro jail wasn't, to my disappointment, a see-through house but had earned its nickname just because it had big windows. Trips to jail were like navigating the school cafeteria, following colored lines on the floor that snaked you here, then there, and then here again, with just as many loud and unruly kids.

"Mind your mother," Robert said. *You're in* jail, I thought.

"Okay, Robert," I said. I'd dropped the "Dad." Neither he nor my mother noticed.

Robert always got out, eventually. We celebrated at Chuck E. Cheese's—*Where a kid can be a kid!* A costumed "Chuck" asked us to leave when Robert was caught stealing rolls of game tokens from other children to keep me playing arcade games.

"Robert's always getting busted by rats, isn't he?" my mother said when we got home. "First, Mickey Mouse, now Chuck E. Cheese!"

"I think both of them are mice," I said.

"God, you're no fun. How'd you get to be my son, anyway?"

For my tenth birthday, Robert drove me to a regular hangout of his, the Hollywood Fun Center on Hollywood Boulevard and North Western Avenue, an all but abandoned husk by the early 1980s, like the rest of the neighborhood. The "Fun Center" was a half-block-long series of dim, smoky arcades that the writer Charles Bukowski described in the documentary *The Charles Bukowski Tapes* as a place where "there used to be cement benches out front and all the insane people would sit there . . . The street people they'd talk to each other all day long." In the street fronts near the arcades, "they used to have women that'd sit in the windows, [and] you could say, 'I want you.'" Across the street was the Le Sex Shoppe porn store, and halfway up the block on Western was Pioneer Chicken, which was "open all night [and] lots of hookers [would] go up there late at night, guys, thieves, murderers, get a late snack at three thirty a.m., get a little bite of something after they've rolled somebody." When Buk talked about these places, you could hear the love in his voice for the "dirty action" and the people like Robert whose sordidness made Bukowski feel alive.

Robert parked next to the transient hotel known as the La Paula Apartments, the first place in Los Angeles where a slumlord was sentenced to house arrest in his own decrepit property. Then Robert dashed into the arcades, giving me quarters that I was swiftly hustled out of by older kids with matted hair and taut skin.

I asked him for more money. "All out," he said, and gave me a money holder birthday card my grandmother's TV repairman friend had sent me. The cash was missing.

"I took you to the arcade with that money!" he said. "But let's stick around awhile."

I wandered the arcade in hopeful circles, and then sat on a bench outside and watched city buses come and go, imagining they were airplanes I could board for distant lands. When I came back in, I couldn't find Robert. It felt like a hide-and-seek prank at first. Was he playing video games? No. At the air hockey tables? Not there. Maybe in the adjacent pool hall? Nope. The men's room was the last place to check. "Don't use them because of chicken hawks," Robert had warned me. *Chicken hawks?* Did he mean that small brown bird that tries to eat Foghorn Leghorn in the old Warner Bros. cartoons? In the bathroom, old men loitered by the stalls, smoking cigarettes. The smoke and eye-stinging piss smell drove me out.

I drifted like scrap paper back to Robert's car. A habitual thief himself, he nonetheless trusted others and never locked doors. I crouched down in the backseat under beach towel seat covers, counting down from large numbers until his return.

He could have been gone ten minutes or four hours—my kid's concept of time was little help—but when Robert returned, he started up the car and took it out of park, ready to drive off, before he saw me cowering in back.

"Hey, there you are!" he said. "Why are you hiding, Son?"

Robert lived with us for almost two years. On the day that he left for good, he spent most of that final morning doing household chores— something that should have aroused immediate suspicion. When he had finished waxing the kitchen floor, he placed the mop handle in the kitchen doorway like a barricade. He shouted to my mother not to walk across the floor.

"I don't want you to break your pretty little head!" he said.

In the bathroom, he padded himself down with soap bars and rolls of toilet paper (he'd already pocketed my mother's emergency cash), went through the back door, jumped a short chain-link fence on the side of the house, and ran down the street.

Robert was gone. What I'd come to call "daddy gone." Not "running from the cops at the front door" gone or "out for three days God knows where" gone. Gone for good. It hit my mother fast how love crazy she'd been. "What the hell was I thinking?" my mother said, shedding her two-year marriage like dead skin. She and my grandmother hugged and cackled at life together again like drinking buddies reunited after a long sobriety. To celebrate, she bought herself velvet hats and Victorian-style dresses and dabbed on her neck hand-blended fragrances she'd sent my grandmother and me to buy at the Mlle. Antoinette's Parfumerie in Disneyland's New Orleans Square. My mother became *my mother* again. We did word search puzzles together; she was brilliant at finding the words, no matter how hidden, snaking, or contorted they were. She'd come into my room and say, "Let's see who can play their stereo the loudest!" Or she'd take the last Shake 'N Bake pork chop off my plate and run while I chased her through the living room.

Then, inevitably, a quiet moment would pounce on her; a ghost whispering in her ear, "You will always be alone." She'd open the shutters to her security-gated window and let a cool breeze swish around the potpourri-scented air in that small bedroom wallpapered with Laura Ashley vertical stripes.

"Bars on the windows and the walls," she'd say.

The cycle began anew: personal ads were reinserted into magazines (or had never been withdrawn), and any trace of Robert was expunged. Pictures were ripped in half, letters crumpled and trashed. I learned, starting with Robert, that when a "father" left, he was never to be discussed again. Between fathers, my "father" didn't exist.

Except that he did exist, inside me, hidden from my mother. Robert hadn't been much of a father. He wasn't even *my* father. But Robert was proof that I *could* have a father every day and—when he remembered to come home—every night, and not just have a father in a letter or on a random Saturday every three or four months. What Robert took with him when he left was the small piece of me that wanted to be a man's son. With each successive father, that piece was regenerated, much larger than before, emerging each time with a tougher casing, a more cynical skin, buried deeper to guarantee its security, though nothing I did kept it safe for good.

Robert was scrubbed so cleanly from our lives, it's a miracle I have one photo left: a Polaroid of him sitting with my mother on her bed. I took the picture, shooting him as if he's slid into the photo for a moment before slipping back out again. My mother and Robert held the picture together as it developed, thrilled to see themselves appearing in seconds. They both hated things that took time.

One Saturday morning, not long after Robert left, my grandmother called to me from the backyard, where she stood in one of her signature extra large impressionist patterned caftans, leaning on my aluminum baseball bat for support, wearing a too-big Dodgers baseball cap, with a catcher's mitt and a softball by her feet. She must have been sixty-four. I hadn't touched my baseball since the game of catch with Robert where I ended up dangling over the neighbor's wall.

"Let's play ball," she said.

I should've hugged my grandmother and said, "Batter up!" Pitched her a ball or two.

Instead, I said, "I don't feel like playing," and went to my room.

Later, when the shame hit me, I peeked through the back door window to see that she was still out there, staring at the backyard, bat leaned against the wall. She sat on one of the concrete planters, but a trick of the sun gave her a silhouette of a much younger woman standing tall.

5

"It was your idea, Brando," my mother said, "for me to become a phone sex operator."

My mother, grandmother, and I were together watching television in the living room. This was before my mother and I had separate TVs in our own rooms: three televisions for three people who couldn't share.

On that day's *Donahue*: "Phone sex operators!" Women who have explicit sexual conversations with men for money. A black silhouette with crescent rolls of vertiginous hair spoke in a digitally graveled voice about the virtues of the job: working from home, lots of tax-free income, power over men.

I turned to my mother and said, "You could do that."

How had I, at ten years old, become my mother's pimp? She leapt from what she called "straight jobs" to sex worker because she felt victimized by a series of menial office jobs, the last of which was at a recruiting office: the ironically named Manpower, where she worked as a headhunter. She "quit" when she was cheated out of a large commission (or, to translate into what she'd call "white man's words," fired for insubordination). There were few work options left to a two-year community college graduate, an amateur unemployed paralegal (via a mail-order diploma course), and a Marinello Schools of Beauty dropout (too many fights with her customers).

Brando Skyhorse

She replied to a tiny box ad soliciting "adult phone actresses" for a company called Inside Moves in Pacific Palisades. It operated like a taxi service. A client called asking for a woman with particular attributes—tall, voluptuous, redhead—and gave his credit card and callback number to a dispatcher or screener. She'd then contact one of the operators, or girls "on call," and give her the client's requests. The girl then called the client collect at the number he (almost always a "he") had provided. When the call was over, the screener would charge the client's credit card based on how many minutes the call had lasted. The girl earned a percentage based on how many minutes were billed; the longer she kept the client on the phone, the more money both she and her company made.

My mother gave an alias for her payroll check. Over the more than ten years that she'd work in the business, she'd cycle through new billing names for a host of reasons: marriage, switching companies, remarriage, eluding obsessive clients, re-remarriage. She accumulated a deck of bad fake IDs to cash checks with no payroll taxes deducted that erased any trace of her Mexican ancestry and spliced together her two fake Indian names: Running Deer Skyhorse, Maria Running Skyhorse, Maria Running Deer, Mia Skyhorse. ("Mia" was a favorite alias.) She fanned them out like a deck of cards.

"I can be anyone I want," she said.

It wasn't easy at first. My mother vomited after her first several phone calls. Then she got the hang of it. After several calls experimenting with various names, ethnicities, and gradations in voice, a clear winner emerged. My mother became "Cara Lee," a twenty-three-year-old Irish grad student from Chicago.

"Straight" sex calls (missionary, no kink) were simple; rape/incest/molestation calls, the toughest, though she could do a convincing mimic of an eight-year-old girl. "Gimme a wowwy-pop," she'd say at the kitchen table to make me laugh, though I knew without understanding that she was never this chaste on the phone. "Golden" and "brown" shower calls (her explanations were useful verbal ammunition for the coming leap to junior high) made her laugh; domination calls were her favorite because they didn't involve graphic sex.

On an ever-expanding Rolodex, she kept a card for every man she spoke to, noting the date and length of each call, where he lived, when his birthday was, his children's names, and whether he liked to imagine Cara Lee—that is, my mother—in black stockings or red lace panties or crotchless. She listened to their insecurities, celebrated their triumphs, commiserated with them over life's disappointments, and acknowledged with handwritten thank-you notes their gifts of flowers, chocolates, and classical music sent to her call center. Her calls could last anywhere from ten minutes ("Get them *off*, then get them *off*") to marathon six-hour therapy sessions, but her therapeutic duties were always second to arousing her clients. My mother scoured pornographic magazines for sexual scenario ideas but was too embarrassed and too tethered to her telephone to buy them. So she sent my grandmother to the neighborhood stand on the corner of Sunset and Echo Park Avenue.

"*Hola,* how are you, Julio?" my grandmother would say.

"*Como estas, abuelita*? Everything good?"

"*Bien, bien*, busy, busy. What you got today?" she'd ask.

"Got the new *Penthouse Forum* you wanted," Julio said, all business. (My mother got her best ideas from *Forums*.)

"How about . . ." my grandmother said, putting on her bifocal reading glasses and looking at a list, "*Juggs* and *High Society*?"

"Next week."

"Then give me the *Forum*, a *Reader's Digest*, and an *Ellery Queen*. I need my mysteries," my grandmother said. "Oh, don't forget the new *Hustler*."

The money my mother earned was good for the early 1980s; up to six hundred tax-free dollars a week, not including her welfare checks and food stamps. With our new fortunes came a cornucopia of constipating middle-class "American" comforts: Hamburger Helper, Spam, Hormel chili, Shake 'N Bake chicken, Hungry-Man frozen dinners. We bought a microwave the size of an air conditioner and a popcorn popper that roared like a military hair dryer. Out with the Kool-Aid, in with Capri Sun and Sunny Delight. Cans, seared foil, and poked-through cellophane replaced fruit rinds and empty flour sacks in our garbage. We graduated from government cheese to Velveeta. I drank whole milk by the gallon and ate so much bacon I broke out in hives.

My mother had packed up my stuffed animals long ago, but now our playacting games moved to the telephone. She read reviews in *Los Angeles* magazine of expensive restaurants in Beverly Hills and West Hollywood where it was impossible to get reservations.

"Do you think you can get us a table?" my mother asked. "Here's the phone. Call them and let's see!"

Maître d's that scoffed at my mother's name softened when they heard mine. We celebrated a nine-thirty table at Spago, party of two, by ordering a pepperoni pizza from the local joint down the block.

My mother had a strict policy at first that I never enter her locked room while she was "on call," but with her home all day, I gravitated toward her like a satellite. Over time the membrane of my mother's closed door became porous, and I could gauge when to leave a tray of food by her closed door or whether I could creep into her bedroom to lay out dinner on her bed. Ever the improviser, she'd wink and smile over how boring a call was or would pantomime a funny second performance for me. One time I brought a salad in a large stainless-steel bowl, and she told her client that she was going to "make a salad in his asshole." ("Tossing salads," anyone?) Then she had me stir the leafy contents for her, making sure the fork scraped hard against the metallic rim. Other times she asked me to slap my palms together to lend flesh-slapping effects to a character she'd created called "the Pampers man," a grown man she kept in her house on a chain who liked to be spanked and diapered.

None of this felt inappropriate to me. We were like two children playing a practical joke on an unsuspecting adult. Perhaps on his end of the phone, he was looking at one of the special advertisement cards Inside Moves had printed up to promote my mother's popular fictional creation. On the card, "Cara Lee" had pouty, deep sea-green eyes, helium lips, ice-pick-sharp cheekbones, 36-24-36 measurements, and curly shoulder-length brunette hair, and wore striped V-cut panties with a tight T-shirt clasped into a sexy knot around her taut belly. In red letters on the shirt: "I am the woman your mother warned you about."

But what if this woman *was* your mother?

Her cushy "working from home" job soon exacted a physical toll from long periods of sedentary activity. Hours were spent on the phone lying in bed or roaming around her eight-by-eight room like a shark in a cramped tank. She had major headaches and in several months added sixty pounds onto her five-foot-three frame. Her voice grew hoarse, her neck and shoulder muscles developed curlicue kinks, her ears chapped until they flaked. She never left the house, not even to collect the mail. For years my mother and I had traveled the country together, as partners, as friends, as adoring son and adventurous, carefree mother. Our backdrops had been stolen glances of pulsing deep-hued skies, open green pastures, and distant craggy mountains. Now I had a maid's-eye view of her bedroom, clearing her food trays while she made two-minute sprints to the bathroom.

I negotiated stacks of glossy office supply catalogues and phone company brochures searching for the right combination of materials for her work space, including padded-ear handsets to ease strain and a pager for her to report back to her house on the rare days she actually went anywhere. One time my mother was attending a friend's AA testimonial at a regional chapter meeting when her pager went off. We made our exit through a sea of murmurs and speculation: "She must be a doctor."

We added a separate phone line when a homework call with my friend cost her a client.

"Call up my boss and fucking apologize to her now!" my mother screamed.

Her boss, hearing me cry, said, "School always comes first, okay? Hey, do you like roller coasters? I belong to a roller-coaster-enthusiast society. Would you like to go to Magic Mountain?"

The boss's phone voice conjured a picture of a giant, statuesque blonde in a tailored business suit; television supplied the only template I had for white women. When she honked her horn, I found at the bottom of our stairs a sweet, frumpy middle-aged woman with stringy, overcooked spaghetti hair named Janet. My mother refused to meet her, insisting you never meet anyone "face-to-face in the business," so I rode off to spend the entire day at an amusement park with a complete stranger who ran a phone sex business.

Janet and I rode coasters and ate corn dogs. I told her my favorite musician was Phil Collins and bragged about the most outlaw thing on my resume: copying friends' computer games onto five-and-a-quarter-inch floppies. I liked Janet but imagined her—my mother's boss—less as a replacement mom and more of an adult whose conversational world I could now navigate with ease. Wasn't that what my mother was doing, anyway, having "adult" conversations?

My mother was growing bored with just talking for money. "Mistress Cara" had become her most popular creation, so she briefly entertained the idea of becoming an actual spanking flesh-and-blood dominatrix. She placed a newspaper ad in the *LA Weekly* but was disgusted by most of the responses.

In a strange coincidence (which in my family is saying *a lot*), a former high school acquaintance named Jerry was one of the men who answered her ad. She set up her only dominatrix meeting with him at our house and had me write out a list of "slave" instructions because my handwriting was more legible than hers. It was a shopping wish list with capital letters, exclamation points, and four-letter words.

"You Are to Buy Me a Bra and Pantie Set You Fucking Worthless Piece of Shit!" I wrote, and then added, "And a Book for My Son of His Choice!"

To insure that he followed her directions, she made Jerry take me shopping with him. She envisioned cachets of money folded into scented envelopes and fancy silk lingerie from Beverly Hills. Instead, Jerry drove his ten-year-old slave chaperone to the garment district downtown and bought bustiers wrapped tight in plastic like kites for seven dollars each. Whenever he checked his side mirror, I thought he was looking at me and smiled.

Jerry's "slave day" consisted of nothing more than buying my mother secondhand lingerie and stealing a passionate kiss from her by the front door before he disappeared. I didn't know he'd vanish, so that afternoon I pretended what kind of dad Jerry would be. With a little work, I could imagine any man—even my mother's dominatrix slave for a day—as my father.

"I hate what she says on that phone," my grandmother said. "You shouldn't be standing around here listening to her. Get dressed. We're going out."

In an Echo Park where drugs or gangs were a routine milestone for children in sixth grade, my grandmother inoculated me with a third option: stories. Musicals, plays, movies, books—whatever could take me away from the neighborhood for a couple hours. What other indulgence was there for a curious boy in a dicey part of town? Gangs? They didn't notice me. Drugs? They never came my way. Booze? It didn't interest me. Girls? See: gangs and drugs.

My grandmother and I saw eight to ten movies a month. *Every-where*. We toured the glorious movie palaces downtown that my grandmother had gone to as a girl. On Hollywood Boulevard, a reliable stream of druggies, hookers, pimps, and johns flowed both outside and inside the theaters, staying out of our way. We went to

Glendale, a suburban haven home to the Glendale Galleria mall and a bucolic main drag of shops, restaurants, and movie theaters called Brand Boulevard.

"So many white people here," she said. "Behave."

I watched as many R-rated movies as G-rated ones, back when ticket sellers actually said things like, "Ma'am, are you *sure* you want your grandchild to see this movie?" We saw the T&A-drenched animated movie *Heavy Metal* and then held court in the lobby after the show with a group of prototypical comic-book geeks who wanted to know how I'd ended up with such a cool grandmother. I knew they were right; she *was* cool, for a grandmother. She just wasn't a father.

There were so many movie dates, I began keeping track, writing movie reviews on the bus ride back home in pencil on notebook paper, complete with crooked check boxes, a line for an overall score, and ample space for thoughtful analysis:

"I really liked this movie! Too bad everybody died in the end." (Commentary on *Scarface*.)

If we weren't watching movies, we were reading—books, magazines, newspapers, comic strips—or making plans to read. We were regulars at the Central Library downtown. The towering corridors and bathrooms of this public landmark were as rough and urine soaked as the streets of 1970s New York; once, my grandmother was almost attacked by a homeless man in the ladies' room.

"I don't like this place," I said.

"Those bad people don't belong here. This is *our* library. We come here so you can understand the value of a book," my grandmother said. "If anyone tries to 'touch' you, slap them hard with your book."

When my mother's phone sex money began rolling in, trips to bookstores replaced the library. There were no bookstores in Echo Park, meaning we had to ride the bus a half hour down Sunset Boulevard to the Crown Books on Sunset near Fountain Avenue, or ride forty-five minutes to Glendale. My grandmother insisted I start my own personal library and left me responsible for my own purchases.

It was just as important that I owned books as well as borrowed them. My first book was *A Few Minutes with Andy Rooney*. I bought it because his segments on *60 Minutes* made my grandmother laugh. I understood the words, but it took me much longer to understand what they meant lined up together.

When homework was done, I'd read books to her aloud. My favorites were the *Peanuts* strips. I read each panel and voiced each character differently except Snoopy, whom I gave my own voice. I wanted to be Snoopy because, just by imagining it, he could turn into anyone. One week he was a World War I flying ace, the next, a world-famous novelist. What power! What freedom!

"You can't be a dog," my grandmother said. "You're more like Charlie Brown." Whenever I held open a door for a lady or helped carry her groceries upstairs, she'd say, "You're a good man, Charlie Brown." I *hated* that.

"He's a loser! I don't wanna be him!"

"No, he always does the right thing. He's a good man. Just like you're gonna be. You're a good man, Charlie Brown," my grandmother said again.

The money for these trips with my grandmother came, of course, from my mother. I didn't understand this then. My mother knew I didn't understand this and hated it. Arguments between the two women raising me were a steady rain, which was building in intensity to a horrific downpour. The closed door between my mother and the rest of the world was like a dam. When it would open in an air-grabbing *whoosh!* I never knew whether what poured out of her room would lift me up to higher ground or drown me.

Between the welfare checks and the phone sex money, my mother's finances were robust. There were token rent and utility payments to my grandmother, but the majority of my mother's money went to her silver buff polish bag "savings" account in her bedroom, a mythical "cash stash" that, with Robert gone, she claimed she would nurture monthly and that would be my inheritance when she passed. The rest went either to my grandmother to spend on me or to my allowance. At the height of her phone sex earnings, I received eighty dollars a month, an absurd amount for an eleven-year-old to spend on himself. Yet I did find a way to spend it. I loaded up on an Intellivision game system that consumed a steady diet of forty- and fifty-dollar cartridges, dozens of Matchbox toy cars, and a gaudy, overpriced Lazer Tag setup—complete with separately sold vests—without realizing that the game required two people to play. When I tried it with a friend indoors (the toys were too fragile and too expensive to be played outside), we ran around the house in pointless circles shooting each other, a boring riff not unlike the one my mother and grandmother acted out daily.

Since my mother's shopping trips were rare, part of being paid such a hefty allowance meant that I'd use a portion of that money to buy "gifts" to give back to her. Some of her wants were simple. Mom's favorite perfume was Tabu, a fragrance I couldn't find in a single department store but that appeared in tall display stacks at the local Thrifty, a drugstore discount chain. (On an old David Letterman clip, Cher said Tabu was a favorite, as it's a smell "good girls don't wear.")

When the department store Buffums announced a pilot program to issue children twelve and older credit cards, my mother falsified my age and signed on as my enthusiastic guarantor despite having no credit history herself. I roamed the creaking belle of a department store, browsing the "gold-inlaid dusting powder set," maxing out my two-hundred-dollar limit in an hour on oversized sunhats, sunglasses, and a jewelry chest in which my mother could store tarnished silver bracelets, turquoise pendants, and cherished boxes of mounted rock collections purchased from the Ghost Town souvenir shops at the Knott's Berry Farm amusement park.

"Rocks stay put and don't talk back like you," she'd say.

What she couldn't send me out to buy she ordered from catalogues and television: a steady column of exercise records, videotapes, and equipment. My mother exercised alone in her bedroom-slash-office, and nowhere else. Through her closed door, *Jane Fonda's Workout Record* played on repeat. The Jackson 5's "Can You Feel It" was over-dubbed with Fonda's direct, never-short-on-breath orders on how to warm up (my mother often didn't get further than that): "*Can you feel it?*—Stomach pulled in, buttocks tight—*Can you feel it*—Really *stretch* it out—*Can you feel it?*—Go for the burn!" She replaced Jane Fonda's album with Jane Fonda's *Workout* video, which was replaced by *Jane Fonda's Workout Challenge*, *Jane Fonda's New Workout*, and Jane Fonda's *Complete Workout*. Then an endless march of UPS deliveries: stationary bicycles, and treadmills, bouncing balls, and rubber bands, step boxes and trampolines, wrist weights, baby barbells, slant boards, and jump ropes. My mother sweated to the oldies, stopped the insanity, and shuffled herself countless losing hands of Deal-a-Meal portion-control cards. She did everything but lose weight.

This was not the first time her body had betrayed her. Because of the blood poisoning scare she'd suffered as a child, she was convinced the remnants of her infection had created an inoperable brain tumor that was the cause of her severe headaches. She'd give us updates on the tumor as if it were an old friend visiting from out of town.

"It's back! I can *feel* it taking up room!" she'd say.

There were other routines. The first and the fifteenth of every month were welfare check days. She didn't need the money—she had plenty from her job—but felt it belonged to her and would hit a hyperbolic panic if she didn't get it *on time*. I was my mother's shakedown man. If I was home from school, I met the mailman at the curb, scanned the mail quickly, and, if the check wasn't there, ask him if he'd "forgotten anything else." If I didn't, I'd be the one that got shook down when I walked through the front door:

"Did the check come?"

"Did you ask the mailman if he had any more mail for us?"

"How did you ask him?"

"You mean you just asked him if he had any more mail and didn't ask specifically if he had a check?"

"What do you mean, he said, 'No, not today'?"

"Are you lying about asking him?"

"Don't you fucking know how to ask questions?"

If I was lucky enough that it wasn't a gray-envelope day—an official summons for my mother to appear with paperwork before a caseworker under penalty of funds being cut off—we'd go to Pioneer Market to cash her check. Hating purses, she trusted her cleavage or the lining of special "welfare check boots" she wore just on the first and the fifteenth.

The money-starved recipients, both legitimate and criminal, swirled together with frustrated, menacing patience in slithering lines, their checks and the just-ripped envelopes that contained them held in balled fists. Hustlers and thieves trolled the aisles to harass, snatch, pickpocket, knock down, and beat up those with the longest string of kids behind them; like the largest of Spanish treasure galleons carrying the most plundered loot, the largest families were sure to have the biggest checks. The thick, caked-on stench of processed sugar and an embalmed scent of fresh bread mingled with the smells of graying meat and spoiled fruit waxed to a purchasable shine. The checkout line belts were loaded with cellophane-wrapped junk that didn't need heat, refrigeration, or a rush to prepare and was exchanged for bright food stamp coupons ripped from what looked like a Disneyland ticket book. (A food stamp "E-ticket" was a coupon worth fifty dollars.) Other families buying a healthy cornucopia of foods played a different game, calculating with each swipe of the cashier's scanner what the total bill would be and would they have enough cash to cover it. Math was a mystery to me everywhere except in the checkout line, where I learned how to guesstimate a shopping cart's contents to within a couple dollars, a trick that my mother and grandmother came to depend on.

When my mother took the check out for the store's endorsement, she slipped it into a sweater's decorative slit pocket instead of asking me to hold it, forgetting that the pocket didn't have a bottom. The check must have fallen somewhere in the hair products aisle; she hadn't gone to any other part of the store.

In the checkout line, my mother asked me for the check. I told her she'd never given it to me. She patted her sides in panic. I cradled a box of Ding Dongs in my arms as if protecting a baby. I realized the check was long gone, long cashed, perhaps at the "No I.D." check cashing place with bulletproof glass dividers a block away. My mother's voice dropped fast. Like a falling barometer, it warned me that an enormous storm was coming. What could I do to stop it?

Panicked, I asked, "Should I put back the Ding Dongs?"

She slapped the snack box on the conveyer belt and then left the store, walking home several lengths ahead of me without saying a word. Seeing us on the street, you'd never have known we were mother and son.

"Can you believe how fucking useless he is?" my mother said, tagging my grandmother like a wrestling match.

"Should you *put back the Ding Dongs*?" my grandmother said. I fake smiled at her laugh. "Good thing you have us to take care of you. You wouldn't last a day on the streets!"

"He only thinks of himself," my mother said. Her anger always rendered me in third person. "How can a smart kid be so fucking stupid?"

My mother had to get a replacement check. She called a cab—she refused to travel to the welfare office any other way—and I heard the familiar stomp, slam, and loud cuss-talking to herself in her room as she changed outfits to leave the house.

I met her at the front door in tears and reached out to her. Hidden behind an almost clown-sized pair of sunglasses, she put her hand on my chest, gave it one swift, firm push—like closing a stubborn drawer—and then slammed the front door.

There would be ten thousand more afternoons where my mother

bellowed in anger, escalating in fury until she'd ransack her room to pack an oversized burgundy suitcase to nowhere, screaming, "Your father got to leave you! Why can't I?"

She had a point, one that through repeated use would dull my love for my mother into sorrow, and whittle that sorrow into anger. This time, though, I ran crying to my window and watched her wobble down the staircase to the street on unsteady shoes, zigzagging amid straight concrete lines in the soft, hazy sunlight.

6

It was sometime during my last year of elementary school that I learned Paul Skyhorse Johnson was not my real father. Inside a faux-oak dresser in my mother's bedroom were colorful binders of photographs glued onto pages of what felt like sticky flypaper, covered with a transparent plastic that when peeled back made an anxious *shhhhh*. It was the right sound: there were secrets here.

"How did you meet my dad?" I asked. There were no photos of my mother and Paul together.

"I was a paralegal and met him at an AIM community meeting," she said.

"Where?"

"Downtown, at the Indian center."

I thought about that. Later I asked, "Why are there no photos of you two together?"

"There weren't cameras on the reservation where we met," my mother said.

I thought about that. Later I said, "I thought you met Paul at the Indian center."

"Pictures steal an Indian's soul," my mother said.

I thought about that. Later still I said, "But here is a picture of Paul alone."

"He had to give his soul to me to keep," my mother said. "He was going off to Wounded Knee to fight and didn't want the white man to have it if he was captured."

I *really* thought about that. Then I asked, "Why would he go to Wounded Knee if you were pregnant?"

"What are you asking me, Brando?"

"Why did Paul leave us?"

My mother thought about that. Then, after months of the same rounds of questions and answers, she said, "Paul isn't your father."

In a photo album was a page-sized portrait of a light-skinned Mexican man with wavy hair, a trimmed beard, and the same naïve, soft eyes as mine.

"Who's that?" I asked.

"This is your father," she said, her voice scary in its even-temperedness. "He lived here with us for a couple years when you were a baby. His name was Candido Garcia Ulloa."

"Was?"

"I think he's dead. He *must* be dead. Or went back to Mexico. He was a wetback. He was your father, and he left you." Not her—*me*. She was quite specific on this point.

"Does this mean Paul's not my father? I'm not an Indian?"

"Of course you're an Indian. Your name is Brando Skyhorse. Paul is your father because he *wants* to be your dad."

"Did Grandma know?"

"Sure. She liked him more than I did."

"How come nobody told me?"

"Why did *you* need to know?" my mother said. "This wasn't any of your business. I'd already given you some fathers. Why did you need any more?"

"Does this mean I'm a Mexican?"

"I raised you Indian, not Mexican. Why, do you *want* to be fucking Mexican?"

"So Candido is my real father?"

"I don't know what 'real' means. Maybe he is, maybe not. I don't *want* him to be your father. So he might not be. Who knows? But he probably is."

"Will Candido ever come back?"

"No, he won't."

"What do I tell people when they ask what I am?"

"Damn it, don't tell *anyone* anything," my mother said. "You act like a white person, telling everyone everything. This is family business, and nobody outside needs to know because they're not family. Try to be more like the Mafia," she said.

"The Mafia? What do you mean?"

"Stand by your *family*. And quit being so goddamn honest all the time."

"This is your father." I'd been hit in the same spot with that line so many times I'd gone numb. There was no impact left in that declaration. I didn't have any feelings about a discovery I wasn't even sure was real. What I had were questions. I wanted the *story*. I'd been raised on my mother's stories and knew how skilled she was in telling them. Now here my mother was, refusing to give me, in essence, my first story. The story of who I was. Why?

"If you want," my grandmother said in a low whisper, "I'll help you write to Candy's parents in Mexico. Maybe they'll have answers."

She'd helped Candido write letters to his parents during the three or so years he lived with us. We began one afternoon when my mother got a call with a repeat client, knowing the call would go long. At our cracked, painted-over layaway dining room table, my grandmother suggested what I should say and then translated it for me to write in Spanish. "They're from the old country and wouldn't understand English. They're dirt poor," she said. I imagined a house with floors, walls, and roof made of actual dirt.

"Candido was a good, simple man," my grandmother said while I wrote. "He liked to scare you by reaching for his belt when you misbehaved, but when you ran and hid behind a table, he laughed and cradled you in his arms."

"That sounds scary," I said.

"No, he loved you," my grandmother said. Only in a family like ours could a story about a man reaching for a belt be considered loving.

"Candido would say, 'Don't be scared, *Pappitas*.' He liked to call you *Pappas*. That means 'potatoes' in Spanish," my grandmother said. "Okay, let's pick the stamps you like for the envelope."

I enclosed some school photographs, part of my allowance to help with the dirt house. At the check cashing place, my grandmother gossiped with the cashiers in a mix of English and Spanish while I slid dollars through the cold metal tray and got back a satisfying array of play-colored twenty- and forty-dollar international money orders.

"You're a good man, Charlie Brown," my grandmother said.

In a couple weeks, I received a photograph of a man and woman in their early sixties standing in front of a green curtain in a studio. Their faces were carved with hard, primitive cheekbones, their skin the color of sun-sopped oak. Their clothes were frayed, their dress shoes new. Their faces were too far from the camera to tell whether their eyes resembled my own, but I could see in them breathless hardships and poverty I'd never know from my home in Los Angeles, a daily grind they never mentioned in their letters, which my grandmother translated.

They were happy to get a letter from me, thanks to God, they wrote, but they had no idea where their cowardly and worthless son, who clearly wasn't a man, was. Thanks to God, they now had extra money to spend on food and electricity. I was welcome to visit them and my many relatives in Mexico anytime and, thanks to God, wished me well in school and in life.

"Why do they keep thanking God instead of us?" my grandmother complained.

Soon I grew bored with letters I couldn't read from people I didn't fully understand how I connected with, spending money on something that didn't show an immediate return. There were movies to see and Transformers toys and video games to buy instead. So I stopped writing. I thought if I simply ignored something I didn't want to deal with, it would disappear as long as I kept pretending it wasn't there.

It worked. For a long while, it worked. I told myself that Candido was doing the same thing I was.

Like father, like son.

Father's Day in a fatherless year became a second Mother's Day. I'd buy cards for my mother and grandmother, sign them with variations of "To the only father I've ever known" or "I never needed a dad" (the cards and signatures my mother's idea), and then listen to both women argue over which of them needed men less *or* hated men more.

Sometimes Frank stopped by. Now when we spent afternoons together, we split our time between things he picked—baseball games, waiting in line for concert tickets, Olympic pin conventions, Spalding Gray spoken-word monologues—and what I picked: theme parks. I loved their perfect "reality" of spotless sidewalks, razor-sharp grassy lawns, junk food on every corner, and a world where kids seemed to be in charge. Frank hated them: having to actually *pay* for parking, and endless mazes of what my grandmother called "sneaky lines" for attractions that lasted minutes or, in many cases, seconds. He felt that theme parks brought out the worst in people.

The Father's Day I was eleven, I convinced Frank to take us to Universal Studios. A kids' promotion handed out "scratch-off" back lot maps that promised a special prize to eagle-eyed children who spotted animatronic characters on the tour and scratched off the appropriate locations on their game card. The tram ride was long, and I got bored. I saw that by scratching a thin line down the middle of each scratch spot, you could find out where the characters were without having to wait to the end of the tour.

Frank was gamely playing along, pointing out a mannequin, when he saw I wasn't hunched over my game card scratching along with the other kids.

"What did you do to yours?" he asked.

He held it up to the sun. My thin scratch marks looked fatter and more conspicuous in the light.

"You cheated, Brando! Why did you cheat?"

"I didn't cheat," I said. "I just didn't have to wait like everyone else."

"No, this is cheating," he said. "You cheated yourself out of a good time. Your impatience ruined the day. God, Brando, sometimes you're just like your mother."

The comeback—"And you're nothing like a father!"—got lodged in my throat and stayed there. I hated Frank, so I punished him with silence on the rest of the tour and the drive home. I'd already demoted him from father, but to what? What was the right word for Frank, someone less than a father but more than a friend? Frank stared ahead, shoulders hunched, muttering about traffic when he dropped me off. He drove away before I'd unlocked the front door.

In my room, I wished that he'd disappear. I got my wish. It would last for three years.

A few months later, my mother's footfalls thundered across the house to my room. She had news. Big footsteps. *Big* news.

"Paul's coming."

"Here? When?"

"Two weeks," she said.

It was early 1985, seven years since I'd last seen Paul Skyhorse Johnson. What would he expect of us? Did he know we weren't Indian? How "Indian" would we have to act? Would Paul confront my mother for raising an "apple": red on the outside, white on the inside?

Since turning to phone sex, my mom's Indian-ness had lost its blush, and any sense of cultural identity I had went with it. She'd stopped leaving the house, so she didn't meet new people to introduce her Indian self to. She maintained her Running Deer identity for her coworkers but had so many faux lives to embody for her calls, her clients gave her the performative space she needed for her own cascading personal narratives. Becoming someone else wasn't questioned or challenged on the phone, it was encouraged and rewarded. My mother could be Cara Lee on one call or an Indian squaw getting raped by a cowboy on the next. She could be anyone on call. Off the phone, she still couldn't be my birth mother Maria Teresa.

I didn't think about being an Indian anymore until someone reminded me of it: well-intentioned white teachers, African-Americans who wanted me to know they were "one-eighth Cherokee," total strangers in search of a good story from their ride on the city bus. For me, being "Indian" wasn't different from what any other kind of ghetto raconteur in Echo Park did: talk fast and hide the truth. Or tell my mother's version of the truth that I had memorized:

"My father is Paul Skyhorse. My mother is Running Deer Skyhorse. They are both full- blooded American Indians. My father was falsely arrested for killing two FBI agents. My mother was a lawyer helping with his defense. I'm the son of a Indian chief and will become a chief one day myself. Any questions?"

Then I went back to my ordinary, homogenized American favorites: McDonald's French fries, video games, Transformer cartoons, and lying. I knew my mother's story about me was total fabrication, but I kept telling it anyway. My mother told me to. My grandmother told me to. Eventually, in his own way, Paul would tell me to as well. Truth is, I'd have kept telling that story even if my family had given me a choice. People smiled when I told them my name. They paid attention to me when I told them my story. The more I told my mother's lies, the less I felt like I was just an extension of her. The truth about Candido seemed like another way for my mother to control me and define who I was. In the shade of absolute falsehoods, I realized I could grow up.

● ● ●

Thirty-nine-year-old Paul Skyhorse Johnson resurfaced in a seniors' convalescent home in Torrance, a town two buses away. Fresh off parole for another undetermined crime and needing to recover from an injury without insurance, he'd been placed in a state-subsidized home to recuperate.

The Paul I'd remembered meeting in jail and in Saint Louis had been a "Thunder Warrior" Indian comic-book superhero hulk with billowing, untamed locks. In Torrance, I found an aged man creaking into his forties with a broken leg and short, thinning hair. His muscular upper body had atrophied into a firm, compact potbelly scarred with slash marks, looking like the tread of an old tire. One of his legs was in a cast up to his hip, and he maneuvered through the bleached flourescent yellow halls in a wheelchair. What I wanted most from a father was a buffer between me and my mother. How would this man stop my mother's hysterical slides off her emotional cliff, when he couldn't stand on his own without a cane?

Had Paul really changed so much in the past few years? Or had I confused him with my brief courtroom memories of Paul Skyhorse Durant, with whom my mother was still in contact? After Durant's celebrated acquittal, he'd been rearrested for armed bank robbery, pled guilty, and was sent in 1984 to the United States Medical Center for Federal Prisoners in Springfield, Missouri, where he underwent a psychiatric evaluation. While there, he filled out a visitors list that authorized only five people: his attorney of record, his brother, his mother, an investigator, and my mother, "Maria Banaga."

Presumably, she had used her real name because, in case of a visit, she'd have to present official ID. My mother was listed as Paul's "friend" and next to her name was a *Q*, indicating a questionnaire had been sent to her that required her signature before she could receive formal approval. The prison's annotation points to her name with the word *money* atop it, which certainly means she'd been sending Durant cash. Her mailing address has been redacted from the visitors' sheet, but my mother kept a PO box in Glendale for many years where she'd collect her phone sex checks and singles ad responses. My mother stayed in contact with Durant because she wanted a backup man, but there was bigger game with him, too. Durant could give her something she never felt she had before: legitimacy. As his potential wife, she could be, unquestionably, at last, an American Indian.

When I met Paul Skyhorse Johnson again as a twelve-year-old, I'd mixed up his CV with what my mother had told me over the years about Durant. He sensed my distance but not my confusion. Our first conversation was about prison fights; he'd been in many of them with both guards and convicts.

"I always get the best of 'em," he said. His laugh burned slow like his Pall Malls, and he made clear, penetrating eye contact over his hump of a bulbous nose.

"Your old dad's a lump head," he said. "Feel."

He ran my little fingers through a mist of blackish hair, across a phrenologist's dream of bumps and ridges. "I was mistaken for dead a lot of times. But here I am, a dead man talking to you."

On his dresser was an arm's-length stack of vintage *Playboy* magazines. "When you get old enough, these magazines will be yours, and you can sell them." My mother and I were silent, each waiting for the other to lead the conversation. Paul was unsettled. "I know both of you can talk more than this. I had plenty of quiet inside jail. Brando, I want to hear how you're doing in school."

"I'm doing good," I said. Pause. "Dad." I knew he wasn't, but whether I was Candido's son or not, it was time to play along. I sat by his side and tried to make conversation with a man who'd abandoned his own son but who was clearly trying to become some *kind* of father to me.

Paul stayed several weeks at the convalescent home and introduced me to several of his ward friends, including another wheelchair-bound patient, a man in his seventies whose head resembled a large snowball with a ring of tufted clouds for hair and chin scruff. When we left for lunch, Paul's friend asked me to sneak him back a small order of onion rings, which he paid for with a gentle appreciation and shoulder hugs. After the fourth batch of rings and hugging, Paul asked me not to bring him food unless he paid money for it.

"He's a child molester," Paul said. "Did time for touching small boys. He won't touch you because he knows I'd 'take care of him,' but I don't want you going near him."

I wondered if he was just lying, the way my mother did. But if he wasn't, why would he have introduced me to a pedophile to begin with?

When Paul was discharged, he moved into my grandmother's house with us. He emerged from his cast with a gimp leg and a permanent limp that made my mother wince when he hobbled too far in one direction.

"He takes longer to get up the hill than I do!" my grandmother said.

My mother said to her, "This motherfucker lied to me. He's much older than I am." They were just a year apart. "If I wasn't going to get a week's honeymoon in Vegas after we get married, I'd kick his ass out."

The wedding, her third, was at the Circus Circus's Chapel of the Fountain on my mother's thirty-eighth birthday, April 7, 1985. My mother, who never divorced any man, applied for a license with an assumed name and a fake ID.

I was the wedding's sole guest when I stood again to give my mother "away" as I had in the Baha'i ceremony with Robert. "No more weddings for me!" my grandmother had said.

In our group picture, I'm wearing a metallic silver suit with a clip-on necktie and white sneakers. My mother looks dazed, dressed in pink, a color she hated, marrying a man she doesn't love. We're posed on a midnight blue shag mat in front of the altar, in front of a cardboard church backdrop, with Paul holding on to both my mother's and my shoulders for support. My hair is long enough to brush Paul's hand. It's easiest here in this picture to see how people would mistake Paul for my actual father—matching long, dark hair, the same bittersweet orange skin tone, and a similar facial structure around the eyes. His, though, were often pinched, narrowed, squinting, as if focused on some faraway mountain peak.

We had another family picture taken in Las Vegas in the fall of 1986 at a showroom in the Frontier Hotel. It was a double bill of oldies acts Paul Revere and the Raiders and the Righteous Brothers. In those eighteen months, both my mother and I have swelled, saturated with a fat that has rounded out our faces and plumped up my mother's arms. (She hated seeing herself overweight; this is the last photo I have of her.) My mother's hair flows to her bust and has been styled with a crimping iron bought from an infomercial, her primary shopping outlet since she grew afraid of "being fat in public." I'm wearing plastic eyeglasses, and my genuine smile from the wedding has dissolved into a saccharine smirk. Paul, originally seated on my left, has since been excised from the photo through a clean vertical rip. What remains is his saddle-tan hand on my shoulder, as if he's offering his condolences or steadying me for a hard, coming blow.

It was ten o'clock on a school night when my mother gave a quick knock on my bedroom door and then barged in. I was twelve years old, hunched over a TV tray loaded with books, reading.

"It's past your bedtime," she said. "Go to the bar and get your father."

My mother wasn't a drinker and underestimated what being an alcoholic meant. She had two glasses of champagne on New Year's Eve and then went to bed until late morning. Paul rotated daily among the half dozen bars within walking distance of our house. Little Joy Jr. on the corner was good for pool hustling and a gay cruising spot. A block away, the Short Stop was popular with off-duty police officers, who, as it turned out, were the easiest marks for Paul to hustle. Stadium Bars #1 & #2 were for Dodgers fans brave enough to park on curbs lined with broken passenger car door glass, as if frozen pools of water had been dropped and shattered.

My mother also didn't realize how much Paul hated living with us.

"I'm in a jail worse than the one I was locked up in," he said to me a month after the wedding. He hadn't once confronted my mother about her phone sex job or me about my "American" upbringing. "This place is run by two hens who want to cut the balls off this rooster. Looks like they already got to you," he told me. My father was right, I thought. My father was also a total stranger who wasn't even my father. How quickly should I trust him?

Paul's local was The Sunset. With its grenadine neon sun signage and marbled brown stucco exterior, it's the first bar seen in the opening credits for Barbet Schroeder's *Barfly*, a 1987 movie written by Charles Bukowski. (When your father's local is the first bar seen in *Barfly*, you *know* how this story's gonna turn out.) Sandwiched like a hunk of bad roast beef between Roy's Market (more *carnicería*— butcher shop—than market) and the Echo Park Trading Post (more pawnshop than trading post), The Sunset was a mix of white and Mexican toughs who'd been softened up by age, disillusionment, and cirrhosis, and out-of-area slummers looking for a dive bar with gums but no teeth. It was here that Paul found his greatest success as a pool hustler, or, as he called himself, a "professional gambler," who earned money through hours-long pool games and tricking people in the hoariest of bar bets. Paul tried teaching me a few of them, most involving cigarettes, playing cards, and number memorization, but I was never as impressed as he wanted me to be.

"Too bad we don't have a pool table at the house," he said. "You could finally realize I'm good at something."

I sat on the curb outside the bar for an hour, blackening my palms and the ass of my jeans, praying that Paul would come out on his own. He didn't. I was more terrified of going back to my mother empty-handed than of whatever was in the bar, so I sucked in air like I was about to dive underwater and then rushed the front door.

Thick, pilled velvet curtains with cigarette smoke and BO trapped in their folds parted to reveal murky blue and red lights undulating over my head. Noise and smoke everywhere, it was impossible to breathe. Then someone shouted, "*Get that fucking kid out of here!*" and I was pushed back out the door and onto the street.

Paul limped after me aided by his cane with a duck bill's head.

"Tell your mom to stop treating you like a dog," he said. "She already treats me like one. Go home. I'm making money for her to spend." If Paul had a good night's winnings, he'd stumble back before midnight. If he lost, he'd drink until close. He was simultaneously an irresponsible drunk and a practical manager of his money.

"What do you mean you left him there?" my mother said. "You can't take on one crippled old man? What the hell good are you? Go back there and *wait* for him."

I sat on the curb outside the bar past midnight, yawning, trying to stay awake. When he came out, tipsy, I drifted alongside, unacknowledged, a phantom son.

The crooked stairs to our house, perched atop a slanted hill, gave Paul trouble sober, so tonight he decided to scale the sliding right angle of our front lawn. He staggered to his feet on the grass, but then he twisted his bum leg, tumbling him through dry, ashy weeds down to a retaining wall like a broken top. His cane flew like a javelin. Finally, Paul let me help him crawl up the hill on his hands and knees. Our neighbors across the street watched and laughed from darkened porches.

A stench of sweat, dead grass, dirt, cigarette smoke, and alcohol floated with us like a noxious fog. "You smell like a drunk," my grandmother said to me and then steered Paul onto my mother's empty bed, where he slurri-naded my grandmother with Ray Charles's and Willie Nelson's duet "Seven Spanish Angels" before passing out. My mother had lost interest in Paul the moment he hit the front lawn and was asleep on the couch. She didn't really want Paul. She just wanted him home.

When my grandmother closed his bedroom door, I asked her why people were laughing at Paul.

"He's a *payaso*," she said. "A clown. Everybody laughs at clowns."

On my sixth-grade graduation day, I plucked out pins from a cellophane-wrapped stabby-collared shirt, tugged at an asphyxiating clip-on tie, squeezed into pinching-sharp dress shoes, and assembled, with a small multiethnic chorus, at the front of our graduating class to sing the refrain from "We Are the World." I was chosen for volume, not ability. When I auditioned in front of our music teacher, Mr. Farina, he said, "That's not singing, that's shouting."

Paul stood and nodded his head when I received my diploma, his face inscrutable. At the edge of the auditorium was a cluster of parents unable to find seats. Who was that man in the corner, holding his fingers up to his lips and going "Shhh"? Was it Frank? Had he figured out when my graduation was and, as if in a Disney movie, appeared when I needed him most?

No. He wasn't there. He either didn't know the date or stayed away because of Paul, but that didn't matter. Like the child of a divorced parent, I started to realize that his being in my life depended just as much on his relationship with my mother as it did with me. I kept expecting him to think like a father. Instead, he acted the way my grandmother said men acted.

"They never do what you want them to do," she said. "Only boys follow orders."

In a warm, shady courtyard, my classmates and I shuffled autograph books among us, signing assorted colored pages with pens that didn't work, scrawling phone numbers and promises to K.I.T. in crooked lettering.

"You can't just sign your name in an autograph book!" a friend told me. "That's just for famous people. You have to write something."

Somebody handed me Nina's autograph book. Nina was Vietnamese, with large, inky black eyes and an unflattering Prince Valiant done at home bowl cut that hadn't changed since second grade. She wore a white and saffron dress, socks with a doily fringe around her ankles, and shined patent leather shoes.

I retuned her autograph book with a signature that overflowed the entire folded paper triangle. "You're not supposed to write a whole book, Brando!" she said.

Nina, along with most of my friends, applied to a gifted and talented program at a junior high in the San Fernando Valley, so I did the same, ignorant of the forty-minute bus trip to Granada Hills. Out of habit, I forged my mother's signature on the school application in the same way I'd signed my own report cards since second grade.

"You don't need to prove to me how smart you are," she had always said, dismissing my grades with a wave and a laugh.

Junior high, I'd learn, was a collection of kids who didn't know who the fuck they were, all of a sudden desperately trying to believe or convince others they knew *exactly* who they were. Those warm months before seventh grade were ripe for summertime Cinderellas. Ugly-duckling sixth graders shed baby fat and stupid clothes, maturing into gawky young adults with too much confidence and makeup. I gained thirty pounds, transforming from cute sixth grader with an Indian name to an overweight four-eyed seventh-grade blob with a mullet. My father's "legal" last name, Johnson, was now my last name too. At my almost-all-white suburban San Fernando Valley school, my records transfer caused Skyhorse to slide to my middle name.

A new "fat" wardrobe had to be purchased, grudgingly. "We already got you glasses," said my grandmother, who'd stopped taking me to the dentist when he told her I needed braces.

Choices for husky kids in Echo Park were hand-me-down Dodgers T-shirts, oversized sweaters, and Dickies dress slacks with pleats, because, a salesman told my grandmother, "Pleats give you extra room in case he keeps growing."

"All the weight I've lost has gone onto you," my mother said and, having graduated from Dexatrim, handed me water pills in a disposable napkin. I knew what water pills were. From the age of seven, I was the only one in the house who could manage the childproof caps.

On water pills, I vibrated around the house like a mosquito, pissed violent jets of colorless urine, and woke up at two in the morning in a sweat glaze, my heartbeat cinched around my throat.

"You can have these back," I told my mother. They scared me.

I did keep "growing" and, to my utter astonishment, was unpopular. Suddenly Nina and my other elementary school friends didn't speak to me anymore. What attention I drew came from misfit bullies: a stocky aggressive dork who copied me video games on five-and-a-quarter-inch floppies and then "claimed" my assigned homeroom seat by punching me in the stomach; or the tall Asian boy with the uncool-even-for-the-era Flock of Seagulls haircut who shoved me into my main locker as kids passed by and grinded his crotch into my large ass in some weird show of sexual dominance. I tried being still and silent in class, so much so that I pissed my pants in seventh-grade math because I was afraid to ask permission to go to the bathroom. In gym, I didn't understand the basic rules of football or volleyball and smiled reflexively when classmates with names like Josh and Alex screamed at me, turning their baby fat cheeks red. I'm pretty sure kids thought I was retarded. Sympathetic, cute, gum-chewing Valley girls with black eyeliner and nude lipstick that I had crushes on whispered to boys *they* had crushes on, "Why do they treat him that way?" How a boy treated me, the class reject, was seen by fawning young girls as a barometer for his empathy, compassion, and coolness.

Nina's dimpled smile, her new, poofy Mary Tyler Moore hairdo, and her exotic appearance and background (this was the mid-1980s in the San Fernando Valley, after all) helped her achieve a popularity that far outstripped what she'd known in predominantly Latino Echo Park. She crushed on a white boy from my homeroom named Jay, a killer Sonny Crockett of *Miami Vice* look-alike—slip-on Vans, turquoise tank top, and a white blazer on Fridays—who volunteered me for all-you-can-eat competitions in the cafeteria.

Despite this, though, Nina and I were secret friends on the bus ride back home, almost as if we transformed there to being what we really were: nerds from a poor neighborhood who'd gotten a chance to go to a better school. Nina and I sometimes walked the same path home, talking about classes and how her parents were going to move away from Echo Park soon because it was a bad neighborhood in which to be Asian.

"When do I get your school picture?" she asked.

The next day, I tried giving it to her in homeroom, our one mutual class. "*Later*, okay?" she said. On the bus home, she asked for my picture again. I handed over a glossy wallet-sized seventh-grade class photo of me in a Le Tigre striped shirt, my sharp canines chewing on my bottom lip like a pork rind.

She flipped the picture over. "You always write so much!" she said and laughed. She was right. I'd spent maybe an hour trying to cram whatever awkward feelings I had for her on the back of two by three inches of glossy paper that didn't take to ballpoint pen. My words were smudged and smeared, like race cars all over a wet track.

"Let me fix the photo," I said.

"You're going to scratch out what you wrote or do something to it," she said.

She handed back the picture, and I ripped it into small chunks that couldn't be shredded further.

"I knew it," she said, even though I hadn't known it myself. It had been an impulsive move spurred, I thought, by her suggestion, but I was furious with myself. I'd acted like my mother and felt exactly the way I did when my mother scolded me. Did my mother feel this way every time she yelled at me? Why would she keep doing it if she did?

Nina ignored me the rest of the ride home. Walking on Sunset Boulevard, Nina's girlfriends from the bus clustered around her in a protective circle. They moved fast, and I struggled to match their steps, trying to find the right moment where I could pull her aside and apologize. I swelled with guilt as each step brought me closer to our paths splitting and the opportunity lost. I challenged myself to stop her outside the market, then the drugstore, then the shoe store. *Hurry*, I thought. *Hurry now, hurry before it's too late . . .*

"Son," Paul said. He was standing outside the Sunset, drunk. It was four in the afternoon.

When I saw Paul, I stopped cold and lost a half dozen steps on her pack. Nina's bubble was floating away.

"Son, where you going?" he asked. Down the street, Nina's group hadn't looked back. It was a stark choice: acknowledge and stand by my father or pursue my enraged, uninterested crush, racing home.

"Stay with me awhile," Paul said and I did. We walked in the opposite direction to the supermarket to buy Pall Malls and, as a special treat, whatever I wanted. I chose a bottle of Flintstone Chewable Vitamins.

I didn't see Nina again. She disappeared, but I was starting to understand that's simply what people you cared about did. Her parents made good on their promise to move out of Echo Park, turning her from an actual person to my forever idealized first crush, an always smiling, always fourteen-year-old girl with now-forgiving eyes and a spring day's playground laugh.

She says, "You always write so much!"

The seventh-grade Young Author's Project was a citywide competition among English classes for which students created their own book, from writing the story, to designing the cover, to binding the book together, culminating in a contest honoring the best entries. It was one of those "long-term" projects with a deadline that always seemed comfortably a few months off on the horizon. Then the horizon was a weekend away. In full panic with no ideas for a book, I asked Paul for help.

"Write about Indians," he said. "I know plenty."

We sat at the dining room table with a fresh pack of Pall Malls, a smokeless ashtray my grandmother had bought him, and my mother's typewriter. There was no story. The hope was that Paul would have enough interesting things to say that would fill out a thirty-two-page book.

"I'm Kiowa White Mountain Apache. Only tribe that never signed a peace treaty with the federal government. You could look that up in a book if the books weren't all written by white people," he said.

"When did you meet my mother?" I asked.

"You're lucky you have a mother," he said, and smoked his cigarette. "I was twelve when my mother died. Her name was Penny Cook. She was gunned down on Mother's Day. Did you get that down? They killed my mother on *Mother's Day*. Police were serving a warrant, and they murdered her." While I typed, I pictured an epic *Bonnie and Clyde* shoot-out at a simple house on a lonely prairie, surrounded by an overwhelming force of armed so-called "good guys," the house riddled with bullet holes as big as pie plates.

"What can people do to help Indians?" I asked.

"Go back to where you came from and leave us alone. 'First come, last served.' We're like the Jews during World War II. Genocide and ID numbers. You know every Indian has to get a number from the Bureau of Indian Affairs? I don't have one because our tribe—*your* tribe, Brando—didn't sign a treaty with the white man. You could get college money if I were registered, but I'm not gonna give you a number."

His answers unfurled in length, complexity, and anger. I couldn't follow what was supposed to be true and what he simply believed; he told stories the same way my mother did.

"Why don't you just let me type what I'm saying?" he asked. "Writing fast is easy for a jailbird," Paul said.

My mother checked on us several times throughout the afternoon, watching Paul type up my months-long homework assignment with furious energy.

"I'm glad you're spending time with your father," she said.

The manuscript was finished in less than a day. What was complicated was manufacturing the book itself. I had step-by-step instructions on how to assemble it, but since I didn't buy any of the materials listed ahead of time, Paul suggested we improvise. He stitched together the pages between two cardboard flaps wrapped in wood-grain contact shelf paper with a pair of dirtied-up shoelaces that were braided along the book's spine. It looked like a frontier journal but was impossible to open.

The title was Paul's idea. Amid a row of books written by twelve- and thirteen-year-olds, with festive cover illustrations of mice wearing superhero capes and happy spacemen, was *The Shame of America*, the title spelled out in vinyl mailbox lettering.

My English teacher, Mrs. Davis, a ghoulish rule lord who wore plum berets and had the formatting instructions for each day's assignments written out in bullet points on the chalkboard before we entered the classroom, read the book and then left a single comment in the margins.

"Brando, whose writing is this?" she wrote in red ink.

Before our books were handed back, she explained how she graded us and what categories each book belonged to, including "one so-called 'analytical nonfiction' entry," which I knew meant me. The first book I'd "written" earned a B-minus. Our class's winning entry was about a frog with superpowers.

"A B-minus, huh? Your teacher's white, isn't she?" Paul asked. "White people don't want to hear the truth."

"I'm getting rid of you!" my mother screamed. She was sending me . . . well, somewhere.

My mother kicked me out of the house at least several times a month, but I rarely got beyond the front door. It was just something she said once in a while, like "Get the fuck out of my face!" or "What good are you if you can't fix my goddamn VCR?" This time, though, she made me pack a bag. I packed a cheap giveaway Dodgers backpack with some underwear and socks, soap and toothpaste (no toothbrush), oranges, and some Capri Sun juice packs. A stuffed animal might make a good pillow, I thought, so I left my Transformers on the shelf and made a *Sophie's Choice* decision to pack Fudgie. He was my first teddy bear, a gift brought to the hospital by my grandfather Emilio when I was several hours old.

Today my mother was kicking me out because Paul had caught me cheating: that is, "conning." I'd shoved a set of vocabulary tests between Paul's face and his smokes, desperate for any of his "before-the-bar" attention. The plan backfired when he saw that I'd rearranged the test papers to make it look as if my grades had steadily improved, when, in fact, they had taken a dip before recovering.

"You didn't think I'd notice the dates on each test, did you?" he asked and showed my mother. "Look at what your son tried to do. He tried to con a con."

"I want him fucking out of here!" my mother screamed. I couldn't figure out why my mother was so upset. She hadn't asked for a report card or looked at my homework since second grade. I didn't understand then that she'd upped her intake of weight-loss pills and was experimenting with speed.

"Why don't you walk around the block for a while," Paul suggested.

I had no neighbors' houses to run to, no friends that didn't live long car drives away, so I carried my bag down to the nook at the bottom of our stairs that was invisible from my mother's bedroom window, next to the old jacaranda tree. This tiny, uneven concrete square was my version of a clubhouse, though it adjoined the sidewalk and the street. I'd sit here after the bus ride home from school, and if the breeze hit the branches just right, bask in a shower of jacaranda flowers before I'd rush into the hot broth of a house dripping with misery. From here, my home looked the size of a castle, enough room for everybody. How could one immense space, so calm and tranquil outside, breed so much anger and rage?

Clutching my Dodgers bag, I didn't picture escape (not yet), but peace, as if I could will it to happen just by imagining it. I was terrified that this time I was being kicked out for real and would be permanently separated from my mother and grandmother. What would I do? These women were my only family. They had created my world, sustained and nourished it; without them, there was not only no world, there was no *me*.

I leaned my head back, felt the blossoms fall on my face like fat raindrops—*plop, plop, plop*—and could imagine the roar of an ocean, feel sandy grit under my palms. I was used to waiting on curbs and had learned some of the magic that came with the practice of patience. Passing cars and the lulls left in their wake became the crashing of waves. The street was an ever-spreading body of water, one not a long bus ride away in Santa Monica but right at the foot of my stairs.

A couple hours later, I crept back up the hill. Nobody had invited me back inside. My mother was locked in her bedroom, her TV turned up. My grandmother, who'd been reading behind her locked door and *never* let a fight get between her and a book, was in hers. Things were "normal" again. Paul was in his own waiting place, perched against the washing machine, back door open behind a locked security gate, blowing smoke outdoors. He ashed into his noisy smokeless ashtray, the glowing end of his cigarette butt a steady buoy light.

"You're not going anywhere," he said. "I talked some sense into her. I was never going to let you be sent away. I would have stepped in and made things right before it ever got that far."

Had a father—*my* father—finally protected me? I tiptoed to my room, afraid that peace in our house was a delicate glass I'd drop and shatter if I made any sound above a whisper, and started to unpack. Then, in the midst of my gratitude, I wondered, why had Paul told my mother about my tests at all? Why not lecture me separately? It took awhile before I fully understood what the lesson was. My father wasn't mad that I'd cheated. He was mad I got caught.

• • •

Paul had been living with us for about a year and a half when he earned enough money hustling to buy a two-door brown Ford Maverick with black plumber's tape trim. It was a car that needed fixing up to become a lemon.

My grandmother hated it. "I don't need cars. I take Brando everywhere on the bus," she said. She knew she couldn't compete with four wheels and a man.

"It's time you got out of the hens' nest," Paul said to me. "Just you and your 'dear old dad.'"

I called Paul "dear old Dad" after hearing the cartoon dog Augie Doggie use that phrase. Paul was the first man I lived with that felt comfortable calling himself my dad all the time. I knew Candido was my biological father, but that revelation didn't change my life at all. The word *father* was something I attached to a relationship, not to any one particular person, and I decided I'd keep using that word on someone until it stuck. Finding out about my real dad that was nowhere in my life didn't mean nearly as much as a fake dad that could be present every day.

Manhood lessons began that summer. We spent late afternoons drifting in the slow lane, eating McDonald's supersized Value Packs for an early dinner, listening to 1950s oldies that Paul remembered from his childhood (the tinkling piano opening of Johnny Ace's "Pledging My Love" moved him to tears), and installing car parts outside the local Thrifty while I fended off the fire ants that swarmed the parking lot. There was rust in the sky as Paul stared off at a concrete wall opposite the lot and reminisced about fun things he did growing up: street fighting, popping off fly balls in the park, shooting his BB gun.

"A boy needs a gun," Paul said. "You ever been in a fight?" he asked, and held up his palms.

"Show me how you'd hit someone," he said. I jabbed with a balled fist.

"Don't do that," he said, motioning to how my thumb was stuck inside my enclosed fist. "You'll break your thumbs doing that. Next time you get in an argument, don't say anything. Take a swing first."

I had shelves of books, games, and stuffed animals, but since Nina moved away, I'd made just one best friend in junior high. Daniel rode the same school bus to the valley but lived in a grittier area wedged between Echo Park, Westlake, and downtown near the shadows cast by soaring freeway overpasses. Dandruff dusted the shoulders of his fake Members Only jacket, and a Milky Way constellation of white-heads inflamed his face. He named his backpack "Anthony" and gave me "thigh crushers" when we sat next to each other on the school bus.

"*That's* the best friend you could find?" Paul asked.

Paul was driving us home when he stopped at a strip mall auto parts store. Daniel squeezed my thigh. He smiled, waiting for me to squirm away in laughter. I threw a punch that glanced off the side of his head. I met Paul's eyes in the rearview and punched Daniel again, this time in the shoulder. Again, I didn't connect. Daniel cowered with his arms over his head, stunned, and waited for me to finish sliding my punches off his back and onto the seat cushion.

We dropped off Daniel a half hour later. He cheerfully waved good-bye without a bruise on him.

"Did you see our fight?" I asked Paul, expecting to check "Get in fight" off my manhood list.

"You were getting some good shots on him," he said. "He wasn't fighting back. You were in control. I would have stepped in if it'd gotten too bad. Maybe we should get you some boxing gloves and go to a gym?"

Gloves? A gym? I hadn't expected to "fight" again, let alone every time I had an argument. I'd sucker pummeled my best friend, done a poor job of it, and was scrounging around for any sliver of the pride Paul felt.

"What do you think?" he asked.

"Sure," I said, and stared out the window. We didn't talk about it, but, of course, I'd never fight again. Next time Paul took me out, he bought me a Crossman BB air rifle.

He set up a cardboard box target mount in the backyard and brought out a folding stool to sit by my side.

"Don't jerk it when you fire. Lean in a little more," he said, his hands gentle as they made tiny corrections. Shooting was boring; practice time with an instrument I hated. Maybe Paul could sense this. He too lost interest after our second lesson. I left the gun leaning in the closet like an old mop.

My grandmother moved the gun to her room, and on nights when couples made out in parked cars under our jacaranda tree, she waved the rifle around on the front porch to scare them away. Then she took the gun on daytime patrols to shoo away people who ate sandwiches at the bottom of our stairs during lunch hour and left their garbage behind.

"You could get shot doing something that dumb," Paul told her.

"Nobody's gonna shoot an old woman," she said. "I'm too old to be afraid."

She was also too old, I decided, to play catch, though she was in better shape than Paul. I had him drive us up to the end of our street and then down a hill to Elysian Park with some gloves and a bat.

"Don't be afraid to pull one," he said. I popped flies that he hobbled after. Later, on a drive to McDonald's, he cut across traffic to park on the side of a busy road.

"Got one coming," he said, and stretched himself out on the backseat as if it were a couch. Paul was about to have a seizure. He'd been having them since he moved in with us. His body gave him a good minute or two warning before one hit. Beatings from sadistic guards, he insisted, had exacerbated his condition. When we picked up his prescription bottles at the pharmacy, I'd read aloud, "Not to be taken with alcohol."

In Paul's front jeans pocket was a tongue depressor made from a pink toothbrush handle with hospital tape wrapped around the brush head. I kept one hand on the stick in his mouth while his seizure rode in like a stampede, trampling his legs, my other hand dabbing rancid yellow foam off his cheeks. When his shaking ebbed, I wiped off the depressor while Paul got a postseizure Budweiser and whisky from the trunk. He drove home tipsy with alcohol on his breath.

We were now spending *too* much time with each other, my mother decided.

"Are you sure you don't see him drinking?" she asked. I hadn't— just saw the empties—but wouldn't have turned him in if I had. I saw him now as a fellow soldier trapped in the same trench. Both my mother and grandmother considered this a betrayal. Their problem wasn't my problem, though. I was becoming a man, I thought, and it was time to take my side by one.

Besides Paul, I stockpiled other men as prominent father surrogates. *Just* in case. Paul drank like a thirsty river. His belly was distended and, like Frank before him, he punctuated the ends of arguments by revving his car's engine and speeding away. So I kept an eye out for other eligible fathers. One was Jose, a thirtysomething Mexican who had a weird maternal crush on my sixtysomething grandmother.

"Jose's too *old* to be a gigolo," she said, "and I'm too poor to give him any money. Maybe he can do something for you." He failed the father test when he took me to a drive-in theater, but I had to pay for our tickets and pizza.

There was Allan, a kind, elderly Dartmouth College graduate I met while he was canvassing our neighborhood for the 1984 Democratic presidential ticket of Walter Mondale and Geraldine Ferraro. My grandmother told him he should talk to her in-house political expert. He looked at her oddly when she returned with an eleven-year-old.

"I didn't realize you followed politics," he said.

"Mondale won't win," I said. "Because of the 'wimp' factor."

After a long discussion about the presidential election, he befriended and hired me as a part-time employee at his West Los Angeles company, which manufactured enclosures for electronic equipment. He drove me out to his offices and back, paying me $4.50 an hour for filing and roaming around the grounds unsupervised. Each visit ended with a paycheck in my own name and, for my birthday, a Commodore 64 home computer.

My grandmother said, "I thought he'd do more for you." There was no gesture she couldn't compound into disappointment.

Then there was Uncle Oscar, my mother's half brother. He'd stop by unannounced a few times a year. My mother would stay in her room with the door closed until he left.

One Christmas, Oscar brought over a BMX bike. "Here's how you ride it," he said, and then hopped on it and pedaled up and down the street. "Now you try."

I wobbled around unsteadily for ten minutes. When I was unable to learn on the spot, he got bored. "You don't seem like you're really trying," he said, and ended the lesson. The bike went into the basement.

"Let me teach you kung fu," Oscar said, and demonstrated some moves. I thrust out my fists at a crooked angle. He was unimpressed.

"If you're not going to take this seriously, I'm not going to waste my time teaching you," he said.

My mother said he used drugs and took money out of her and her mother's purses growing up. For a while, he was a member of the Reverend Jim Jones's People's Temple branch in Los Angeles but dropped out when he realized he would have to hand over all his money and possessions. He lived in a small, junk-cluttered Silver Lake bungalow and sometimes brought over tall, leggy, beautiful white girlfriends with strange, exotic names like Renee who stroked his hands while he and my grandmother argued on the couch about everything. When he was alone, they argued about his father, Emilio.

"You never treated Papa right," Oscar said at the dining room table. My grandmother sat on the opposite end. I sat in the middle, spectator to a Ping-Pong match between a father figure angry about his dad and a mother figure angry with her son. "You cheated on Papa and lied to him. You hated him," Oscar said.

"Papa hated you too," she said. "You didn't visit him once in the hospital before he died. You only showed up at the will reading. You were always an ungrateful child."

"How about all those women you used to bring over here into your bedroom?" Oscar said, his voice trembling. "Me and Maria had to sit here as little kids and see a parade of women come through the house when Papa was working."

"Okay, so I was a bad mother that gave you a rotten childhood and you turned into a rotten human being. We're not going to get anywhere talking like this all night."

"I concur," Oscar said.

"What does 'concur' mean?" I asked.

"It's a fancy white man's way of saying, 'You're right,'" my grandmother said.

One afternoon Oscar showed up in a gray hoodie and sweatpants. His face was gaunt, his eyes sleepless. His sweats drooped off him like curtains. He was itchy, bouncing from room to room, confused by Paul's presence. It was the first time Oscar had visited since Paul moved in.

Oscar asked my mother if he could borrow fifty dollars. "I'm not giving that asshole shit," she told me. "He's using again."

When he got into an argument with my grandmother, Paul asked Oscar to leave.

"Who are you?" Oscar shouted. "This is my mother I'm talking to! I don't know who you are."

Paul stepped in front of my grandmother in the living room and tried to push Oscar toward the front door. Oscar pushed back, and Paul went into a defensive fighting stance. Oscar assumed a kung fu pose. Paul's bum leg sent him stumbling backward while Oscar punched air. What should have been an old-school rumble became a slap fight, their heavy fists punching the empty space between them.

It seems comical now, but it was terrifying then. I was sobbing when I grabbed my baseball bat and, clutching it to my chest, screamed, "Get out!" Here I was, thirteen years old, with a chance to defend my house and my mother. My grandmother could handle herself, but I'd once been my mother's "little big man." We both knew that I'd since become a fat, wimpy, smart-mouthed nerd. I hadn't grown into Al Pacino from *Scarface*—my mother's favorite movie character—meaning she still couldn't find, or create, a man interested in or capable of protecting her. That broke off the first part of her heart. I knew I wanted to guard the parts that were left. I just didn't know how.

Paul knocked Oscar off balance toward the front door. Oscar looked at me and said, "See what they're doing to me, Brando? They'll do this to you! This is what these women are going to do to you!"

My grandmother grabbed the bat and leveraged Oscar out on the porch, but he yanked the bat from her as we slammed the door closed behind him. He swung the bat hard at the door's glass-and-wood middle section, splintering it into large chunks. A large flapping shade kept the glass from spraying on us.

Then it was quiet in our house. The sound was so unfamiliar it was deafening.

Oscar drove away. My grandmother and I collected the largest glass shards. This was the second time, along with Robert's smashing through the sliding glass door, a window shade had "protected" us. The next week, my grandmother would install shades on every available window and leave them drawn day or night. We debated whether the police should be called, but the one thing my grandmother wanted her son charged with—theft—was moot when the bat was found tossed at the base of the hillside's retaining wall.

My grandmother turned on Paul. "You didn't land a single punch on my son," she said. "Didn't you fight in jail?"

Paul said nothing. My mother shifted her fury to me. "Do you know how much that fucking front door is going to cost?" she asked. "Do you think Oscar's going to come back and pay us for it?"

"Brando doesn't think anything through," my grandmother said.

"Could you have gotten away with shit like this when you were a child?" my mother asked my grandmother. "Acting like a pussy *and* costing your mother money?"

"Are you kidding?" my grandmother replied "My mother would have beat me from here to Hollywood if I hadn't protected her!"

My mother said to me, "You're turning into a worthless man, just like the rest of them."

I stood silent, ashamed, incapable of acting. I hoped my mother would exhaust herself lashing out at me. Or that Paul would step in and do something. Anything.

He went to the laundry room to smoke.

Later I thought about what Oscar had said before he'd grabbed the baseball bat. "These women." It was the same thing Paul had said to me, too. Oscar had just bashed in our front door, but the danger, he said, was inside the house. Were Oscar and Paul right? What *would* these women do to me?

Though I'd had enough experience and should have seen the warning signs by then, whenever a "father" left, it always came like the jab of a needle: a white-hot flash of intense pain and the dull, alcohol-rubbed ache left behind. My mother was surprised, too, though by now she had come to expect abandonment over security. With the strength of a thousand arms, she held on to these men she hated from the first moment they walked through our front door, but when they were ready to leave, it made no difference. Men always traveled toward unseen constellations, pulled by the force of their own gravity.

And they always remembered to take the car with them.

Paul's last night was in early 1988. On a rare "family night out," we drove to La Pizza Loca, a sub-Domino's chain, just to bring the food back to the house. When Paul went inside to order, some young cholos swaggered from across the parking lot, sat on the hood of our car, and started rocking it. They cursed and chugged from forty-ounce bottles.

My mother, from her customary spot in the backseat, yelled, "Can you stop bouncing our car up and down?" Her voice was a nervous crackle.

"Fuck you, *puta*!" one boy said. "Come out here and make us, you fucking bitch!"

My mother told me, "Don't just fucking sit here. Do something!"

Cholos and I didn't see each other in Echo Park. I pretended I couldn't see them while they tagged walls with indecipherable characters or drank forties on street corners at three thirty on a Tuesday afternoon. One time I stood several feet from a fat one as he snatched a woman's purse on the corner where I waved to my grandmother every morning and did nothing as he huffed off in escape. Cholos were better than the white bullies in junior high, though, because cholos left you alone if you knew how to do the same. They ambled down the street at a crooked angle to lean into you, spoiling for a fight. So I gave them plenty of space on the sidewalk, crossing the street to avoid posse clots down the block. I was great at avoiding confrontations and fights *outside* my house. But these cholos I couldn't avoid. My mother wouldn't let me.

I crept out of the car. The plan was to hide with Paul. Head bent over, I sulked past the gangbangers. None of them was old enough for facial hair. One of them said, "Hey, he's gonna snitch on us."

I told Paul what was happening. He glanced out the window and said, "Let's wait for our food."

We emerged arms laden with "feed a family for eight dollars" pizza and two-liter soda bottles to see the group shambling off, their cursing and bottle slinging an echo that now made them seem like harmless teenagers.

"They were just kids," Paul told my mother.

"You two hid inside like pussies!" she screamed, but she could have been talking about herself too. Her days of being a badass exotic fake *chola* were long gone. She couldn't talk to cholos the way my grand-mother could have and was as out of touch with gangs as she was with the rest of the neighborhood, having lived the past several years of her life inside a phone sex bunker.

Paul and my mother argued until they got home. He said, "I'm not listening to this anymore. I'm going for a drive."

My mother followed Paul down the stairs, screaming. She had never fought in public, feeling that violence against loved ones was a private matter. From my bedroom window, I saw in the dank yellow front porch light my mother and Paul fight at the bottom of the stairs next to the jacaranda tree, the same place I prayed every day for some kind of peace in this house.

Paul sped off. My mother burst through the front door.

"He pulled a knife on me! He cut me!"

"Where did he cut you?" my grandmother asked, skeptical. "I wanna see these stab wounds for myself." Paul carried a buck knife, but I couldn't tell from my bedroom whether he'd pulled it on my mother. She gathered us around and showed us a faint nail scratch on her wrist.

"That's not a cut," my grandmother said. "I'm going to bed."

By the next morning, Paul hadn't come back. He'd never stayed away overnight before. My mother ransacked the house, totaling up subtle clues that only a con, or someone who had been conned enough by cons, should have caught but didn't: Paul's bare clothes hangers shoved to the back of the closet. His bathroom cabinets emp-tied. The telephone unplugged. Paul had planned to leave that night. He just needed an excuse.

I kept a vigil by my window at night for his car and counted off each day that he was "missing." My mother said I was wasting my time. When a week passed, she filled several garbage bags with his letters and the cutout shapes of Paul's face and body from mangled photographs.

"Paul's dead," my mother said. "That's what you tell people now. Your father is dead."

• • •

"It's a dead man talking to you," Paul's voice said when I picked up the phone. It'd been several months since he left. My mother was in her room working, this time on shift-based per-minute-billing 976 and 1-900 sex lines. My grandmother was grocery shopping.

"How's my son doing?" It hadn't been that long, but I hated that word *son* now. Hated the way Paul used it so freely, the way it required no effort to say it, no commitment to weight it with value or meaning. I didn't feel like his son anymore. I didn't want to be any man's son.

"I'm fine," I said, my voice controlled.

"What have you been up to?"

"Nothing," I said, and answered his follow-up questions in pleasant, monotone, monosyllabic answers. He shared no details of where he'd gone or what he was doing.

"Don't you have anything to say to your dear old dad?" Paul asked.

"Nope."

"Okay. You'll never hear from me again. Good-bye!" he said, sounding almost upbeat. He hung up.

I was five when I'd clung to Paul's legs like a tree and called him "Daddy." I was fifteen when the father I'd waited ten years for, the one father I'd believed in, or thought I'd had a right to, abandoned me, just like the others. Hadn't my other fathers—Candido, Frank, Robert—been building up to this one father whose name I shared? Who was supposed to stay for good? Was I no longer a Skyhorse? I was still "Indian," closing yearbook signatures the way I had in seventh and eighth grades, "May the Great Spirit guide you," the same signature Paul used in his letters. If I wasn't a Skyhorse—the only part of my identity I felt was "me"—then who *was* I? A Mexican who had no idea what being Mexican meant, pretending to be an American Indian in name only? An abandoned son mourning his dead father who wasn't dead and wasn't his father?

To my mother, these were stupid questions, really. Paul said he was a "dead man" when we first met in Los Angeles and the last time we spoke, but that didn't mean who my mother and I had become would die with Paul, too. We were Skyhorses now. To every white person we met who said, "You're Indian?" my mother said, "Did you think you killed us all off?"

7

"Don't ever do this, Brando," Frank gulped, holding in pot smoke. "Do as I say, not as I do."

Inside the duplex mountain "cabin" in Lake Arrowhead, California, Frank rolled joints and helped my naked, shivering mother operate the whirlpool tub. The weekend trip was meant to be a vacation from her own bedroom, but instead Frank ferried my mother chips, soda, and takeout all weekend because she didn't want to leave the room. My mother indulged its middle-class amenities like wearing bathrobes baked on the heated towel racks and climbing up and down an indoor staircase just for fun.

"You've got stairs at home, babe," Frank said.

"I know, but these stairs are cute, and they go to my room!" my mother said.

Watching Frank and my mother together more than ten years after they met was like watching a comedy team whose timing was just a little off, with older and somewhat gentler versions of their young, dream-weighted selves now capable of acknowledging how silly their roundabout arguments were—at least until their fighting flared up like a chronic, asymptomatic rash.

I had grown less forgiving of Frank's visits with my mother, which included an afternoon tryst at a local motel, and less forgiving of him. It had been three years since we last saw each other, and that time had aged us both. He tired more easily, was grayer, and seemed fatter. I was older, crueler, and less satisfied with his episodic parental routine of swap meets and Sunday live-theater matinees; tired of waiting out in parking lots for concert tickets to bands I didn't like; and wandering convention trade shows where he tracked down Olympic pins and Beatles memorabilia. His souvenir habit branched out into collecting autographs that would turn his childhood home into a hoarder's fantasy. In his car trunk: a bag of fresh, white baseballs that he asked celebrities to sign, believing that a signed Tom Cruise baseball—which he has—will be more unique, more valuable, and harder to lose than a cocktail napkin. I despised his generic excuses for his long absences, his hypocritical pot smoking, and his cheapness. For my junior high graduation, he took me to Sizzler for a celebration lunch.

"Cheapest steakhouse in town," my grandmother complained. She was right, I thought. Why wasn't I *worth* more to him? I'd been taught daily that money equaled love. Sizzler *wasn't* love. Sizzler wasn't even friendship!

Over lunch, Frank asked me, "So, is that man that was living with you Paul Skyhorse?"

"How do you know?" I asked.

"One day I stopped by the house while you were at school. I was just in the neighborhood." I thought, *You were in the neighborhood only while I happened to be at school?*

"Some man came to the door. I didn't know Maria was living with someone. It was an older gentleman with a limp and a cane. I told him I was a census taker, then left. Was that Paul from the Skyhorse-Mohawk trial downtown? Was *that man* your father?"

"*I guess,*" I said.

I was a sardonic fifteen-year-old tired of humoring my . . . well, what exactly *was* Frank in my life? We hadn't used the words *father* and *son* since grade school. He was uncomfortable with being called "Dad"—he felt he hadn't earned the title, since he didn't marry my mother—and I was disinterested in being his son. I wanted Frank to humor me, take me to do the things I wanted to do. The fact that I had no idea what those were didn't matter.

When he dropped us back home, Frank said to me, "I'll see you soon, pal." Soon, it turned out, would be another two years. I didn't say good-bye when I got out of the car. By now I knew our routine. The tide goes out, the tide comes in; Frank leaves, another stepfather enters.

My mother went back to the singles ads. Since I refused to miss school to travel, we were now limited to short hit-and-run excursions during vacation breaks. I knew these trips weren't to find me a father. They were to land my mother a man. We weren't partners anymore. I was her companion solely because she wouldn't travel alone. Through my teenager's eyes, I revised memories of our buoyant, picaresque, cross-country "father-man" hunting adventures into a playing deck of awkward instant friendships with pathetic men, filthy shower stalls, lumpy couch beds, and eggs in greasy spoons for breakfast—weeks I spent watching my mother playact patience and kindness with other people's children hungry for affection.

Still, I helped with the singles ads. I sorted through my mother's responses and handled the enclosed photographs like trading cards, convinced that this time I could limit my involvement to a scouting report.

"Here's one owns his own home and lives near Vegas," I said. "But he's way too old." Elmer was an enormous pot-bellied man in his fifties with two preteen boys, Phil and Dil. He enclosed a Polaroid of him topless with the words "Dare you to send me one like this" written on its back. She didn't, but she asked for and received two prepaid round-trip train tickets. I didn't want to go.

"It'll be like old times," she pleaded. It wouldn't be, but my mother needed me.

It turned out that Elmer lived in Henderson, a good drive away from the Strip, or what my mother considered "real" Las Vegas. On our first day there, we drove out to a fish pond where Elmer's energetic, sandy-haired, blue-eyed boys and I fed loaves of day-old bread to glistening fat carp that hopped and skimmed for food across the water's surface. My mother stayed in the car.

"I didn't come to Las Vegas to feed a bunch of fucking fish!" she said.

Next, the Hoover Dam. My mother stayed in the car.

"I'm not climbing a bunch of fucking stairs to see *water,*" she said.

The boys dug out an unused chess set at home, and I showed them, in the firm, guiding way I imagined an older brother might, how to move the pieces around the board. We were laughing and having fun until Elmer got home from work.

"Pick that mess up off the floor," he said.

We never made it to the Strip, gambling instead at a casino in Laughlin, ninety miles south of Vegas, where Elmer said the prime rib and slots were cheaper. We dropped off Phil and Dil at an arcade, while I wandered around by my mother's side as she played quarter slots for ten minutes.

"I'm done," she told me. "Get Elmer so we can get the hell out of here."

I found Elmer shuffling by the roulette tables.

"My mother says she's ready to go. She's out of money."

"Well, I've got money!" he said and gave me the car keys so the rest of us could wait in the parking lot.

"What the *fuck* did he say?" my mother asked. "*He's* got money?"

My mother fetched his kids, and we sat in his darkened car while she told them stories about us being Indians. They laughed and asked bright questions, oblivious to the serrated edge in my mother's voice that offered the one clue as to how furious she was at their father.

"How was it out here?" Elmer asked when he returned an hour later. He turned on the radio. "Had a good time?"

"We learned about Indians!" the kids said.

My mother said, "Can you turn off the radio?"

She was seated behind Elmer. I saw her in silhouette, as if her hands

136

were prepping a garrote to slice through his wattle. She said nothing, though. At his house, I taught the kids the card game Uno while Elmer begged my mother to stop packing her suitcase. She decided we were returning to Los Angeles the next morning, a week ahead of schedule.

On the train platform, his kids gripped each side of my mother as if she were a fresh-baked cookie they could split in two.

"Please write us!" Phil and Dil pleaded

"We'll be back," my mother lied.

I saw myself in these boys who wanted a mother—*any* mother— with the same hunger I'd wanted Paul, who had left his own child fatherless yet had tried to be a piece of a father to me. I wanted to push them aside, warn them not to attach themselves to my ruthless exaggerator and liar of a mother, but those boys didn't want my protection. They wanted what they thought they could sense spilling from my mother's pockets, what their father was too old and exhausted to give them, and what I no longer believed any adult— mother, grandmother, or father—could give me. They wanted love. When they wrote my mother, they got silence.

"Do you mind if I write them?" I asked my mother.

"If you want," she said, "but we won't be seeing them again." I sat with a pencil and crumpled pages containing only three words: "How are you?"

There were new letters to read. Bob was a divorced father of two girls from San Luis Obispo whom I cleverly called "San Luis Obispo Bob." He set up a bedroom for us for a week's stay in his mother's converted garage. My mother introduced herself by sending him a decade-old photograph. A rectangle of picture was missing next to her waist where my four-year-old self had been trimmed out.

"Dear Bob," she wrote on the back, "this was with someone else."

Bob had the misfortune of being my fourth assigned "father" in as many months, and I'd had enough. He was stunned to learn that my mother had a son but treated me with a warm, steady kindness. I rewarded him by sulking in restaurants if they didn't serve Coke and French fries.

"*Thanks* for this seafood burrito," I said.

Meeting Elmer's sons had been the best part of that trip, and I wanted that same connection with Bob's tween daughters. I'd sometimes turned residents of my stuffed animal kingdom into younger sisters whom I protected from the ineffable waves of my mother's wrath. There were fictional older brothers, too, absorbing most of the anger meant for me, but brothers felt too much like fathers and therefore more difficult to imagine. With Bob's girls, I saw myself as an older, wiser version of the clingy, father-hungry boy I thought I no longer was. I asked them questions about school and suggested books I thought they'd like, but when they saw my roiling "I'm fatherless" anger lash out at their dad, they kept their distance. Like my mother, I was learning how to want too much too soon.

My mother told Bob, "We'll be back," but Bob took her at her word and, a month later, showed up at our front door in a station wagon with his two girls. They were packed for an extended stay.

"I think you misunderstood me!" my mother said and reached into the wagon to play with his girls. They talked for about ten minutes.

"I'm sorry, Maria," he said, and then gave my mother a good-bye kiss. "I'll see you both next week, then?" he asked. Then he got in the car to drive three and a half hours right back to San Luis Obispo.

My mother performed a soldier's wife's wave good-bye.

"Are we going up there next week?" I asked.

"Yes. We're going to get married," she said.

"Really?" I asked, both skeptical and uncertain.

While Bob did a three-point turn, my mother caught my eye. Then, as his car sped away, she elbowed me and laughed. I kept smiling and waving.

Some months later, my mother said that Bob had kidnapped his daughters and gone on the run.

"Really," I said again, the statement perched atop a question mark's scythe. I worried about his daughters but wouldn't take the conversation bait. What little time we spent together now was in front of her television watching movies. On slow work days, she'd leave her door open a crack, and I'd sit on the bed with her. No matter how far along she was in a picture when I arrived, I'd stay with her, laugh when she laughed, egg her on to talk back to the screen, and watch through to the end. She'd speculate on what happened to the characters in a movie after the credits rolled, in particular if it was a love story with an ambiguous ending.

"Do you think they make it?" she'd ask, and in her eyes was an earnestness that pleaded, *Tell me* you *have the answers I need, Brando.* She knew I didn't want the answers my mother had for me anymore.

My father figures and stepfathers were magicians, able to appear or disappear at will. When I was fifteen, my fourth stepfather, Pat, materialized at our house with a U-Haul trailer towed behind his car. He had driven straight from his one-bedroom apartment in South Lake Tahoe, Nevada, and just showed up at the front door around midnight—another man like San Luis Obispo Bob, ready to move in, an instant father; just add a fake marriage license.

Pat stood around six feet, with murky Santa Monica Bay green eyes and short blond hair, and was younger than my mother by several years. He rode a motorcycle, and his 265 well-proportioned pounds occupied space like a couch perched upright on one of its arms. He leaned as if he could topple onto you any minute.

When we'd visited him in Tahoe for a week—"It's like Vegas in the mountains!" my mother said—he showed up two hours late at the airport.

"Go search the airport and find him!" my mother ordered, panicked. I walked outside the tiny one-terminal airport, looked around, and then waited, as far away from my mother as I could.

Pat arrived in a limousine with cheap roses and a bottle of celebratory champagne we never opened. He *loved* to talk. His voice curved high like a contrail, and he claimed to know everybody in town. A vengeful maître d' who gave us crappy seats at a Dean Martin show would "get what was coming to him," and Pat casually tossed out the fact that he personally knew one or two guys listed in gambling's infamous "Black Book," men who were banned from entering any casino. My mother, unhappy with Pat's stories taking up all the space in the room, explained our Indian heritage as she refused to take the customary boarding photo before a paddleboat cruise because "photos rob Indians of their souls." (Her weight problem made her avoid photographs altogether.)

Two nights before we left, Pat went out for a motorcycle ride around ten at night. He left behind his car keys and a full fridge. Pat didn't return the next day, didn't call, nor did anyone stop by to check on us. He didn't return the day after that. For the first time in our years of traveling, we were marooned.

"I'm not going to worry about a man I'm not even married to," my mother said. I can't remember whether she said "yet."

We concocted various getaway fantasies that, because neither of us could drive a car, ended at his front door. We ordered pizza because neither of us knew how to cook. My mother ransacked his apartment, first for money and then for clues as to "who this man really is." She found neither. An honorable discharge certificate confirmed his story about being in the navy but everything else was a mystery. What had happened to him? Had Pat wiped out on his bike? Was he in a hospital somewhere with a memory-sapping concussion? My mother, faced with legitimately mysterious circumstances that could have spelled the trouble she seemed to love chasing, backed off, and we flew home.

The choppy flight back spooked my mother, who'd never fly again. "I haven't noticed any turbulence," a stewardess snapped at my mother. She wasn't used to traveling with a teenager and not an adorable attention-getting child. It was difficult to watch how terrified she was. I thought about what might comfort her: some conversation, a joke, holding her hand. But I was so used to absorbing her fear and anger in silence, it was automatic to say and do nothing. My own terror of a panicked mother had jelled into numbness. Now I spoke when spoken to and made only the tiniest of gestures in her presence, unable, or unwilling, to protect her from her own fears.

There were messages from Pat on my mother's answering machine when we got home. What Hail Mary explanation had Pat offered to explain his disappearance and continue the relationship?

"I'd wiped out on my bike and didn't know how to reach you."

"He couldn't call his own apartment?" I asked my mother. "That doesn't make sense."

My mother said, "It's none of your business." Once meant to dissuade me from my past, "none of your business" was how my mother handled my increasing curiosity about our shared futures.

Three months after Pat had disappeared in Tahoe, he reappeared, like magic, at the bottom of our front stairs by the old jacaranda tree. In the spot from which my biological father and two of my three stepfathers took their first steps into flight, I shook Pat's hand in tentative friendship. Two weeks later, I shook his hand again, celebrating his first marriage while I "gave away" my mother at her fourth—that is, her fourth marriage ceremony. (Official paperwork was sent in with a false name or not at all.) It was her third marriage without a divorce in less than ten years.

Pat's mother, Jane, lectured my mother on her wedding day about the importance of dieting—"A moment of temptation in your face, a lifetime on your waist!"—and gave Pat a wedding card that he opened at the outdoor altar. There was a fifty-dollar bill inside. My mother gasped. When the yelling started their honeymoon night, at the same Lake Arrowhead hotel where Frank had taken my mother and me less than a year earlier, I realized her gasp had been stunned disappointment.

Pat was kept oblivious about us being Mexicans so that we could benefit from what my mother called "white man's guilt." That made no sense, I told my mother. Wouldn't whites feel guilty about how Mexicans are treated too?

"Are you fucking serious?" my mother asked.

Pat found a job as an assistant restaurant manager in the San Fernando Valley, but then the car he drove down from Lake Tahoe collapsed in an asthmatic attack on the highway. There wasn't enough money for a replacement.

"I see that I can take the bus to work," he said. "What's that like, Brando, taking the bus in Los Angeles?"

Public transportation was a lot like my house on wheels, really: ridden by the poor, the minority, the working class, and the sometimes crazy.

"I think you'll get used to it," I said to Pat.

To a white man who'd never known the indignities of squeezing into a Spam-can-tight seat bench surrounded by "loud and angry blacks," as Pat described it, the daily commute was four hours of sheer punishment. He'd come home and try to quietly unlock the front door security gate. "Sounds like I'm opening a prison cell," Pat said. "Can't we get rid of this door? You don't need it anymore to be safe. I'm here."

Those metal clangs summoned my grandmother and mother to the living room, where they pounced on him:

"What took you so long to get home?"

"Where is your paycheck?"

"What do you mean there's nothing left after taxes?"

"What kind of dumb fuck works so long for so little?"

Despite all this, Pat maintained a never-dimming attitude that was positive, cheerful, easygoing, compassionate, and, most important, sober. I'm not sure how he did it. His was a linoleum personality that wiped clean after each spill. I wasn't as strong. In the face of a similar battery of questions when I came home from school, I hid behind my room's semifunctional lock, like my mother, and gorged myself on one large platter of food at a single sitting. Pat took over cooking duties and cooked navy-style portions that I'd eat and eat until the food was gone.

"You like beef Stroganoff?" my grandmother asked in disbelief. "He makes too much goddamn white food."

It was a sick pattern of dinner binging without the purging meant to limit how much time I spent with my family and to fit into my own high school uniform: rayon print shirts that resembled Moroccan wall tapestries and Z. Cavaricci slacks—tapered at the ankle, wide at the hip—with an identifying white brand label down the fly.

"Dude," my male friends asked in earnest, "do you have an eating disorder?"

A shift change at Pat's restaurant a couple months later meant that he came home around midnight, after my grandmother had turned off her television and my mother had gone to bed. I was still sleeping in my grandmother's bed, and my burning bedroom light frequently led him to rap on my door and strike up conversations, but I'd shut him down with teenage detachment and distance. I had decided that, at fifteen, I was now too old for a father-son relationship, the same way one reaches a certain age where it's too late to start playing a sport with an eye toward reaching a professional level. I'd welcomed Pat to the house with two basic rules: do whatever my mother says, and leave me alone because I don't want a father anymore. The first part Pat had down cold; during arguments with my mother, who came up just to his shoulders, he bent his head down so she could jump up a half foot and slap his face.

"I had to want to be hit for her to reach me without a stool," he said with a smile. The other half, leaving me alone, was harder for him to accept. One night Pat came with a gift.

"I asked at the record store who the lead singer of that band you like was," he said. "He said I should buy this." Pat handed me a long-boxed copy of Morrissey's first solo album *"Viva Hate."*

"I don't know Spanish, but that title means 'Long live hate,'" Pat said. "He looks like James Dean. What could *he* have to hate about life?"

I laughed. "Yeah, I guess I like him because he sings what I'm feeling."

"We both have growing pains here, don't we?" he said.

Before I could answer, he said good night and closed my door with a respectful click.

How safe was it to get close to a man who'd shown a capacity to materialize from nowhere or, worse, *Northern California*? (All that fog-shrouded "losing myself to find myself" scenery up there.) Yet here was a sincere attempt at alliance that, unlike my other stepfathers, didn't involve pitting my mother against me. It was flattering, and, as often happens when you're being flattered, your longing to be embraced overrules your sense of caution. Pat saw us as POWs in the same prison camp, and it made sense for us to pool our resources, to trade each other's trivialities, the things that we held dear to us when no one was looking—things that he said would bond us together to survive "in a house filled with men-hating women."

Given the time Paul spent drinking, the days Robert vanished, and the gaps between Frank's check-ins, Pat's day-to-day presence gave him a familiarity and a legitimacy my previous fathers never earned. I saw for the first time the punishing treadmill of life of a man who wasn't my grandfather Emilio, who had to leave the house every morning and come home at the same time each night. On weekends, Pat was exhausted but took over cooking duties. He lobbied for a new sectional sofa and loveseat with a pullout mattress that folded out onto the floor, so that at sixteen I finally had my own bed to go with the room that had been mine since my grandfather's death. I'd shared a bed with my grandmother for fourteen years, longer than she'd slept in one with her husband.

"An older boy needs his own room and his own bed," he said. "Besides, Grandma," he told her, "this way he won't wake you up when he climbs into bed after staying up late doing his homework."

A television Pat had brought in the U-Haul, an old Nintendo game system, and a VCR completed my hermetically sealed setup.

"Don't stay up too late watching cable. Sometimes they have naughty movies on," he said, winking.

We rented movies together, and he watched me play video games. He applauded when I vanquished Zelda II, where, upon rescuing the princess, the hero receives an embrace behind a curtain.

"All that work for a hug?" Pat asked. "Just like real life," he said, high-fiving me with a conspiratorial man-to-man grin.

Pat and I helped each other find a safe place in our own harsh and confusing worlds. I told him where to sit on the bus on his ride home from work so that he wouldn't get hassled for being white: closest to the exits, nearest the driver, never in the back. He showed me how to knot a necktie.

"You can't wear a clip-on to your office job," he said. "Put the skinny end near the fold of your inside elbow. Like this," he said, and leaned down to help. Pat's meaty hands tied a gentle knot around my neck. One of his fish stick–sized fingers brushed my throat, and I jerked back a bit—a dog on a leash wincing at the sting of my mother's strangling me in Nakome's trailer.

"It's okay," he said, and I knew in this one small moment that it would be.

"Thanks, Pat," I said. The word *Dad* cowered on my tongue's tip, a groundhog too spooked by shadows of fathers past to emerge.

Pat earned his promotion to "father" with consistency and time, the two things a stepparent can't force. Riding in on a wave of pubescent testosterone was severe disfiguring cystic acne that distended my back, chest, face, and earlobes with boils as heavy as gram weights.

"I'm not taking you to a doctor," my grandmother said. "The neighborhood's filled with quacks. I had acne, and I turned out fine. You don't need any medicine."

Time grated my cheeks down to miles of bad road. My back crinkled into skin mistaken for second-degree-burn tissue. I'd wear undershirts that at school day's end had shoulder-to-shoulder bloodstains resembling birdshot. Pat brought home clean Hanes T-shirts and medical pads to tape across my back.

When I'd caught a persistent cough, my mother drowned me in NyQuil and music.

"This will help you sleep," she said, and played the Doors' self-titled debut album on repeat. I liked her effort to be maternal, but the Doors and NyQuil were a horrifying mix. I'd drift in and out of consciousness, waking up sweat drenched during Jim Morrison's oedipal howl in "The End" and seeing large black dogs at the foot of my bed.

My grandmother's approach was different.

"You want me to *eat* the Vicks VapoRub?" I asked. "It says 'external use only' on the jar."

"I've eaten it all the time, and nothing bad's ever happened to me."

"*External* means you don't eat it," I said.

"God, I loved it more when you weren't able to read," she said.

When the weeklong cough developed into walking pneumonia, Pat stepped in. "You can't solve this with NyQuil. Either I take Brando to the doctor's today or I'm not coming home tonight."

In the pharmacy parking lot, Pat said, "Wait here in the car." There was the comforting sound of the car door locking behind him, his confident "taking care of business" stride while he got my medicine. Gripped in a delirious sickness where you surrender to wherever help comes from, I put my fingertips on the cool windshield to touch him and said, "Okay, Dad. Okay."

Just when my mother stopped pressuring me to accept a man as a father did it at last feel right. I trusted Pat. It was impossible to untrust him now.

To my other dads, even my real one, I'd been forgettable, easily abandoned, a distraction, an acceptable sidekick, a transparent sponge to soak up their tastes and desires, and not able to express my own. Now, with my fourth and sure to be last stepfather, perhaps some alchemy could turn us into men, together.

Presto, change-o, *alakazam*! A visible son, at last.

• • •

A work truck filled with tree trimmers wielding poles and chainsaws arrived to trim the jacaranda tree out front, bringing to an end my grandmother's decade long letter-writing crusade to have her tree trimmed. She'd written numerous letters to every California public official for help: LA mayor Tom Bradley, Governor George Deukmejian, Senator Alan Cranston. She'd even enlisted officials who weren't from our same state.

"Ted Kennedy represents Massachusetts, Grandma," I told her.

"I voted for the bastard when he ran for president!" she said. "He's supposed to help old women like me."

The tree trimmers stripped the branches above my favorite place, a nook at the bottom of our staircase that couldn't be seen by anyone in my house, down to stumps. My grandmother had robbed me of my clubhouse. By high school, her charms seemed vulgar and grotesque; my high school friends, of course, thought she was a total badass. My mother, too, was "awesome." When she wasn't locked in her bedroom working as a phone sex operator, she befriended my teenage buddies, our high school's only multiethnic alterna-music-loving collective. She peppered profanity into conversations. At first they encouraged her to curse; then struggled to keep up. ("What's a 'reverse butt plug'?") She learned their likes—which became my likes, of course—and soon had copies of the Cure's *Disintegration* and Depeche Mode's *Music for the Masses* sitting next to her Buffy Sainte-Marie cassettes.

She was the "cool" parent you could talk music or sex with. Asking questions, though, meant that you had to shut up and listen to her, too.

"Did you know I'm dying?" she'd say, and tell stories about her numerous health maladies: the temporary blindness, the blood poisoning, the ingrown toenails, and the "inoperable brain tumor": that pernicious beast that shadowed her for years, routinely bursting into her head DEA-drug-bust style and then vanishing like an ice-cream headache. My friends trusted my mother's stories; one friend's sincere greeting whenever I saw him was, "So how's your mom's tumor?"

No topic was off-limits. Nothing, that is, except her job.

"Doesn't your mom ever come out of her room?" one friend asked me.

"When she's not working."

"It's ten o'clock at night."

"She's a telemarketer."

"What does a 'telemarketer' do, anyway?"

"She's in sales."

"What does she sell?"

"Office supplies," I said.

"Who buys office supplies at ten o'clock at night?"

"Someone who . . . really needs paper." (I wasn't as swift on my storytelling toes as my mother was.)

My friends were old enough to poke holes in this and my other gaseous tales, but one thing that had to remain secret was our identities as Mexicans. I sure was inventing some tall tales of my own to keep that part of my life hidden, though:

"My father was an Indian chief. Yes, that means I'll take over the tribe one day."

"My name Skyhorse means 'great warrior.' Yes, just like a Jedi from *Star Wars*."

"Yes, these blond highlights my mother got for me at the Edward Boye' Salon in West Hollywood are consistent with my Indian upbringing. Indians put sand in their hair as part of their ascent into manhood."

Not that any of it mattered to my Mexican high school friends, who were more interested in seeing the Cure at Dodger Stadium or hearing the latest Morrissey single than speaking Spanish and discussing our mutual "*cultura*." We talked of getting Depeche Mode tattoos and lusted after what we called KROQ (pronounced K-Rock) chicks: white and Asian girls named for the local alternative music radio station who wore wispy black dresses on ninety-four-degree days or jean shorts with black tights and combat boots. Our shared culture was English pop music, not *la raza*.

My mother, who was still playing her deck of bad fake ID cards with interchangeable versions of Running Deer Skyhorse, acknowledged being a Mexican only when playacting on the phone with her clients. When my mother's best friend in the phone sex business (her only friend that I knew of) was out of town, the friend's boyfriend wanted some action. Instead of calling his girlfriend's service, which would have let him talk to someone for free, he dialed my mother's service and spoke to her for eight hundred dollars' worth of charges. When my mother's friend got the bill a month later, she asked her boyfriend why he did it.

"I wanted to speak to somebody Latina," he explained

His girlfriend told him, "The joke's on you, dummy. You were talking to an American Indian."

"Who are the roses for?" Pat asked. I'd stashed them in the fridge and told my mother and grandmother that they were a gift to a teacher leaving staff. They believed me.

"Roses for a teacher," Pat said. "Uh-huh. She must be very . . . pretty."

I'd crushed for over a year on a casual friend who worked at the student store, but I had no idea what to do next. Buy her something nice, express my feelings in the most over-the-top way possible, and pray that my feelings are reciprocated, right? At her best friend's suggestion, for Christmas I bought her college sweatshirts: soft-hued Nordstrom knockoffs to soften how weird and masculine these gifts were. I wrapped them in shiny foil boxes that I stuffed in my backpack and paired them with a dozen roses I carried to school upside down in a plastic bag like a bouquet of inverted balloons. On the last day before winter break, I assembled everything on her homeroom desk then asked her for a date. Out of sheer embarrassment, she said "yes."

She found a way to say "no" a couple days later on the phone.

"So what did the flowers you gave me mean?" she asked after an hour-long conversation.

"They mean, I guess, that . . . I love you." She didn't hear the question mark I ended the sentence with in my head.

"I think we should just be friends," she said. I was devastated, but by now it was a familiar feeling. This heartache played in a minor key compared to what I felt when a father left. Pat spotted that my sullenness was not, as my mother feared, a defiant act of rebellion.

"Why are you turning into an asshole?" she asked me.

"He's okay. He just misses his teacher." Pat patted me on the back and yawned, clinging to the kitchen sink. His bus commute was exhausting, but he was stuck, since my grandmother refused to have "another man in my house with a car."

Surprisingly, my mother, a long ways from her passionate defense of Robert, stood up for Pat. "Maybe it's time for us to go, then. Pat wants to get us a place of our own. I really don't want to die in this house," she said, convinced that her tumor was acting up again like a pulled tendon.

"A new broom sweeps clean," my grandmother retorted. "You aren't going *anywhere*."

Sharing a house with my mother and grandmother had always been like shuttling between two divorced parents. They drifted apart when a husband arrived but came back together when he left, two land masses forever separating and colliding. No one had ever seriously threatened—or encouraged—us to move out before now. Pat's work ethic meant that he might be a man my grandmother had to take *seriously*.

"Let Pat support us if he wants," my mother said. "If he can't buy himself a car with his own damn money, it's time for us to move out on our own." My grandmother backed down. That was the easy part.

"You see this here?" a salesman told Pat. "This is a 'red flag.' You have three of them on your credit report."

When the salesman left, I asked Pat, "What's a red flag?"

"Oh, it doesn't mean anything. My report should have been cleaned up by now. It's an old college loan thing. I took care of everything in Tahoe," he said. His reply was itself a red flag, but before I could respond, he patted my shoulder and said, "We'll get there, Brando."

Pat at last found a "new" used Subaru with power windows, power locks, power antenna, power sunroof. It was the most extravagant four wheels our family had ever, or would ever, own.

"Would you drive this car?" Pat asked me with a wry grin. I was exhilarated to ride in a not-piece-of-shit car. Could our family *afford* this?

"My parents will wire transfer me the three-thousand-dollar down payment," Pat said. "We can take it home today."

We drove off the used-car lot under a bright sun, a clear spring Los Angeles sky with the power windows and power sunroof open. I tuned into my favorite radio station just as it played my favorite band Depeche Mode's new single—and thus my new favorite song—and Pat high-fived me. Being sixteen, I thought that life's happiness came from lining up as many of your favorites in a row as you could. Here they all were, together, with my new favorite father.

The next day, a Saturday, Pat gave me my first driving lesson in the rambling paved valleys of Dodger Stadium's acres-wide parking lots. The car was a feather-touch automatic, and Pat, a patient, encouraging teacher, but I was still the slow learner I'd been when Oscar had tried to teach me how to ride a bike.

"We'll go out again next week," he promised.

Three days later, I ditched school with permission from my mother—who warned me to "be safe and take care of myself" if anything bad happened, and whose habitual premonition for catastrophe I shrugged off—and got into a line with a group of four friends and over three hundred other kids at eight in the morning to earn

Depeche Mode autographs at a record-release in-store signing. In that pre–cell phone era, we passed the next thirteen hours listening to the new album on state-of-the-art CD boom boxes and dispatches from the radio station organizing the event. We made cardboard *Honk If You Like Depeche Mode* signs that we waved at confused motorists and had awkward, parrying conversations about who we liked in school. I wandered through the bright, clean aisles of the Beverly Center mall across the street with Cristina, a new crush, not talking, and imagined us sitting at a food court, sharing deep secrets while her black tights and Doc Martens brushed against my ultra-cool Zodiac shoes.

Nightfall swelled the waiting crowd to an estimated fifteen thousand people. The line became a surging, bottle-throwing sea that carried me several feet off the ground and dropped me hard against a concrete shore. The signing, unbeknownst to us, was canceled. We'd waited hours for nothing and were stuck in an angry mob. My friends didn't want to leave, but my mother's survival instincts kicked in. I fought through the crowd and called Pat from a pay phone a block away. Where that instinct to call him for help came from, I don't know. It might have been desperation or a sincere belief that here at last was a father figure I could turn to when I was in need.

"Stay safe," he said. "I'll come and get you as soon as I can." It took him almost two hours, but Pat found us, materializing from around a corner.

"There were police barricades on the street, so I had to park a few blocks away," he said.

"How did you get past them?" I asked.

"Oh, I have my ways," he said and smiled. He drove me and my friends to the restaurant he managed. It was past closing time, but he opened up the kitchen, sat us at a booth, and took our orders like a waiter. Starved and dehydrated from waiting all day in line, we wolfed down sizzling hamburgers coated with shaved onion rings and swallowed oversized glasses of delicious, ice-cold sodas.

"You have, like, the coolest dad ever," Cristina said.

"She's right, Brando!" Pat shouted from the kitchen.

Pat crammed us into the car—there wasn't enough space for us, so Cristina sat on my lap—and drove each of my friends home. We pulled up to our house around three in the morning.

My mother let me sleep in late and miss school the next day, too. Pat was home early, the car cutting almost an hour and a half off his commute. When I joined everyone for dinner that night, there was this eerie peace; a sense of joyous calm that settled over the table.

"I'm glad you're okay," my mother said. "It must have been like the sixties for you out there!"

"I should've listened to you to be careful," I said.

"Pat was there when you needed him," my mother said and stroked his arm.

That dinner, there was joking without cruelty, laughter without maliciousness. Some kind of spirit was there in that dining room binding us together, protecting us all from unexpected misfortune that had nipped our every step for years. Good things *could* at last happen to us. We were *going* to make it.

Two days later, Pat called from the restaurant.

"I'm coming home late tonight on the bus. Somebody stole the car."

"Let's see you steal this one," Pat said as he attached a theft protection club to the steering wheel of a crippled 1970s yellow Honda hatchback that with his seat pushed way back put Pat's knees right under the steering wheel. The car lost power at odd times and filled with engine smoke when put in reverse.

"This is only for a while," Pat said. "I'm expecting another wire transfer."

When the new round of transfers cleared, the Honda was traded in for a large Pat-friendly Ford Bronco SUV. He found new work at a family-style restaurant chain that let him take home "overstock" food destined for the trash and crammed our freezer with steaks, burgers, and chicken breasts. An "asshole manager" from his old job who had accused Pat of a nebulous financial impropriety found his car damaged.

"Instant karma," Pat said.

The red flags were thick as wildflowers, and yet I can't remember a time when we, as a family, were less alert or more content. I'd never see my mother happier or watch her anger dissolve faster. She cared less about the plight of American Indians and more about new patio furniture and aromatherapy. My mother let Pat string Christmas lights around the security bars on our front windows as he tortured us with a high-pitched rendition of "Grandma Got Run Over by a Reindeer."

"Invite your friends for Thanksgiving dinner," he said. "I want to cook for them."

When my friends arrived, Pat set out a spectacular multicourse "overstock" feast catered with large restaurant-sized cartons of steak and lobster, along with five different whole pies for dessert. Sitting himself with my mother and grandmother at what he called the "kids'" table on the back indoor patio, he served me and my friends in the dining room wearing his chef's whites.

I'd invited over my newest crush, Sofie, a Vietnamese girl who'd been a friend for almost six months. My mother and grandmother were completely oblivious to my feelings for Sofie; Pat wasn't, and courted her with extra servings.

"Make sure she's comfortable," he told me. "She's not just here for the food."

After dinner, my friends played board games while I sat next to Sofie and counted the times we accidentally brushed against each other. On the patio, the adults sipped wine, cussed without malice in a tryptophan afterglow, and listened politely as my mother spent the entire Thanksgiving dinner talking about a concert she and Pat were going to in a couple weeks. The tickets were for Fleetwood Mac, but they actually were a passport for my mother to meet her "Goddess": Stevie Nicks.

I'd saved up enough from my summer job at a stock brokerage house to buy her and Pat twelfth-row floor tickets. The concert would be my mother's first "night out" in a year. She idolized Stevie Nicks, whose smoky voice was like a drug to help Mom escape from her life. My mother deputized herself a high priestess in Stevie's faux Wiccan army; if Stevie had formed a country, I'm sure my mother would have found a way to make us citizens.

Mom went to a beauty salon for her hair and nails, and then spent the afternoon in front of her closet interviewing potential outfits. Pat bought a gold box of long-stemmed roses that my mother was to use to get to the stage. During a darkened encore break, a security guard let my mother approach the barricade. There, for about thirty seconds, my mother became the rock star she had wanted to be her whole life.

She could hear a lumbering roar float up from the front of the stage, rise like a wave to the back of the arena, cresting up in the cheap seats, and then snapping back down to her. Why all this cheering? Were they cheering, she wondered, because she'd made it up to the barricades? Were they cheering for *her*? (Oh, *Mom*.) She didn't see the band's silhouettes slide across the stage. Leaning over the metal barricade, my mother shoved the box of roses onstage just as the stage lights came on. My mother was ten feet from Stevie Nicks.

"I love you, Bella Donna!" my mother screamed. Stevie flip-twisted her hair and smiled, and then cradled the gold box of roses and handed them off to a roadie. She mouthed the words "Thank you."

My mother had looked into the eyes of her Goddess. And it was good. She recounted that story for a week and a half—and, uncharacteristically, told it the exact same way—wanting to stretch that moment out to experience it every day.

"I'll never forget what you did for me, Brando," she said. "You really do love me."

She'd forget, of course. But she remembered that night.

• • •

On New Year's Day, 1991, Pat and my mother invited Sofie and me to Disneyland. Sofie and I had already been on several platonic dates, and this was the day I'd hoped we'd consummate our relationship with a kiss. Having breakfast together on Main Street, U.S.A, in the Carnation Café inhaling piped-in candy-cane-scented air, we could have been a bad barroom joke: a large Irish man, his Mexican wife and stepson masquerading as American Indians, and a young Vietnamese girl walk into the Happiest Place on Earth and order breakfast. But this time there wasn't a cruel punch line. No stuffed Mickeys were abducted, no messy entanglements with undercover Disney police officers. My mother had a content, tranquilized glow about her. She was feeling safe and secure with Pat, and also taking new diet pills. My mother was genuinely happy, but years of seeing her miserable had made it difficult for me to tell. It was easy to mistake what happiness looked like at Disneyland.

Pat and my mother split off halfway through the day so that Sofie and I could spend time alone together. We rode the Skyway from Fantasyland to Tomorrowland. Sofie was facing me, looking back at Fantasyland and what we were leaving behind, while I looked ahead to Tomorrowland and what was yet to come. It's a perfect metaphor, sure, but it's hard to see us in that moment here, knowing what was about to come: for us, for my family, for me. If I could take that ride again, I'd sit next to Sofie with her hand in mine and my back to the future too.

Sofie sat on my lap in the backseat on the night ride home.

"I think we should be *together*," I said.

"I do, too," she said, and we kissed. Over her shoulder, I saw Pat eyeing us in the rearview mirror, grinning. When he dropped her off, he said, "I knew she liked you. Now all you have to do is keep her happy so you don't lose her. That's the hard part. There's a lot of little things and tricks to keeping a woman happy."

I waited for my mother to chip in some brutal, acerbic comment. She had fallen asleep in the passenger seat. Pat looked at me in the rearview and mouthed "See?"

"You didn't get either of us *anything* for Valentine's Day?" my grandmother asked. It didn't take my mother and grandmother long to figure out they wouldn't be getting their customary sweetheart cards.

"You have a *girlfriend*?" my mother asked. "You sure you aren't gay? You'd be so much more interesting if you were."

My parents soon realized how valuable a new person to talk to would be. Drawn to Sofie's sweetness and naïveté, my mother tried being my girlfriend's girlfriend. When Sofie came over, my mother took off her sweaty phone headset, roped Sofie into her bedroom, and stunned the poor girl with her ribald, adolescent vigor. Sofie had never heard the words *skinny* and *bitches* used as a compound phrase before.

"This is what speaks louder to a real woman than any fucking thing," my mother said, and pulled a rolled-up ball of cash from her cleavage, fanning it. "You must get your 'men' to pay to be around you."

My grandmother had noticed how much time Sofie spent with my mother and wanted to see if she, too, could connect with her.

"Did I tell you about my worthless son?" my grandmother asked. "I've left him one dollar in my will. He's never getting this house!"

Or: "Don't you think Pat makes too much food?"

Then: "Why is Brando such a horrible grandson to me?" Like Pat, Sofie found it odd that I'd just now graduated to my own bed, and the wet kisses my grandmother gave her when she walked in the front door made her uncomfortable.

Pat was Sofie's safe zone. He told G-rated versions of Andrew Dice Clay routines and sang goofy songs like "Stray Cat Strut" while he led Sofie and me into the kitchen to watch him make restaurant-sized omelets with fat chunks of fresh "overstock" lobster and blueberry pancakes smeared with peanut butter.

"Sometimes it seems like Pat's the only normal one here," Sofie said.

Pat had lived with us for close to two years when he revealed that he was in the running for a senior management position at his chain restaurant's corporate headquarters in Northern California.

"Starting salary is ninety thousand a year," he said, a staggering amount to our family. His mantra repetition of that sum just made it seem more unreal.

"Think, Brando," he said, "you could have a *real* bedroom. Big enough for an actual bed. With only three of us, you could have two rooms, one when you come home from college you could use for your studies, like an office. Wouldn't you like that?"

Was it safe to imagine a middle-class life outside of Echo Park provided by a man who disappeared from his own apartment? Or whose new erratic work schedule led him to stash white burlap money sacks with rolls of coins under my mother's bed? ("It was too late to visit the bank," he said. "I'll deposit them tomorrow.")

I never stopped to ask because I was dreaming of an escape to college. I'd been identified a gifted student in second grade and took advanced courses throughout junior high and high school but didn't know how realistic my dreams were. I carried my college catalogues—Harvard, Yale, Stanford—everywhere, as if they'd disappear like my fathers if I let them out of my sight. I woke myself early on test days, hitching rides to test centers with friends, and stayed up late playing MTV with no sound, teeth chattering while I wrote bad college application essays and struggled to fill in tiny, precise spaces with a moody electric typewriter. I pictured me and a multiethnic group of friends smiling outdoors on a sunny patch of grass, *just like in the glossy pictures*! I saw Pat lugging a heavy steamer trunk—something I didn't even *own*—up a narrow flight of dormitory stairs on a hectic orientation day, winking at me when a cute girl said hello. It was like the playacting I did with my mother, except the stuffed animals were gone, and I didn't need my mother as a partner to pretend anymore.

I didn't discuss what schools I was applying to, campus tours, or how I'd pay for it all, because no one I knew had ever gone to college; my mother had some community college and beauty school. It was just assumed I'd go *somewhere*.

"That's what smart kids do," my mother said. "You don't need my bullshit to interfere."

"We'll mortgage the house if we have to," my grandmother said.

Later my mother said, "Don't expect her to do that. Figure the money out on your own. If you can't afford it, remember you don't have to go to school. You don't have to go anywhere," my mother said. "But I know you will."

I kept the college process away from my mother. I was just ready to get *out*. The problem, of course, was Sofie. She'd become far too important a part of my life, and I couldn't imagine what would happen when—*if*—I went away to school. Pat was the only one who seemed to understand our relationship. Maybe I could talk to him about Sofie. I joined Pat on a rare afternoon spent on the living room couch watching my grandmother's television. It was just the two of us.

"About time I got to do *something* in this house outside of your mother's room," he said. He didn't seem himself. There was a war movie on cable.

"Those 'gooks' are really dug in," he said.

"Hey, Sofie's Vietnamese," I said. "That's a really racist word to use."

"I know about your girlfriend," he said. "I wasn't talking about her."

"You should apologize."

"What's got into you? You know that's not what I meant," Pat said. "You're making something out of nothing, just like your mother."

There was that slap to my face again: "just like your mother." Was

I just like her? What did that mean, exactly? How many of my fathers had said that to me?

I stormed off to my room. *Just like my mother would have*, I thought. Maybe he was right. I knew he didn't mean to insult Sofie. Why hold an Andrew Dice Clay fan to a higher standard than my mother or grandmother, who spouted racist, sexist, and ethnic stereotypes every time they opened their mouths? What I didn't understand was why he wasn't backing down this time, the way he'd done in every disagreement. His standing his ground was as much a betrayal as was my singling him out as a racist. We never cleared the air, just sort of dropped the discussion. He had other things on his mind.

The next week, I was called out of my fifth-period economics class to take a phone call in the guidance counselor's office. There were rumors among my college-bound friends that you were pulled out of class when you were accepted to a really big school. Was this how my new future would begin?

At the office, someone said, "Your father's on the phone."

"I got the job," Pat said.

"You did? That was fast. Wow," I said, unwowed. Maybe this wasn't certain yet. Maybe the job would fall through.

"Ninety thousand a year," he said. I already knew that. Why keep repeating what I knew?

"I have to go to Northern California to their corporate offices to begin the paperwork. I wanted to call you before I left." I hadn't talked to him about Sofie. How had I run out of time with Pat already?

"You're going right now?" I asked.

"I want to get a jump on the traffic."

"Oh," I said. "Do you want to stop by here so you can say good-bye on your way out of town?"

I heard what sounded like the receiver shuffled around. "There really isn't time, but I'll call you when I get up there. I'll be sending for you and your mother in a week."

"Okay," I said.

"Ninety thousand a year," he said. "I'll see you soon!"

That afternoon, I left school in a daze. I didn't want to leave the house I'd known my whole life. There were so many *good* memories here—weren't there?

At home, I tried calling Sofie but couldn't get a dial tone. The phone wasn't dead; someone had unplugged it.

Pat fled Los Angeles with some of the restaurant's money and the Bronco—my mother claimed it was ten thousand dollars. The restaurant gave him the option of returning the money—and then getting fired—instead of facing prosecution. There would be no bedroom of my own or an office to do my college studies, just as there was no ninety-thousand-dollar-a-year job in Northern California. It seemed that our Thanksgiving dinner and the many pies and boxes of lobster and steak that filled the freezer weren't all "overstock." At least some of the bags under my mother's bed were restaurant deposits Pat never made. The Subaru he bought the year before had been repossessed when his check bounced. There wasn't a single emergency wire transfer from his parents, who, when informed of Pat's deceptions, responded with a brusque, officious air of incredulity that we'd been suckered in the first place. (Removing physical traces of Pat was easy; there was nothing to throw away because by then my mother had stopped posing for pictures.)

I was seventeen with four past "fathers"—Candy, Robert, Paul, and Pat—not to mention Frank and the chain of temporary boyfriends. They were all "count 'em off" scratches on a wall now. It had seemed possible for a while that one steady man could steer us to a "normal" family life of barbeques, father-and-son road trips, and a nice house in boring middle-class suburbia where your dad rose and slept under the same roof. Pat's lies cracked that dream apart. It was time to rid my house of *every* lie. I had to "come out" as a Mexican.

It had been three or four years since I discovered I was Mexican, yet I was still acting out the same Indian charade for strangers, for my friends in school, for Sofie. We'd been dating only a couple months, but my teenage black-and-white thinking made me certain I'd marry only once and that Sofie was *the one*. She'd been absorbed into my family drama so fast, and had become such a necessary brace and validation for how I survived in my world, I decided that Sofie deserved the truth.

My mother drilled me never to tell anyone "outside the family" about our real backgrounds. "It's none of their business," she'd say, warning me I'd be disappointed with how people would react.

"Nobody gives a shit about another ordinary Mexican from Echo Park," she said. "Nobody will care who you are."

More lies to protect a lie, I thought. By telling Sofie, I hadn't planned on "embracing my Mexican roots" or learning Spanish. I wouldn't change my name to Ulloa, because why swap the name of a father who had abandoned me for *another* father who had abandoned me? I'd thought Paul was my father for years and lived with him as his son. I'd earned the right to be called Skyhorse. What I didn't have a right to was telling people I was Indian. It seemed simple to me. This wasn't about losing one set of cultural roots and replacing them with another or swapping one set of politics of the oppressed for the other. I wasn't interested in being *just* an Indian *or* a Mexican at seventeen. I wanted to be *me*—someone who wasn't an Indian or a Mexican *first*. My mother was telling me that if I didn't want to lose people I loved, I had to be *her* version of me. I knew she was wrong.

"What do you *mean* you're not American Indian?" Sofie asked. "I don't understand."

"I'm Mexican," I said. "My father was Mexican, but I was raised as an Indian."

"You've been lying to me? What about your mother and your grandmother? You're *all* Mexicans too?" It hadn't occurred to Sofie once that my family was Mexican. Sofie saw my mother silence my grandmother whenever she spoke Spanish so often it had briefly occurred to her that my grandmother could be Mexican, but of no biological relation to my mother.

"Well, yeah. I mean, it's no big deal. I'm the same person. Is this a problem?"

"Yeah, it's a big problem. I feel so sick." She was in tears. "I'm sorry, I can't be with you, Brando. I can't see you anymore."

When Sofie told her family what happened, one of her sisters asked, "Why are you upset? Date a nice white guy."

I was devastated. My friends were confused. "What happened? Who dumped who?" By way of explanation, I "came out" one at a time to a rainbow coalition group of friends: white, Indian, Asian, and Mexican. (How much easier it'd have been to announce a "race change" as a status update on Facebook—*Hey guys, I'm Mexican now. Olé!*) I prepared an elaborate array of explanations and defenses for why I'd hidden the truth for so long. I thought my white friends would ask me endless rounds of questions I couldn't or didn't want to answer. My Mexican friends would call me a traitor.

"Oh, you're Mexican?" each of my friends said. "Weird. But whatever."

Sofie and I were broken up for two days; a month in high school time. She was contrite when we reconciled.

"It's my family," she said. "I'm not supposed to like Mexicans. They threw rocks at my house when I first moved to America. The girls teased me about my flat chest and my hairless forearms. In elementary school, they threatened to jump me in the bathroom. A Mexican mugged my brother and stole the one BMX bike we all had to share. Every Mexican I've met is the same. That's why I couldn't understand how you could be one too. You're not like any Mexican I've met," she said, and then added, "I'm sorry you had to tell everyone your secret."

I believed *secret* was the right word. This was information I'd have to protect when I went to college. How could I risk that anyone new in my life would offer the same kind of understanding and acceptance as my friends? Being a couple again, I saw things that confirmed Sofie's view of the world. In Chinatown, we received long, hostile glares when we held hands, and weren't seated in restaurants. On a bus, a light-skinned Hispanic woman said as she stepped off, "You two are disgusting!"

My own mother's and grandmother's reactions were just as hostile, but they were mad for a different reason.

"She *dumped* you?" my grandmother asked. "What the hell did you *think* would happen when you told an Oriental girl you were Mexican?"

"Why the hell did you snitch to anyone outside the family?" my mother asked. "Didn't you learn *anything* from being my son?"

I'd broken my mother's omertà. I repaid her with my senior class yearbook quote: "Thanks to my friends for EVERYTHING! Thanks to everyone else for NOTHING!"

"What the fuck did your friends ever do for you?" my mother asked.

It was a good point. With Pat and his paycheck gone, I didn't need friends. I needed cash. What I'd saved from my summer job wasn't close to covering senior year expenses. It was money I had to fight my mother to keep.

"How come you aren't like black kids that give all their money to their mothers and the house? Why are you so fucking greedy? You live here rent free and don't contribute shit!"

"This is money for college," I said. "And I pay as much rent as you do. Zero."

"Fuck you! Get the fuck out of my house!" Thunderous steps, a slammed door, an earthquake under my feet.

My acceptance to Stanford University, arriving a couple weeks after Pat abandoned us, was a parenthetical aside that didn't merit enough interest in the house for a closing bracket.

"Of course you got in, you're smart!" my mother said. "But are you smart enough to fix my VCR?"

Pat left at the worst time imaginable. Who would pick up where he left off? Who would help me with expenses for the prom? Who would help pay my enrollment deposit for college? I hated the fact that, for the moment, I thought more about Pat's wallet than his fatherhood, but my mother had taught me a simple thing throughout my life so far: money equals love.

"Take this," said Frank, pressing a roll of hundred-dollar bills into my hand. He'd do this twice that year—once at prom and again when he dropped me off at college. Unlike money that had come to me this way in the past—in warm, moist clumps—I knew how long Frank had worked for it, knew he hadn't stolen it, and knew he'd never ask for or steal it back.

I'd summoned Frank like a genie, but granting wishes came with new tests of understanding for both of us. He seemed confused about the man I was becoming: a man modeled on him in so many ways that we both didn't yet realize or understand. He drove Sofie and me to a concert and took us to dinner before the show. When Sofie went to the bathroom, Frank asked, "So who likes this band, you or her?"

"We both do," I said.

"Pet Shop Boys," he said. "I only know that one song of theirs. 'The East End boys and the West End girls.' What does 'Pet Shop Boys' mean? Are they a 'gay' band?"

"I don't know. I guess they're gay."

"If they're 'gay,' they're a 'gay' band. Do they have any songs about being gay?"

"No, not really. They're not like Bronski Beat, which has this song about coming out and being gay."

"That sounds sick," he said. "How do you know about this music? Do they play that song on the radio station you listen to?"

"Frank, I'm here with my *girl*friend."

I was angry with Frank for not being Pat, the same way that I had been angry with my other dads for not being Frank. Being a kid had helped me forget that anger *and* forget Frank fast, but I was too old to forget resentments anymore. I hated Frank's filthy Birkenstocks, his boring seventies rock music, his preconcert ritual of weed and drinking a six-pack of Heineken. When Frank took my mother, Sofie, and me to see Stevie Nicks, I sneered at the "Bella Donna" wannabes in the parking lot holding their arms aloft with chiffon shawl wings while they swirled in circles to music coming from cars.

We sat in the picnic area, Frank with a six-pack of Heinekens.

"How many beers is that?" I asked.

"This is my fourth and last one," he said.

"I think it's irresponsible for you to drink while you're driving us." I was the coming-of-age "son" standing up to my "father." Strip away the quotation marks, though, that connected us as father and son, and I was being a spoiled shit to my mother's old boyfriend, since I had no way of lashing out at any of my other dads or my actual biological father.

"We'll be here for a few hours. I can drink four beers, and it doesn't affect me. I'm a big boy."

"You're being selfish," I said. "And you're embarrassing me."

"Do you think I'd jeopardize your safety?" he asked. "Or Sofie's? Or your mother's?"

My mother sat quiet. It was a public space. "This is between you two," she said.

The four of us had two pairs of tickets on opposite sides of the outdoor amphitheater. From the other side of the theater, Frank waved and then stood and gave a clenched-fist salute. After the show, Frank asked, "Did you see how I held my hand up? Just like Jackson does?" He called singer Jackson Browne by his first name, as if Jackson were a casual friend.

I nodded and said, "Yeah, I saw it." There was a genuine, hopeful look on his face that said, "Let's move past this fight."

"Who's Jackson?" Sofie asked.

"You know, Jackson Browne," I said. "'The Pretender.'" I said those words like I was singing a song Frank taught me, using the same tone of voice and intonation he'd used for years. Neither Frank nor I caught it then, but if both of us had listened close, we'd have heard Frank's imprint upon my speech so clearly and distinctly, you wouldn't have been able to tell our voices apart.

I was in the living room around midnight, leaving with Frank for an all-night drive to Stanford. I'd had dinner and a slow dance with Sofie in my tiny bedroom earlier that night, where we promised to stay together no matter what. We'd been having sex with each other since the spring, but that night we just huddled close on my small couch, as if coiling ourselves together would keep the future from striking us too hard.

"You're the best thing that's ever happened to me," she said. "I want for us to get married one day. And for your parents to not be there."

My mother gripped me in a fierce hug. My grandmother said, "C'mon, the men gotta get going! Let your son go and be happy for him." But my mother didn't let go. When she released me at last, she said, "You don't get a vote on what happens here now. You don't live here anymore."

"I know," I said, and exhaled an eighteen-year-old sigh of relief.

"You're seventeen, and we're running up one-oh-one!" Frank sang as he drove north on Highway 101 throughout the night, blasting Jackson Browne's "Running on Empty" to stay awake. We hit campus before sunrise and found an empty parking lot, where Frank pissed on a tree. Then he moved my things in—a CD boom box, some clothes, an electric typewriter with a floppy drive and a four-line pre-view screen—and passed out on my roommate's bed. I watched his belly rise and fall, his snores blending with the crushing wail of ori-entation freshmen screaming outside. It wasn't the first day of college I'd pictured with Pat, but I was away from home at last.

I looked out the window. Outside was a morning auburn fog, the eerie kind of light found in display cases of sacred texts. Now what?

I would spend the next four years wandering through that fog, desperate to connect—it took an entire week to find a student who knew exactly where the financial aid office was—and distinguish myself, resigned to becoming a nervous, introverted, black-clad stereotype that I *knew* wasn't me any more than the other sons or ethnicity I'd been playing my whole life were.

I got a phone call to join the Stanford American Indian Organization. "We heard you were kind of a radical," the caller said. I blew them off out of shame and then spun the invitation into a macho story about asserting my individuality.

"I didn't leave the ghetto to stick myself in another one!" I'd say, and maybe score a couple cheap laughs. Then I'd throw in a fabricated story about witnessing a drive-by gang shooting or the time I saw someone shot point-blank in the head on the mean streets near my house. I made few friends but excelled at hating everyone and everything for every reason.

I would have major arguments with Sofie, who stuck it out with me but hated our long-distance relationship. She'd gone to a commuter college and continued living at home. Without Facebook, Skype, unlimited cell phone minutes, or even regular email access, we blamed each other for our lack of companionship and our enormous phone bills. On my vacations home to Los Angeles, I would fly into panicked searches for temporarily missing college documents or have severe car-key-throwing anxiety attacks over what the parking situation would be at a movie theater or restaurant. I didn't know how to fully become any one of my fathers but had learned how to be my mother's son.

I would legally change my name to Brando Skyhorse and steer clear of El Centro Chicano, Stanford's Latino student center. The name change was a faux stab at independence from my biological father's name based solely on embracing the persona my mother had invented for me. I was as much in her thrall now as I was when we shared a house, since my college life revolved around avoiding her and keeping her howling anxiety at bay.

I would join the long line of men who'd abandoned my mother, but unlike her husbands, she wouldn't let me go. She called ten to fifteen times a week, sometimes multiple calls a day. We spoke for hours, racking up two-hundred- or three-hundred-dollar monthly phone bills. If I ended the conversation to study, she'd hang up on me or call back to hang up on me if I'd hung up on her first. Every call, early morning or late night, was an emergency. Every emergency required my immediate attention and could be resolved only by me. Every failure to respond led to more calls and more angry messages on my answering machine. Studies and exams weren't considered valid excuses; she called minutes before I rushed off to take tests, or during midterms, or every day during finals week. I was excommunicated as her son dozens of times and then reembraced when her fever had passed. Once, there were seven messages, each over five minutes long, left during a one-hour period in which my mother had an entire conversation with herself:

"Where are you, Brando?"

"You are fucking worthless, Brando!"

"Forgive me, Brando?"

"I have no fucking son! Go fuck yourself, Brando!"

"Really—please—where are you, Brando?"

I would do poorly at Stanford, sometimes dropping classes on the last day before finals. My English major classes weren't too hard; I was just always exhausted or out of time. My mother, not my studies, swallowed whatever free time I had, and it was never enough. Whenever she called, I was strangled by a constricting depression and lost consciousness, sleeping away the hours in bulk. When I mentioned my depression, she'd say, "You inherited my madness," and then warn me to be on *her* death watch. There was her brain tumor ("I can't let them cut off all my beautiful hair to open my skull," she said), her failing eyesight, or her blood poisoning, all of which were jeopardizing her fragile health. She wanted to say "good-bye," since every conversation could be her last, and wanted to know if I had anything to say to her before it was too late? If not, *why the fuck not?*

Frank would visit Stanford once more, sophomore year.

"How are your grades?" he asked. They were adequate. How could they be anything else?

"Do they have magna or summa cum laude here?" he asked. I didn't reply.

"Nah, I bet they don't even have that at schools like this," Frank said, his way of giving me an out.

In an exit interview with my Stanford freshman advisor, he said, "You never did quite find your place here."

When I hear the word *Stanford,* I see a clear picture of my arrival on campus and wince. There's a part of me that still thinks I can warn that boy I was on his first day and say, "Disconnect your phone. Don't rise to anger's bait. Cut off ties if you have to." I can't reach him, of course, the same way that nobody at Stanford—friend, girlfriend, professor, counselor, or "father"—could reach me.

The fog outside had lifted when Frank woke up an hour later. "I gotta hit the road," he said. "I only got one day off from work."

"Do you want to get some breakfast? Maybe walk around the campus?" I didn't want him to leave this soon.

"I really have to go," he said. "But I can come back. We can walk around and check things out then. As long as your mom says it's okay and she's not with anybody that might think it's a problem, you know where to find me. I'm always there if you need me, Tiger."

I was four when Frank first held me up in the air and called me Tiger. Now I was seventeen and living away from my mother, the excuse that Frank and I both used for why we didn't stay in touch. Were we ready to be each other's father and son? Or would we dance around the holes we were waiting for the other to fill?

We'd dance.

We'd wait.

We'd age.

We'd forget about each other sometimes. We'd grow embarrassed over how much time passed between phone calls. We'd let so much time pass we went beyond embarrassment right back into that nostalgic buzz you feel before ending a long estrangement that says, "We'll make it work this time." Then Frank would pick up the phone.

"Hello."

"Let's do something."

"That was fun."

"Love you, too, pal."

"See you soon."

Disappear.

Repeat.

I returned home freshman winter break to a doll's house, everything grossly reduced in size and painted over in loud, unfamiliar colors. When had my house sprouted giant foundation cracks, grown yellow and red paint skin boils, and pitched its front stairs at hunchback angles? When had it gotten *old*? The Christmas lights Pat strung last December were left up the whole year, coated with dust. (They would stay hung, untouched, for the next eight years.) The rooms seemed smaller and darker; windows that Pat had cracked open were weatherproofed shut, with the shades duct taped to the walls.

My mother had made vague threats before I left for college about finding someone new. In the span of three months, she had met, moved in with, and gotten engaged to a man from a homeless shelter who had replied to my mother's Christian singles magazine ad. (My mother had never been a Christian, nor was she ever technically "single," since she had never legally divorced any of her husbands.)

Before, whenever I met a new father, he made the house feel alive, enormous, full of life, even if I didn't like him at first. My fifth step-father, Rudy, brought with him barricades to the outside world that shrank the house's dimensions, making plain to me how small and petty our family really was. We weren't a castle bathed in light on a hill, the way I'd seen our house from the street as a child. We were a dying Golden Rain tree, one of the common street trees lining blocks in Los Angeles, thirsting for a breeze in the autumn shadows.

These shadows said, "At least it's never boring."

8

"You have to sleep with the man you're living with. It isn't right," my grandmother said. Ignoring how she'd exiled Emilio from her bedroom for years, my grandmother and my mother were arguing about what to do with Rudy. When Rudy moved in two months after I left for school, he got a temporary job as a security guard and surrendered his pittance of a bimonthly paycheck in exchange for a spot on the couch or my empty bedroom. Now that I was back from school, where would he sleep?

"Why can't he stay in Brando's room? He doesn't live here anymore," my mother said.

"I'm here right now," I said, "and I don't want a stranger in my room."

"*You're* the only stranger here," my mother said.

"Stop it, you two," my grandmother said. "Don't you love Rudy?" she asked my mother.

"Of course I don't!"

"Then what the hell is he doing here in *my* house?" my grandmother asked.

"I can't find anyone else," my mother said. "I don't want to be alone."

"Then take your future husband into your room."

"I don't want to sleep with a dead lay!" my mother said.

Rudy had ended up in a homeless shelter by following a woman to Los Angeles. One morning he awoke in their motel room to find the woman and his money gone, with a scrawled message in lipstick on the mirror: "Limp Dick." Later my mother's version of the story had Rudy as an obsessive phone sex client who had migrated west to woo her.

"I don't want any more men in my house," my grandmother said.

"He wants to be my husband," my mother said. "He wants to be a dad to Brando."

"I don't want anything from Rudy," I said.

"I don't see *your* father helping you out," my mother said. It was hardly worth wondering anymore which father she was talking about.

My grandmother and I nurtured an escalating defiance to each consecutive stepfather's introduction into the house, a familial hazing that unified us until the man asserted himself and I eventually "adopted" him as a real potential father. Whenever my mother pushed one of her men—often, literally—there was a certain amount of pushback that she both rebelled against and craved. Even Pat's chattiness and constant stream of positive energy was in itself a kind of challenge to my mother's relentless anger and negativity. He refused to let her get him down.

Rudy, however, offered no resistance. He was an absolute blank slate. With a cherubic face, jagged smile, stout body, tufted crown of clown's hair, and a hiccup of a laugh, Rudy resembled a giant Robin Williams balloon in the Macy's Thanksgiving Day Parade, guided by my mother's tethers, drifting whichever way she pulled. He laughed at every joke at his expense, posed no challenge whenever his opinion was invalidated, and made no defense of himself when my mother and grandmother gored him with some weeping dissatisfaction of theirs or confronted him with his own pathetic backstory.

My first night home at the end of freshman year, my mother called me into her room and said she'd been contacted by the woman Rudy claimed had swindled his money.

"She said Rudy screwed *her* over," my mother said. "She sent me letters Rudy wrote while he's lived with us."

We convened a family tribunal in the living room. My grandmother actually shut off the television. This was serious business. I sat and listened while my mother presented the letters.

"You don't get a vote, remember?" my mother told me.

"I am with a family of Indians that live in a manshun," Rudy wrote. In his illiterate hand, he detailed his elaborate plans for wresting the house from my grandmother once he'd married my mother. Then there'd be the honeymoon.

"'I want to tie a red ribbon around my dik while we fuck 69,'" my grandmother read aloud from the letter, adjusting her bifocals. Rudy stood in the center of the room while we spoke about him in third person. "God, he's even less of a man than I thought," she said.

"She asked me to write those letters, Grandma," Rudy said. "I don't know why I wrote those things. I won't speak to her again."

My mother encouraged thuggish behavior from her men, but this wasn't Pat taking food from his restaurant to feed us. This was madness. Our family was falling backward into a Jerry Springer abyss. Wasn't it just a year ago when Pat was working toward buying a house (apparently on stolen funds) to move my mother into a place of her own? Yet Rudy's steady paycheck of $218 every two weeks meant that my mother could—nay, *would*—look the other way, and I had to look with her. Rudy could stay, and the letters were not to be brought up again.

I was furious he'd been let off that easy. But that didn't mean amnesty for everyone. At least once during every school break, my mother would cackle, "Remember the time Brando lost my welfare check and asked, 'Should I put back the Ding Dongs?'"

"Why are you doing this?" I asked my mother. "Kick him out. You can do better."

"You're not giving any money into the house," she said. "You're just taking money out of it. Rudy and I are supporting you at school, and you haven't called him 'Dad' once."

Rudy never asked me to call him Father, nor had he complained about the money he'd sent me at college throughout that first year—about a hundred dollars total. An important token contribution of his total earnings, but not really support. My mother's college contributions—aside from a bike and a stereo bought from a catalogue on her Spiegel credit card—went into her silver cloth money hoard bag that, depending on her mood, was either for "my future" or "escaping from this fucking madhouse." She'd reduced her phone sex business, forced out by a never-ending roster of number prefixes (976 begat 1-900) that my mother said emphasized "quantity over quality," and had stopped receiving welfare and food stamps, but her overhead was low. She lived rent free in my grandmother's house for years, and grocery money was optional. How big had her stash bag grown?

"That's none of your business," she told me. "But when I die, you'll see how much money was in there and know how much I really loved you."

Over summer vacation, I woke to the sound of Rudy dry heaving in the bathroom. For thirty minutes every morning, an undiagnosed condition left him vomiting clear bile into the toilet while my mother mocked him in the hallway.

"You hear this, Momma?" she asked my grandmother, laughing.

"Take some Tums and go to work!" my grandmother shouted through the closed door.

Rudy worked as an unarmed security guard for nine dollars an hour. His salary, he told my mother, would double—*triple!*—with a "gun card" that somehow just remained out of reach for reasons that were neither consistent nor logical.

"Rudy seems confused," I said. "I think he's lying."

"I believe him more than I believe you," my mother said. "What do you ever do for this house except criticize it? Why don't you try making Rudy more a part of your life? You finally got a father in the house that isn't going anywhere. Isn't that what you always wanted?"

There wasn't much free time for Rudy and me to talk alone. He worked long hours and came home exhausted. At dinner my mother worked Rudy like a puppet, ordering him to "shut the fuck up," or getting him to retell her favorite story of his about how he evacuated his security post at a Smart & Final food warehouse during the recent LA riots without permission.

"They started looting the place," Rudy said, "so I called my boss and said we have to get out of here. He said, 'Yeah, do what you gotta do.' And I got out of there!"

"You couldn't remember to grab any shit out of the store for us, you dumb fuck?" my mother asked. Rudy laughed along with her laughing at him.

I loathed Rudy's shady patheticness but felt some kind of small urge to stand up for him. I just didn't know how. Can you defend someone who is impossible to offend? What was he like? What *did* he like? I had no idea. I couldn't engage Rudy in any meaningful way like I had Pat and couldn't have a single conversation that didn't get stuck in silence. However, he went to work every day and was predictably docile in every encounter with my mother, an anti-"Terminator" programmed for complete submissiveness.

One afternoon there was a soft *tap-tap-tap* on the front security gate. My grandmother and mother were sitting in the living room chatting, watching the sun move a rotund shadow across the drawn shades that covered our porch windows.

"Who's outside?" I asked.

"Shhh," my mother said.

"We don't know who it is," my grandmother said.

"Why don't you go to the door and see?"

"I don't feel like talking to anybody today," my grandmother said. *Tap-tap-tap.*

"Maybe it's Rudy," I said. "Did he lose his keys?"

"He doesn't have keys," my mother said. "He hasn't earned them yet. Don't go to the windows and see!"

"When is Rudy supposed to be home from work?"

"About now. He had to work a sixteen-hour graveyard shift."

Tap-tap-tap.

"It has to be Rudy. Can one of you please open the door?" I asked.

"What do you care? You don't live here anymore, and you don't like Rudy anyway," my mother said.

I sat with them on the couch for a minute. Rudy never called out, raised his voice, or moved from the spot he stood in. He just tapped on the front security gate, like a pebble shook in a tin can.

"Why don't *you* open the door?" my mother asked.

The best way of challenging my mother, I thought, was to not challenge her. I left Rudy on the porch, went to my room, closed the door, and plugged into a pair of headphones. That was how I solved problems at home, the way Paul had when he'd retire to the laundry room and smoke. I knew I was capable of acting better than this—so why couldn't I at home?

Tap-tap-tap.

I told myself Rudy would get in somehow, but I also knew my mother *wouldn't* give in, content to sit on the couch and see just how long he'd stand there knocking. Who'd break first? I played songs for maybe an hour or maybe the rest of the afternoon, and in the silence between each track heard the faint *tap-tap-tap* of Rudy's knocking, like the steady drip of a leaky roof just before it gives way.

My mother married Rudy under the name "Maria B. Skyhorse" the following year, in June 1993, at a quickie wedding chapel on Wilshire Boulevard. It was her fifth marriage; I gave her away for a fourth time. I invited Sofie, whom I'd been dating for two and a half years. She was the wedding's sole guest, acted as a witness, and signed the cardboard printout "license" that my mother treated as if it were real. My mother and Rudy had been "engaged" for about eighteen months, though there seemed no difference from their engaged life to their married one.

The priest asked my mother about her name after the ceremony. She said she was originally from Arizona.

"Oh, whereabouts?" he asked. "I've spent a lot of time on reservations over the years. What tribe are you affiliated with?"

"I don't remember," she told the priest. Where her fantastical explanations would once have dazzled me and silenced any skeptics, she didn't have the energy to defend her lies anymore and was unable to spin herself out of the corner she was in. I snickered at her then, unaware that my mother was showing me what shedding your dreams looked like, one broken hope at a time.

We drove to our wedding reception dinner following the ceremony in Rudy's "new" car, a 1985 cream-colored four-door paraplegic Buick Skylark bought from a lot that sold used cars to illegal immigrants and bad credit risks. The car had one tinted rear passenger-side window, as if it were being customized on layaway by a drug dealer, and a host of mechanical problems that Rudy had no idea how to repair, including a broken gas gauge. The car died several times in the freeway's fast lane while I was driving, the steering wheel locking, its pedals unresponsive. On three occasions, I was seconds away from a major rear-end collision.

"Rudy's never had any problems driving it," my mother said. "For a Stanford student, you sure are fucking dumb sometimes."

Robert's wedding banquet had been a rowdy family dinner at a Love's Bar-B-Que; Paul's, at a fancy Vegas steakhouse. This meal was in the parking lot of Pink's Chili Dogs. Four chili cheese dogs each for my mother and Rudy, and two dogs for me and Sofie eaten out of greasy cardboard boxes. We drove back to the house with two cold chili dogs for my grandmother, who, once again, had refused to attend the ceremony.

"This is all you brought me back?" my grandmother asked. "Did everyone only have two hot dogs?" she asked Sofie.

"I think Mom and Rudy had four," Sofie said in complete innocence. How could she think that a mother and a daughter would fight
over hot dogs?

"You and Rudy had four hot dogs apiece, but you could bring me
back only two?" my grandmother asked.

"It's my fucking wedding day!" my mother screamed. "You're actually fighting with me because I had two more hot dogs than you did
on my wedding day?"

"You've had five wedding days!" my grandmother shouted. "How
many more weddings do you need?"

"I feel really bad for your mother," Sofie said to me later. "I thought
you invited me so I could see what our wedding day might be like. If
this had been my wedding day, I'd have killed myself."

"Our wedding day won't be like this," I said and laughed. "This is
Rudy's fault," I added. How did my family devolve into this hellish
caricature? Had they *always* been this way? "We're in this together,"
I said.

"I know," Sofie said. Then she said, firmly, "If we have kids, I don't
want your family anywhere near them."

That summer break between sophomore and junior year, Sofie asked
to move in with me. She'd had a fight with her parents and thought
this would be the best way to make her stand.

"It'll be like what our life is like when we're married," she said. "It'll
be fun!"

"You only see a part of who my family is when you're here," I
warned. "You *don't* want to live here."

"Your parents can be bad sometimes," Sofie said, "but I think I
know how to handle them."

"*Mi casa, su casa*," my grandmother told Sofie. "That means 'My
house is your house.'"

What this actually translated to, though, was that Sofie's showers were timed, her bath towel usage and food eaten from the fridge (even the groceries she bought) tracked scrupulously. Using the phone, sitting alone in the backyard, or playing with the dog without including my grandmother were all off-limits. Sofie sat alone in my tiny room all day waiting for me to come home from my summer job the same way that my mother sat by herself in her room. I'd come home to a storage facility: my grandmother, mother, and Sofie each in her own room behind a locked door.

"Your girlfriend's really antisocial," my grandmother said.

My girlfriend was also, in my eyes, turning into my mother. Our relationship let me invest in the naïve dream that I'd choose a woman unlike my mother in every way and wouldn't copy her romantic choices. *One girlfriend, one relationship that leads to one marriage!* Of course, insisting that I'd never be with anyone like my mother led me to a woman just like her. Dramatic emotional swings—Sofie's and mine—that too closely resembled my mother's made me feel Sofie and I were incompatible. Or *too* compatible. We both had to win arguments, both needed the last word, both heard anger at decibel levels louder than expressed. Our moods were like flights of stairs we shoved each other down.

My mother saw potential in Sofie and enlisted her in a prank call to Frank. Mom's calling Frank wasn't new: for years he got hang-up calls on Friday and Saturday nights that he assumed was my mother checking to see if he was out with someone or at home. When Sofie moved in, my mother told her that Frank was my biological father and gave Sofie a written script to read on Frank's machine: "I just wanted to let you know that Brando doesn't need a father anymore because he's about to become one. You've always been a part-time father, but now Brando's going to become a full-time dad. We're going to get married, and he's going to be the father he always wanted you to be but never could. Bye!"

Frank was offended that I would have my girlfriend tell him I was a father like *this*. He stopped calling me. When I heard what Sofie did—what my mother asked her to do—I thought, good! Why

181

wouldn't Frank call me if he thought I *was* a father now? He knew how many different father figures I had and how incompetent or incomplete they were. This is when I'd need his counsel and guidance the most. Even when he was twice removed, he still couldn't handle the full-time responsibilities of a child. Why would he let me handle fatherhood alone?

I stopped calling Frank. We'd lose contact for two more years.

Sofie didn't realize how destructive that one call was. She thought my mother's schemes were fun, like one of my childhood playacting games. She was sweetly oblivious to what she was participating in or to how she was enabling—like we *all* were—my mother's growing reclusiveness. Sofie planned takeout dinners with my mother and, since my mother hated calling restaurants, phoned in the orders. They watched long blocks of television shopping programs together: QVC for "Indian" southwestern turquoise jewelry and the JCPenney Channel for going-out blouses and skirts my mother would never wear "out." My girlfriend also helped her choose items, as well as signed for my mother's packages.

"I think the UPS lady has a crush on me," my mother said by way of excuse. She sucked her thumb and forefinger together out of anxious habit, watching for the truck by creasing moist puckers into the window shades. The truth was that my mother was less afraid of the driver and more and more afraid of the outside world.

One summer afternoon, the UPS truck arrived while Sofie and I were having sex. When my mother saw the truck, she drum rapped on my bedroom door to get Sofie and then shoved her way inside, the flimsy lock giving way. Realizing what she saw, my mother snapped awake and shut the door.

"I didn't see anything," she lied. "I'm so sorry." My mother signed for the package and then retreated to her bedroom. I couldn't remember when my mother last apologized in earnest.

Sofie cringed out of embarrassment as she went to my mother's bedroom to ask for forgiveness. My mother said, "You and Brando should eat dinner together. Let's get takeout. I'll pay for it, but call the restaurant for me. I don't want to talk to anyone new on the phone."

My mother was a revelation to Sofie as a parent compared to her conservative Vietnamese family. "All she wants is someone to take care of her," Sofie told me when my mother and I collided daily over petty slights. "She's like a big tornado. You have to know when to duck. She's not like your grandma. Your grandma's a black hurricane. She scares me."

Once, while I was gone with Rudy and my mother was working, my grandmother invited Sofie into her bedroom and sat her on the bed. The shade was drawn and the lights off.

"I've been in this room a long time," my grandmother began. "I had a girlfriend that lived with me right here," she said. "We loved each other very much." Sofie didn't know what a lesbian was, never having heard the word before.

When June was in her thirties, she fell in love with a Spanish woman in her forties named Eleanor. There had been before, and would be again, other women in June's romantic life, relationships conducted through rendezvous in Spanish-language movie theaters that sometimes led back to the Portia Street house where a confused little Maria and an angry Oscar and Emilio watched from their bedrooms. Eleanor was different. Young June moved her into the house and nicknamed Eleanor "Tata" (Spanish for "nanny"). Their closeted relationship resulted in Emilio's moving out for a time—though he continued to make the mortgage payments—and Tata became a kind of surrogate parent to both my mother and Oscar, albeit one prone to hysteria, melancholy, and botched, alcohol-fueled suicide attempts. One evening Tata wanted to watch Mexican wrestling on TV. My eight-year-old mother wanted to see a special about Disneyland's grand opening. June sided with my mother, so, while little Maria watched a black-and-white vision of the Happiest Place on Earth, Tata retired to the bedroom she shared with my grandmother and hung herself in the closet.

My mother believed that June blamed her for Tata's suicide. June believed that Tata sought vengeance from her from beyond the grave. After Tata's death, my grandmother heard over the next few weeks a series of late-night knocks on the sliding glass patio door. The sounds stopped whenever she went to investigate. One night she ran to the patio and saw a floating blob of golden light.

"Go home to the dead!" June shouted. "We don't want you here! I don't love you anymore!"

The knocks stopped, but Tata's painted portrait remained in a living room archway for years after, her short brown hair, stabbing cheekbones, needle-thin red lips, and pink-haloed background a mysterious yet unchallenged cipher. When I was old enough to ask who it was, my grandmother removed the portrait and hid it in her bedroom.

"Eleanor killed herself, right here in this very room," she now explained to my seventeen-year-old girlfriend. "It was in that closet. Sometimes at night, I can still see her shadow swinging in there."

Sofie said nothing, desperate to hear me walk through the front door.

"Go on and look in the closet," my grandmother said.

"No, that's okay," Sofie said. "I'll do it when Brando gets back." She considered it impolite to leave a room while any adult was talking, but she excused herself and ran to my room, where my mother found her. Sofie told her what happened.

"We like *men*," my mother said. "Grandma isn't like that."

Sofie lasted two weeks before she moved back home. "I'm sorry I didn't believe you, Brando. I'll never doubt you again," she said.

"Sofie's welcome back anytime," my grandmother said.

Sofie and I kept dating, but she wouldn't return to the house until the holidays to help me wrap presents. When I was eight, my mother made me the house's official gift wrapper, and the job stuck. For years

I knew what I was getting before Thanksgiving, plucking my presents straight from the Sears Christmas *Wish Book* catalogue, breathing in the smell of those pages, like uncapped markers left in the rain. How cool was my mother! When her unexpected turns of heart worked to my advantage, I loved her capriciousness and embraced my unique situation as her child.

Then I became her teenager, which made it easy to curse her borderline behavior.

The ritual of opening up presents that contained no surprises for me made the day a chore. My mother already hated Christmas. Her maybe-real son Shane had died, she said, on Christmas Eve, so she'd stay locked in her room watching *Scarface* on repeat, pausing to check a TV channel for her favorite part of *It's a Wonderful Life*, where Jimmy Stewart loses his shit on Donna Reed and his kids.

"Why isn't the whole movie like this?" my mother asked. "*This* is how Christmas feels for everybody."

Presents were a good distraction for my mother—as long as she got the most gifts. If she didn't, she'd sulk, rage, scream, or retreat back to her room with a paper plate of my grandmother's Christmas meal.

To fix this, I stretched out my mother's gifts by wrapping things separately. Four pairs of panty hose were wrapped in four different boxes. I laid out the presents under the tree throughout December so she could count how many gifts the three of us (or four, if I had a father that year) got. If someone was ahead of her in the present count, my grandmother rushed to neighborhood stores on Christmas Eve to buy my mother more things. It wasn't uncommon for Santa to bring my mother seventy to eighty gifts. Then, on Christmas Day, amid rivers of festive red and green paper, stick-on bows, and loose tinsel, we feasted on a briny holiday ham to honor the American Indians.

"The Pilgrims ate turkey," my mother said, "and the Pilgrims are what led to the Indian genocide."

"Fine, we don't eat 'white people' food," my grandmother said. "I still don't understand why I'm the one who has to spend all day in the kitchen cooking a goddamn ham."

When Pat moved in, my grandmother stopped cooking Christmas dinners and then didn't start again when Rudy replaced him. My second winter break back from college, Mom asked Sofie to order pizza for dinner. One pizza for her and Rudy (she finished his portions), a second for my grandmother, and a third for Sofie and me. Three pizzas for five people. My mother hated sharing her food but hated more the thought that others had to share theirs. When we finished eating, she started a Monopoly game with Rudy.

"Do you want to play, Grandma?" Rudy asked.

"No, your wife cheats and gets mad when she loses," my grandmother said, watching TV.

"How about you, Brando? You want to join us?"

"I need to drive Sofie home," I said.

"Oh that's right, you can't spend time with us on Christmas," my mother said. "This is just a hotel to you. We don't need you. You're not really a member of this family anyway."

A kind crinkle in Sofie's eyes said, *Walk away*. She wasn't being magnanimous. Throughout our relationship, I'd often be on my way out the door to pick up Sofie when my mother called me into her room to ask a "quick" question:

"Brando, why are you such an asshole?"

She'd call my grandmother in for backup. An hours-long conversation unfurled, clotted with roundabouts of blame. Sofie would wait—outside of bus stations, on street corners, on elbows perched on her room's windowsill—craning her neck for my car that was sometimes three hours late. She waited for me with that same eagerness, and then dashed hope, I once had when I was a child, sitting by an open bedroom window and waiting for Frank's car to turn down my street.

"Why can't you just walk away from them?" Sofie would ask, furious, teary. "They just have the same conversation over and over! They make time stand still in that house. They want time to stand still for *you*. What do you *talk* about with her?"

Sofie didn't understand I wasn't talking at all. I was waiting for my chance to *speak*, to tell my mother about *me*. I was in pain. I had an expanding list of maladies that I felt with a growing discomfort could be traced right to my mother. I wanted to stick my hurt out at her like a black-licorice-coated tongue. See my constant queasy physical nervousness that makes me airsick sitting in a chair when you raise your voice. Look at my abject fear of new experiences, my explosive tantrums at Sofie, my attention-grasping sudden departures whenever I feel anyone "challenges" or "insults" me, my terrified crabwalk around your rules—their one constant being their inconsistency and the punishment for violating them being your incantations that send me to hell or the abortionist's claw. *Here is the son you raised, Mom.*

I didn't want to cling to our fraying arrangement anymore, sandbagging for waves of rage that threatened to kick me out of the Portia Street house, a promise that had hung over me like a loose stalactite from the first time I heard it, when I was five years old. Every "argument" with my mother was building to the one confrontation where I'd argue back.

That Christmas afternoon, Sofie picked up her bag and strode to the front door. *Walk away*, her eyes and smile urged me again.

"We aren't a family," I told my mother. "We share a roof. We're *barely* a family." My voice shivered like leaves in a Santa Ana wind.

"You want to show off for your girlfriend, don't you?" my mother said. "God, I know Shane would have been a better son to me than you."

"When I see a mother, I'll act like a son."

My mother set down her Monopoly money and scraped her chair on the floor away from the table. She stared at me, just as curious as I was about where my words were coming from.

"If you don't like it, there's the door," she said.

"The door you never let me leave?"

"Get the fuck out of here!"

"Now, wait a second," my grandmother said. "It's Christmas Day. Do we have to have all this fighting and cussing on Christmas Day?"

"Fuck you, Momma!" my mother screamed. "And fuck you, too, Brando! Get the fuck out of *my* house! Don't *ever* come back!"

"It's not *your* house," my grandmother said, "it's *my* house, and nobody's kicking anyone out. Not on Christmas Day. Wait until he gets back to college, *then* kick him out. See, this is why I don't play Monopoly with you."

The joke didn't defuse the tension. My mother and I stood maybe ten feet apart. "Get the *fuck* out of this house," she said.

"No," I said. "I'm not going anywhere."

She stormed up to me, her face an inch or two from my chest. "I hate you!" she screamed. "You should have died and not Shane! I wish I'd aborted you! I'll kill you!"

"Then kill me!" I shouted. Here at last was the rage that had been boiling inside me for years. "Here I am! Quit being a coward and kill me!"

My mother ran to the kitchen. I heard her rustle through the silverware drawer. I looked at Rudy. What would he do to stop this? Each father had been a loose seawall for my mother's rage. None offered complete protection but sometimes blunted the storm. I was nineteen years old but still looking for a father to shelter me. I'd been forced to call Rudy "Father" since he moved in but was ready to drop all my resistance and embrace him like an actual dad here and now in exchange for one moment of protection.

Rudy sat motionless at the dining room table. He said nothing and stared blankly at our Christmas tree. If he didn't speak or move, he became invisible to my mother. This was the same technique I'd used to survive my house for years.

My mother appeared in the kitchen doorway with a long butcher's knife in her hand.

"Brando, we should go," Sofie said. "Right now."

"No!" I shouted. "I've had enough of this bullshit!" I flinched from cussing in front of my grandmother. "No more!" I screamed. "Let her come and kill me so I don't have to be her son anymore!"

My mother walked halfway through the living room with the knife in her hand before my grandmother rose from her chair and placed herself between me and my mother, just as she had stepped between Candido and my mother's knife when he abandoned us. It was my grandmother—not a stepfather or any man—who protected me.

"Get out!" my grandmother told me. "Go!"

Sofie and I drove off. I had nowhere to go. I thought about calling Frank, but we hadn't spoken in so long. Besides, what could he do? What could *any* father do?

"Don't take me home yet," Sofie said.

We went to a movie, ate fast food for dinner, watched the sunset at Santa Monica beach, and drove in long, aimless circles through the Los Angeles night until Sofie fell asleep.

When I dropped her off, she said, "You can sleep on our couch. My dad won't like it, but I can explain."

"I have to go home," I said.

"I hate that place," she said. "Stop calling it 'home.' It's not."

I snuck back into the house after midnight. The Christmas lights had been left on. I crept to my room, braced the door with a chair, and stayed up until morning, waiting for my mother to come into my room sometime during the night and slit my throat.

Routine is uninteresting to recall and often unmemorable to record. My mother's apology, if there was one, was much like the ones before or the ones that came after. I never confronted her again. Drift and disappearance were my protection now; I was just another man running to get out of my mother's path, much like Frank driving away when he saw a fight coming. I handled my mother by setting myself in a plaster cast of a personality, rigid and safe. I gave her pieces of a son and in return saw her in fragments: a glimpse of me creeping by her door so she wouldn't catch me and call me into her room where she watched endless loops of TV. Or a snatch of conversation on the edge of her bed where I sat upright like a bookend, answering her questions with "Yes," "No," or "We'll see," which to me translated to: I wish you'd disappear.

"We've been getting along well, don't you think?" she asked. "Are you going to move back home when you're done with your rich white school?"

"We'll see," I said.

My senior year of college had been one long, drawn-out nails-clawing-on-the-edge-of-a-cliff struggle to stay at school and not return home. For the fall quarter, I studied overseas at Oxford University. A kind, gray-haired English administrator named Pat fell in love with my last name.

"The mailman came by and said, 'You got another letter for Chief Crazy Horse,' and I told him, 'There's nothing crazy about him!'" (Oh, if she *only* knew . . .)

A common phone line in the house on High Street meant that my mother had no direct access. It was my best quarter academically and personally.

My mother and I spoke just once.

"All I wanted you to do over there," she said, "was to buy me videotapes of Tod Slaughter in *Sweeney Todd* and those other movies where he's killing people, and buy me hats from Laura Ashley. What do you mean they use a different *kind* of videotape over there? You go to Stanford, don't you? Aren't you smart enough to figure out how to get what I want? And what do you mean the hats are the same there as they are in the Laura Ashley stores here? I *know* they're different 'cause I saw them on TV! They send the shitty hats *here* and keep the good hats in England!"

During my four months at Oxford, Frank visited my mother one day while Rudy was at work. In his van, they had a conversation free from blame or guilt. They checked into a nearby hotel, made love, and in the warm skin-on-skin bliss of a perfect day reminisced about when they were young together and how Frank had spent torrid evenings sopping moonlight out of my mother's waist-length hair.

Later they spoke on the phone, and my mother dredged up cheating accusations from a decade ago.

"You drove me away from you," she told Frank. "Everything bad that's happened to me since we broke up is your fault." She hung up on him. There would be more hang-ups between them. There wouldn't be any more words.

I sent my mother and grandmother postcards as I traveled through Europe, drinking seltzers at a rowdy Dublin bar with Friday-night drunks who at first mocked my avoidance of alcohol. Then they were touched by it, after I explained that I couldn't take a drink without picturing my "father"—Paul Skyhorse Johnson—rolling down my front lawn. I was almost mugged in Paris and Florence and ran into a pair of drunken racist skinheads at a doner kebob truck in Oxford, acting like a deaf mute until they stumbled off. In Geneva, I bought my grandmother an authentic wooden Reuge music box in honor of her father's Swiss roots.

"You bought the cheapest-looking piece of shit music box in Switzerland!" she said.

When I returned to Echo Park in December, I learned that my grandmother and mother had changed just a couple facts about my Stanford-in-Oxford studying-abroad program to their friends in the neighborhood.

"A Rhodes scholar!" a salesman at our local clothes store exclaimed. "When do you meet President Clinton?"

When I got back to campus, I learned—or could no longer ignore the fact—that I wouldn't have enough credits to graduate in June. Financial aid didn't cover fifth years in college. I'd dropped so many classes to prolong this miserable college experience of mine that, *damn it, I should have savored,* I was in danger of not earning a degree.

I'd also broken up with Sofie after almost three years and a hundred "This is the *last* time" breakups. Remembering my grandmother's trips to the corner magazine stand, I sent a new girlfriend to buy Asian-only porn I claimed my mother needed as research for her phone sex. I tried to throw myself out of a friend's truck in (slow) traffic. There was a slapstick plan to commit suicide romantically inspired by Kurt Cobain that got as far as the local Target to price shotguns before realizing the store didn't sell firearms. I prayed at the altar of my eighties music CD collection for a miraculous intervention of alcohol or drug addiction, to succumb to junkiedom solely for the narrative it would create and the pity it would arouse. But I didn't know the cool drug kids at Stanford (were there *any?*) and was too poor to sustain a cocaine habit. Even in the grips of a total breakdown, I had to stay practical about how to destroy myself.

My mother called one late spring afternoon and said, "I'm back in touch with Pat. He called me, and he's sorry. He's living in Northern California and wants to know if he can visit you."

"I'm not sure," I said. "I don't think it's a good idea. It's my last quarter at college, and I don't want any distractions."

"I already gave him your number," she said.

Pat's voice was as bright and high pitched as I remembered from four years ago. Now, though, his agreeable, pleasant tone made me sick with a nauseating impotence. Here was someone I still loved but was unable to speak to the way I once did, with the easy, blind air of security. I ushered us into setting up a reunion, figuring a quick visit would be the fastest way to get him in and then out of my life. I chose as a meeting place the Oval, Stanford's official entrance and a public location with lots of people around, because I had a grandiose fantasy that Pat might kidnap me. But how could I be kidnapped if I *wanted* to leave with my kidnapper?

Terrified of moving back with my family *and* being a college wash-out, I'd collapsed into a severe depression. I had panic nightmares, wore sunglasses everywhere day or night, pretending I was some drug-addled character from an eighties teen movie (forgetting I wasn't rich, white, and, aside from my peyote trip as a five-year-old, had never done drugs), ditched classes, and was afraid to leave my room and collect the dining hall trays a friend left outside when I skipped meals.

I was wearing my sunglasses when Pat pulled up in a large SUV.

"Didn't think the day was bright enough for shades," he said. "You look cool, though!"

I picked a restaurant off campus that I knew I could walk back from if Pat excused himself during the meal and drove off before the bill came. I adjusted my sunglasses, which stayed on throughout the meal, did my best "I don't care about you" slouch, and said in a dis-affected *The Breakfast Club* voice, "So, where have you been all this time?"

"Lived on a houseboat for a while near the Russian River, north of San Francisco," he said. "I grew a beard. You can tell I've gained some weight. How's Sofie?"

My next girlfriend after Sofie, a brief relationship, had been a light-skinned Mexican girl.

"You're making a big mistake dating one of them," my mother had said. "I know. How could you dump Sofie after how much she stood by you? Where did you learn to treat people this way? I thought you weren't anything like me at all."

Pat nodded. "Your mom didn't mean that. And I'm sorry to hear about Sofie. I know she loves you very much. Sometimes love isn't enough. You know how much I loved you and your mother."

"Is that why you didn't say good-bye?" I asked.

"I wasn't leaving you. I was leaving because I had to. I wanted to say good-bye, I really did. There wasn't time."

"Why did you steal the money?"

"It wasn't as black-and-white as it was made out," he said. "I wasn't stealing from *you* guys. How could I tell you what I was doing? My heart was in the right place," he said.

I heard my grandmother's voice: *Too bad his hands weren't.*

"Why didn't you write?"

"I wanted to, but I didn't think you wanted to hear from me. I was ashamed." Our dialogue sounded so much like ex-lovers, it was hard to believe this was the language men used when they had too many secrets and not enough courage to come clean.

"You know," Pat said, "you don't need your sunglasses on in here."

"I'm fine," I said.

"You wouldn't wear your glasses at the movies, would you?" he asked. "Want to go see one?"

"The closest movie theater is in Mountain View," I said. "I don't know the way back on a bus."

"You think I'd leave you there?" Pat asked.

"Yes."

"Brando, I've done some bad things, but I wouldn't do that. You know how I feel about your mother. And *you*."

"There's no reason for you to be here," I said. "We have nothing connecting us. I can take care of myself."

"There's no age limit on having a father," he said. "Unless you already have one in Rudy?"

I had tried accepting Rudy in the role of a father and a contributing part of our family even when his contributions didn't add up or sometimes went missing. He was still on the hunt for the elusive gun card that would raise his salary tenfold and magically transform his and my mother's lives. He was still pocketing my gas money to fill up his car with the malfunctioning gas gauge that magically drifted to *E* whenever I drove it. ("I *swore* I filled up the tank.") Our "dates" together were easy and unmemorable. I invited Rudy to "father and son" steak dinners where the sound of our knives scraping the plates substituted for conversation. He sweltered on summer days wearing Stanford sweatshirts I'd bought him as Christmas gifts.

"He's proud of you," my mother said.

"It's just for your benefit," I said. "He's showing off."

"Why shouldn't he?" she said. "He's paying for most of your education, anyway." (Stanford's financial aid package was a generous mix of scholarships, grants, and loans. Rudy's total college contributions equaled maybe five hundred dollars.)

Rudy offered movie dialogue as a stand-in for insight or comment, which seemed appropriate, since I'd just learned how to shave properly from a touching father-son scene in *Lethal Weapon 3* instead of asking him for help.

My mother: "Brando would make a great lawyer."

Rudy: "*You can't handle the truth!*"

Rudy wasn't a father. He was a Big Brother volunteer matched to an angry, unreceptive inner-city young man who had been told one lie too many. Rudy hadn't reached me because he couldn't. Pat had closed that door. Only Pat could walk through it now.

"So how about a movie?" Pat asked again. "Anything you'd like to see?"

"I like *Pulp Fiction*," I said. I'd seen it five or six times. It was the one piece of entertainment that gave me any joy or happiness during my insidious black depression. I took off my sunglasses and watched Pat watch the movie. He laughed in the right places, scoffed at the medical inaccuracy of the stabbing-the-hypodermic-needle-in-the-heart scene ("That's not how it's done; I used to be an EMT") and shifted uncomfortably in the final diner robbery scene. An older overweight restaurant manager—someone Pat could physically resemble in a few years—was pinned on the counter with a gun to his head. I laughed loud enough that it was obvious I imagined it was Pat.

"I was in a restaurant robbery once," Pat whispered. I felt a blush of shame before I realized Pat had also robbed a restaurant himself, though without a gun.

On the drive back to campus, Pat said, "I'd like to come to your graduation. Is that something you'd feel comfortable with?"

I had no reason to trust someone who had lied and abandoned me, but I couldn't help myself. I missed Pat, what he taught me, what we shared, and the life he promised me: one free from the burdens of having to be my mother's full-grown man when I hadn't even learned how to be a boy. More than Frank, Paul, or Candido, I saw Pat as a victim whose good intentions had been hijacked through circumstances beyond his control. My mother had pushed him into an impossible corner. Hadn't she done the same thing to every single man in her life, including me?

"I don't know if you should come," I said. "Rudy will probably be there. My mother said Frank might come too, but I haven't spoken to him in a while, so I don't know if she's telling the truth."

"Your mom can be a little flexible with facts," Pat said. We both laughed. Then I heard my grandmother's voice again: *So can Pat. Don't give your trust so easily just because he's a man. All men lie.*

"So what do you say?" he asked. "Can I come?"

"Let me think about it."

"Brando," he said again, "you're never too old to need a father. Don't miss out on having one because of pride."

He was right. He *had* to be right, I thought, because he was still some kind of father to me. He knew just what to say that would hurt the most, a gift that biological and stepparents have in common.

He also knew what to do that would hurt the most, too.

Pat's phone was disconnected a week before graduation. Every day, I'd redial at a different time, sometimes as many as three or four calls in an afternoon, hoping he'd pick up and knowing he wouldn't. How could I let myself be heartbroken and disappointed again and again by men who were just half a father?

The day before graduation, Frank left a message. He sounded distant, stilted. I couldn't remember the last time I'd heard his voice.

"I thought about coming up," he said, "but I don't want a fight with your mother to spoil everything." It was the first graduation he'd miss since sixth grade.

"Remember, I'm proud of you, Tiger," he said.

This time I felt there wasn't anything to be proud of at all. I'd "walk" my graduation ceremony and finish up my last college credits in summer school. Instead of three fathers rooting for me when I made my processional entrance into the football stadium and onto an immense green field to collect my empty diploma case, there was Rudy, an unfather, somewhere in a blurry sea of cardinal red. And yet, I couldn't stop craning my neck deep, looking for *all* my fathers— Candido, Paul, Robert, Pat, and Frank—imagining a row of ghosts way up in the stands, each man rooting for the son I was to him.

"There he is," each of them would say proudly. "*My* son."

9

"Turn the wheel," Frank said. "You gotta turn that wheel, Tony."
Tony, the used-car salesman, backed up to the car lot's entrance. I'd asked Frank to come car shopping with me, since he was the one adult I knew with a credit history good enough to be a cosigner. Counting his graduation message and Sofie's prank call about me becoming a father, we'd "spoken" twice in about three years.

On the drive to the car lot, he asked, "So she was never really pregnant?"

"No."

"Then why did she call me?"

"Mom asked her to."

"Yeah, that's what I thought," he said. "I didn't think you'd get a woman pregnant like that. You're not that irresponsible." He paused. "You know about condoms, right?"

I almost laughed, but then Tony opened the passenger side door of the Toyota Corolla for Frank. He had to squeeze into the backseat.

"You understand, Frank," Tony said, "that I gotta ride up front with Brando. It's their rules, not mine."

"Of course," Frank said.

While I drove, Tony asked Frank, "What line of work are you in?"

"I work for the state of California," he said. Frank played with the holes in his sneakers and stroked his graying goatee. He dressed and looked like a man fifteen years younger than he was.

"What do you do, Brando?" Tony asked.

"He's a college graduate," Frank said quickly.

"Ah," Tony said, "nothing beats a great education."

We drove under a bridge. "Let me turn off the air conditioner," Tony said. "So you can hear the engine."

"Sounds like a good engine," Frank said.

"So how were you planning to pay for this?" Tony asked me.

"Well, I was gonna cosign for him," Frank said before I could answer.

"You know, Frank, it would really be better for the both of you if you bought him the car. I'm sure your credit is better than his," Tony said.

"I have excellent credit," Frank said. "But I'm just here to cosign for him."

We drove back to the lot. "Okay," Tony said, "Let's see how excellent that credit is."

Tony led us through a series of offices with no doors and floor to ceiling windows. He set down a stack of carbon-copy forms at his desk and then turned his back to me.

"So, Frank, are you gonna buy this car for Brando?"

"You know, Tony," Frank said, "I really just came here to cosign. He really wants to buy the car on his own."

"Yes, I know, but this is the reality," Tony said. "You have the job, you have the credit. If you buy this car for Brando, you'll have smaller monthly payments. He can pay those to you. Nobody cares as long as the monthly payment gets made. Also, when you buy insurance for Brando"—Frank flinched when he heard this—"the payments will be a lot smaller."

Tony looked at us and said, "I'm just trying to help you guys out."

"Sure, Tony," Frank said.

"Now, remember, if you do buy this car, it has nothing to do with him," Tony said, and brushed his hands at me. "This will be your car, and you'll be giving it to him."

Frank glanced at me, rubbed his double chin. "Yeah, let's go ahead and do it like that."

"You wanna do it like that?" Tony asked.

"Yeah, sure," Frank said, and pulled out his wallet. Tony pushed over a long form. "Okay, I need you to fill this out, here, here, and here," he said, making large blue *X*s on the sheet. "Frank, I'm gonna pull your TRW report." Tony pushed back his chair, clicking a ballpoint pen. "Are you Brando's father?" he asked Frank.

Frank and I blinked at each other. Then we blurted out together: "Yes," Frank said. "No," I said. Then we flipped our answers.

"Hey, yes, no, it doesn't matter," Tony said, taking it in used-car-salesman stride. "You two will figure it out."

I was twenty-two years old. I'd known Frank as some kind of father for eighteen years. We still froze whenever anyone asked if we were father and son. We were still trying to figure things out.

The average shelf life for a stepfather was two to three years. Yet Rudy was heading into his sixth year without any signs that he was leaving. My mother was enjoying the delusional tranquility of her fifth and longest-lasting marriage.

"Rudy's loyal," she told me. "You could learn something about loyalty from him. Every day you become less and less my son."

For her forty-ninth birthday in April 1996, I treated her to an expensive restaurant she'd read about in a magazine. It was a reconciliation dinner. I was living an hour's drive away in Irvine, California, attending a creative writing graduate program I started right after college. She was furious that I hadn't moved back into the house and commuted, and we'd had a series of increasingly bitter phone arguments that led me to cut off communication with her and screen all incoming calls. First, there were angry voice mail messages, followed by ten to fifteen hang-up calls a week over the next two months. Then one morning I found a manila envelope stuffed under my car's windshield wipers. In it was a collection of short stories I'd written in college. My name was written in my mother's hand on the envelope.

She had Rudy drive her forty miles to tuck the package on my car and then had him drive her back home. I couldn't tell whether the gesture was an attempt at reconciliation or a threat.

There in the restaurant, out of the house, out of her bedroom, away from my grandmother and Rudy, I found a woman who was funny but not crude, vivacious but not loud, smart but not caustic. She flirted with our waiter, drank good white wine, and ate Cajun pizza. She listened as often as she spoke.

"Rate me," my mother said. "On a scale of one to ten, how good a mother was I?" She asked me this now each time we talked.

"A seven?" I answered, unsure. I saw her as a ten when I was a child. Now in my twenties, she was a two or three, tops. Truth is, she *was* a seven that night.

"I would have gotten mad before if you didn't say I was a ten," she said. "But I think you're being generous. Why couldn't it have always been like this, the way it is right now?" my mother asked. "This is nice."

That night, she wrote to herself in her long-gestating memoir: "For a while, I felt normal. Even though I know I can never be normal. Never. As you know by now, I'm dying, and for the first time in a long time, I cried for my position. I've always read about people dying in books, and now I'm writing my own. I have blood poisoning that's made a tumor that's exploded in my brain . . . I know *nobody* believes me, but it's true."

Her book, called *The Beginning*, had been in process since Robert lived with us. She'd been typing up her fears on a Sears manual typewriter with a sleek plastic lid that let her carry it from room to room like a suitcase, filling up pages margin to margin without paragraph breaks or spelling corrections. The writing had brought her happiness in a way that few other things did, but her journal entries, prose poems, and chapter fragments had now degenerated into amorphous paragraph blobs intended to "say good-bye" and "make amends" to the people in her life because she believed she was dying. She wrote Sofie a letter apologizing for her behavior and telling her how much she loved her. The rest of what she didn't tell Sofie, she wrote in her book: "I miss her and love her. I hope she forgives me because I was a fucking cunt, acting like I had some kind of power over her I didn't have."

She spoke to my grandmother and Rudy daily about how she'd "die young" like Kurt Cobain and AIDS educator Pedro Zamora from MTV's *The Real World* and urgently shared the deaths of famous celebrities as if updating me on the family business. Her life was confined to a single room with a telephone and a TV—this information *was* the family business.

My grandmother told my mother, "You know what happened to the boy who cried wolf, don't you?"

For some reason, probably simply because she said so, Rudy was convinced that Maria, in her late forties, was pregnant. He "felt movement" in her. She wasn't, but she now carried over 230 pounds on her five-foot-two frame. She'd stopped exercising and refused to take walks with my grandmother down the hill, complaining of excruciating migraines, severe exhaustion, foot trauma, and failing eyesight. When I took my mother out for Mother's Day, she was walking alongside Rudy arm in arm on their way to his car when she stumbled on a flat sidewalk and crumpled to her knees. She walked off the fall with a laugh and a jittery sluggishness.

At my grandmother's birthday dinner a few weeks later, my mother, belligerent and disoriented in public—something I'd never seen—challenged June to shut up for being too boisterous. In the round-robin slotting of alliances, I took my grandmother's side.

"Maybe you should have taken her out for Mother's Day instead of me," my mother said.

"Are you kidding?" my grandmother said. "You would have *killed* me if Brando had taken me along, even though I've been as much a mother to Brando as you."

"Do you see what you started, Brando?" my mother said. "You're the most selfish person I've ever known. I wish—"

"You wish what?" I asked. "Are you going to storm off and leave me here?"

"I wish I had left you like your father," my mother said.

"I wish you had, too," I said. "I might have had a chance at a normal childhood."

"Fuck you," my mother said.

"Oh, for God's sake, I don't know who the bigger baby is, you or Brando," my grandmother said. She hailed a waiter. "Give me a grasshopper fast, so I can get my fucking birthday party started."

Round and round it went—it would *always* go—and then: apologies and laughter.

More than once I'd succumbed to fantasies where my family disappeared—gone in some Disneyfied plunge into a dark chasm where the ground wasn't visible—but I assumed this was simply what parents did when they aged, finding new ways to embarrass and mortify you by revealing, but not acknowledging, their limitations.

"You have to keep this between us," Frank said. "The news would devastate your mother."

Frank was getting married, and I was invited. It felt sudden, though the last time we spoke, he'd alluded to a having long-term girlfriend. He didn't share too much out of fear I'd report back to my mother. Being out of the house made it easier to keep things from her, like my having moved in with a girlfriend named Kitt. We met in my writing program, which she'd joined after leaving her job in New York City.

I brought Kitt to my house for dinner just once. It was so . . . *quiet.* Our family didn't do quiet. Intimidated by Kitt's education and age, nine years older than me, my mother said nothing. In our house, my mother's silence could blow out your eardrums.

My grandmother served Shake 'N Bake chicken on reused paper plates to save water. "I don't ordinarily cook 'white' food," she told Kitt by way of half-hearted apology.

"I had Shake 'N Bake growing up, too," Kitt replied and smiled.

I promised Frank I'd keep his marriage a secret. "Any woman in my life has to accept you too," he said. "That's the deal. Nothing's going to change between us."

He meant well, but the fact that things *hadn't* changed was the problem. Who would I be to Frank now that he'd have a wife? How would we introduce me to Stephanie? In front of others, we scrambled to define what our connection was, but our answers were never consistent. Sometimes Frank called me a "close friend"; other times, after a couple beers, I was "the son I never had." Frank was, to me, "an old buddy," "my stepfather," or, on a rare night, "my father." We switched up what we called each other depending on the social situation: the more august the ceremony, the "higher" we elevated the other in rank.

At the wedding reception, Frank worked up a great beer buzz fast. He walked out to the street in his tuxedo with a Heineken and sat on the hood of an unoccupied LAPD car. When he came back inside, Stephanie brought him over to my table.

"I'm so happy to finally meet you," she said and hugged me. "It was really important to me that you came."

"I'm glad to be here," I said, and then looked at Frank, hovering over Stephanie's shoulder. *What do I say?*

"I know exactly who you are," she said. "And you're always welcome in our house."

Frank and I said nothing, both of us relieved. She knew who I was even if, after close to twenty years, Frank and I didn't.

"You're moving to New York City?" my mother asked. "I don't know how you're going to make it. You've always relied on me for everything."

"I'm done with my writing program. Kitt got a job offer there," I said. "A long- distance relationship won't work."

"A long-distance family won't work either," she said.

My mother couldn't see that we'd already become a long-distance family. In the two years since I'd moved an hour's drive away, I visited her and my grandmother maybe four or five times, while ignoring about two or three dozen of my mother's "emergencies." Every visit ended with the two of us in a fight. I'd race down the stairs and drive off in the car Frank and I bought together, running away from my mother the same way that Frank did when I was a child. One Christmas I mailed my family their presents instead of driving an hour and spending the day with them. That's what my family had become: a "them."

When the time came to move to New York, I signed over my car to Rudy for a dollar so he could get rid of the deathtrap he drove my mother around in. I didn't feel comfortable with Rudy possessing the title, but he had lived with her now for six years, longer than any of my stepfathers or even my *actual* father. How could he possibly pull a Pat after all this time? Or a Paul? Or a Robert? Where was he going to go?

"You really don't have *any* plans to come home again at all, do you?" my mother said. She was right, but I couldn't tell her that.

"We'll see," I said. *Please disappear*, I thought.

On the December night I left Portia Street, my grandmother clutched me by the porch railing she had leaned on a thousand mornings watching me walk to school. When she had seen me off for college, my grandmother christened me a man and encouraged my mother to release me. Then she showed my mother how it was done. My grandmother shouted my name and clasped her hands together over her head like a prizefighter. How she let me go was a gift.

I walked down the stairs that night with Rudy and my mother. With Pat's Christmas lights turned off, my grandmother's silhouette blended into the web of jacaranda tree branches she'd spent years trying to amputate. I was around the age my biological father, Candido, had been when he left me. Had he known he wouldn't see me again? Was this the last time I'd see my grandmother, or my home? Did he look back the way I was looking at the house now, his guilt tempered by a sense of liberation and joy? Did he sprint down the stairs with the same lightness in his feet I had in mine?

"Take good care of my mother," I told Rudy, because it sounded like the kind of thing a protective son would say instead of good-bye. It was a feeble attempt to be menacing; I knew there was nothing I could do from across the country.

Rudy and I embraced in an awkward pat-down. Then I hugged my mother.

If our good-bye had a hint of dramatic tension or anger, or a portentous exchange that foreshadowed the future, I'd have done a better job of remembering it. It was a simple "See you soon" and a hug. It was a hug, in memory, that seemed to go on forever, one that clung around my neck like a weighted anchor.

Driving off, they—my family—blended into nothing but darkness. I exhaled a comic-book bubble sigh of relief, confident it'd be a long time before I had to see them again.

I was out of contact for a month while my girlfriend and I lived at her brother's place in Hoboken waiting to move into a high-rise waterfront apartment in Jersey City. Within minutes of getting a live phone connection, my mother called, and we talked for an hour.

"Here's what I want from New York," she said, and rattled off a list of souvenirs I pretended to write down. When I ended our call, she said, "All right, Brando! C'mon, New York City!" She sounded upbeat, animated, as if she'd saved up all her energy from the past few weeks for this one phone call with her son.

Sometime that evening, a Saturday, she came down with the symptoms of a mild cold.

On Sunday the symptoms of her cold worsened, and she stayed in bed. At some point, she used the phone and pressed "record" on a machine she'd purchased to tape calls. She recorded one side of an unintelligible conversation that I'm convinced was with herself. When I listened to this recording later, her voice was muffled, drugged, almost deranged, like sleep talk. The tape ends with the only word I understood: "Good-bye."

Late Sunday night and then on Monday, her condition worsened. She sprayed Lysol in her crotch instead of changing her days-old underwear and staggered out of bed several times, complaining to my grandmother about the temperature in the house.

"I'm cold, Momma," she said. "Why am I so cold?"

My grandmother gave her a stack of musty Southwestern pastel bedspreads and a jar of Vicks VapoRub, and then made her some soup. On her stereo, my mother played not her beloved Stevie Nicks but Julia Fordham. (Her CD player would spit Fordham's *East West* out the next time it was plugged back in. The first track is called "Killing Me Slowly." The album sits unlistened to in my record collection.)

"I'm coming to the end of my life," my mother had written several months ago. "I don't even care or give a fuck about the pain that will be inflicted. Sure, I will be screaming at the top of my lungs, but I feel, or fear, that pain is normal."

My mother was quiet the next day, Tuesday. She hadn't left her bed. My grandmother checked on her in the afternoon and asked if she wanted some soup for dinner.

My mother said, "Yes, Momma. I'd like some." My grandmother closed my mother's bedroom door behind her, out of habit.

"There has to be something more than my closed door and my room," she wrote. "I wonder what AIDS patients think of. What is everybody's last moments like?"

• • •

On Tuesday, January 6, the same date my great-grandmother Lucille had died at the age of thirty-eight, Rudy left a message on my machine: "Brando, I need you to call me back right away. Okay? Call me as soon as you get this message."

My mother had left hundreds of similar emergencies on my machine, so I avoided this one at first. I didn't want her to feel I could be paged three thousand miles away. There was a crackling fear in Rudy's voice, though; an insistency that sounded like backbone. The previous year, a college buddy had called to tell me a mutual friend had died in a Yosemite hiking accident. He had that same edge and crackle in his voice, as if the words were stuck in his throat and he had to use all the strength in his stomach muscles to dislodge them, like a bit of food blocking your windpipe. He had to force the words out before they choked him.

When Kitt came home from work, I played her the message. "Either my grandmother fell down the stairs or my mother died." I said this with a flippant, macho laugh, though I don't know why.

Rudy picked up the phone. "Your mother is dead, Brando."

I leaned over to Kitt and parroted, "My mother is dead." She covered a gasp and put her head on my shoulder. I stiffened, shrugged her head off, and listened impassively. Rudy passed the phone to my grandmother.

"The paramedics tried for half an hour," my grandmother said, sounding chastened. "And the cops were so nice. I'll never say anything bad about 'pigs' again," she said.

My mother had been acting erratic, it's true, but nothing seemed wrong. "You know how she always complained about everything," my grandmother said. "I thought she was faking. She just seemed a little sick. How could I know anything was really wrong with her?"

I didn't blame her. My mother feigned so many illnesses over the years, how could my grandmother distinguish a fake malady from a real one?

An autopsy determined the cause of death as "dilated cardiomyopathy." A flabby heart. No blood poisoning, no brain tumor, not a trace anything else was wrong save that her heart was too weak to support the strain of her weight and sedentary living. She was fifty.

My grandmother scoffed at the report's wording. "Obese?" my grandmother said. "She wasn't obese. They act like she was some kind of carnival freak." Later, she'd find the speed and a hoard of illegally prescribed fen-phen in nonchildproof jars that my mother had been cocktailing to lose weight.

I had years of practice losing fathers. I had a lifetime to learn how to try to live with my mother. I had a day to learn how to live without her.

Then another day.

And another.

And another.

And another.

10

"You sound like something bad happened, Brando," Frank said. "Are calls this late at night ever good news?"

"No, I guess not."

I told him my mother had died.

"What?" he asked. "That's impossible. I *just* talked to her. I mean, I'd just gotten a few calls where someone hung up on me. You never told her I got married, did you?"

"No," I said.

"Good. I didn't want her to know that. Did I ever tell you how we met?" When he finished, he said, "God, she was *such* a babe. That is how I'll always remember her. I can't believe I was fortunate enough to have known her."

My grandmother asked me, "When are you coming back for the funeral?"

I'd promised I wouldn't run home the first time my mother asked because I'd never return to New York if I did, and yet here my mother was, "asking" me to come this one final time. The house in Echo Park felt like a point where space and light collapsed around it, swallowing lives whole. Returning home meant helping my grandmother "for a few days" that would turn into weeks and months, maybe years. Would I take my mother's place in the house? I'd have to end my relationship with Kitt. Worst of all, I'd have to share a house with Rudy. I knew he wasn't going anywhere now.

I sent a bouquet of flowers—the path of least inconvenience—and then tried to cheat my way out of guilt by reconnecting with Sofie, asking if she'd attend the service.

"You meant a lot to her," I said. "She'd want you there."

"I can't do that," she said. "We're not dating anymore. Besides, wouldn't she want *you* there?"

I told my grandmother I wasn't coming to the funeral. "If I go back to LA now," I said, "I know I won't return to New York."

"This is about what I expected from you," she said.

My grandmother sent funeral service announcements that gave my mother's name as Running Deer along with two of her married ones. She listed my mother's real name as a pseudonym.

"She always wanted to be an Indian," my grandmother said. "Now she gets to be one."

About twenty mourners came to the service and offered their memories of my mother. My half uncle Oscar said, "She helped me with my alphabet."

"What kind of dumb fucking thing is that to say at a funeral?" my grandmother asked afterward. She praised Frank for showing up and his heartfelt eloquence. "I never realized how good a man he was until now," she said.

Frank phoned me later. "It was a lovely ceremony. I'm sorry you couldn't be here with us."

The late-night hang-up calls that plagued him for years stopped when my mother died.

My grandmother searched for my mother's mythical "cash stash" that she'd bragged about for years and claimed was somewhere in her room—a room she had lived in for forty-five of her fifty years. The one plausible hiding area was her bookshelf of true-crime biographies. I pictured dozens of flopped-open, face-down books with their spines cracked around my grandmother's feet like a pile of dead birds. Amid those pages, she found a single fifty-dollar bill. (The state of California holds an additional $62.64 in my mother's real name, waiting for me to claim.)

Both Rudy and my grandmother said they'd wait until I came home to spread my mother's ashes. "No matter how long it takes," my grandmother said. "We want to do this when you're ready."

A month later, my grandmother had waited long enough. She and Rudy scattered my mother's ashes illegally somewhere into the San Pedro Harbor.

I didn't cry over my mother's death. I couldn't cry because I was incapable of crying. When my tears came at last, I cried because I'd been deprived of a chance to lash out at her for my pain. I was stricken with a paranoid depression more brutal and unforgiving than my college bout, leaving me incapable of leaving our thirty-first-floor apartment. I couldn't collect the mail during the day because I thought the elevator cable would snap. I gained fifty pounds and grew my hair out for an entire year down to my waist; my mother had liked my hair long, so to rebel I'd always cut my hair short instead of growing it out. I listened to the wind howl against the sides of the building and imagined jumping from our window, wondering how many seconds I'd have in the air before I hit the sidewalk. I turned away from Kitt whenever she touched me because I *couldn't* respond to her touch. I wasn't *feeling* a thing for the woman I loved. I sat in a single spot on the couch from the time Kitt left for work to the time she came home, cataloguing the passing hours based on the way sunlight moved through the apartment. She would shout out to me from the front door every day she arrived from work, desperate not to hear the whooshing sound of an open window, dreading a suicide letter cocked on an end table jutting out at her like a spoiled tongue.

I didn't want to live or to die. I was afraid to do either.

I started therapy to combat the depression. On my way to a session,

I was distracted by the Stevie Nicks song "Landslide" on the radio and almost got slammed by a car running a red light.

Running low on money, I asked Rudy if he could send me a few dollars to help me out.

"I don't want you to sell my car," I said. "I just need a little help until I feel better."

"I can do that," he said. "Your mother wanted me to take care of you, and I gave her my promise I would."

We'd never speak again.

"Rudy is a good man to take all this crap. I would have been gone a long time ago. I realize I will never love him, but I do like him as a dear friend," my mother wrote in her unfinished book. After she died, my grandmother found a xeroxed copy of my mother's ornamental marriage certificate to Rudy. On it, my mother wrote: "Nov 26th, 1996, at 9:42 P.M. Rudy asked me for a divorce." Rudy then signed his name under her note.

My mother had never legally married anyone except Candido, so a divorce was impossible, but it was the first clue that Rudy had envisioned a life without my mother. Now that she was dead, my grandmother saw what his idea of that life was. She said he stopped coming home right after work. He stopped eating dinner with my grandmother. He stayed out for several days at a time, stopping by to shower, change clothes, and sleep. Confronted by my grandmother one night, Rudy said, "My bed is cold. Do you want to join me?"

"I don't take my daughter's lovers," she told him.

It's conceivable this happened. Rudy may have thought that this was the one way he could stay in the house and perhaps inherit it. My grandmother wanted to evict Rudy but said she couldn't do it on her own.

"You need to help me move Rudy out," she told me. "With force if you have to."

Seeing catastrophe stalk every decision I made, I opted not to fly and bought a cross-country train ticket. Kitt sat with me at a TGI Fridays in Penn Station before I left and talked me through why I was going back home. What did I hope to accomplish out there? What could I do that my grandmother couldn't do by changing the locks? Would I come back? Wasn't my life with her now?

She was right. I called my grandmother and cashed in my ticket. When Rudy came home and found that his keys didn't work, he didn't *tap-tap-tap* on the door but tried to force his way into the house. He yelled, screamed, and kicked at the security gate. My grandmother threatened to call her now-beloved "pigs" if he didn't leave.

"At least let me have my clothes, you fucking bitch!" he shouted. She kept the door shut and called the police. Rudy stormed down the stairs and didn't return.

A few days later, a repossession officer gave my grandmother the rest of the story. Rudy used the car I signed over to him as collateral to borrow money and secure a number of credit cards he couldn't have gotten with his bad credit record. These cards were all maxed out. The officer gave my grandmother his business card in case Rudy reappeared, but I knew there was no chance of that. I'd been through this four times before. This time a father's leaving wasn't a shock, or a heartbreak, or a betrayal, or a loss of innocence. It was a cure.

In a memoir, a day of your life can be a long chapter; a month a single line of prose; a year can be a text break or an entire blank space. Time doesn't work that way. It forces us to give each moment we embrace the same amount of room as the moments we want to forget. Here, on these pages, it's easy for me to cover in a few words the year and a half between my mother dying and my grandmother getting sick. I can ignore the months that passed where my grandmother waited in her house for my phone call, or the weekend I set aside my fear of flying to attend a friend's wedding in Los Angeles but didn't drive up to my grandmother's house to spend a few hours with her. Back then I had to outrun memories of my grandmother to pretend I hadn't turned as callous as I was acting. I called what I was doing "protection."

Without my mother by her side to heckle at life, my grandmother had no more errands to run, no more arguments to fight. A year and a half after my mother died, my grandmother fell ill. An incorrect diagnosis of gallstones kept her in the hospital; the correct diagnosis of terminal cancer would bring her home. We spoke on the phone before she checked out of the hospital.

"I haven't heard from you in a long time," she said. It was a shock to hear my grandmother now sound like the seventy-nine-year-old she was.

"I've been busy with work," I said, and then decided to make the leap that a year of therapy had suggested I take. "And I didn't want to fight with you anymore."

"Yeah, fighting is bad," she said. "I don't like the fighting."

"When we fight, Grandma, it's hurtful to me," I said. "I would really like if it you didn't yell at me anymore, because you're my grand-mother, and I love you, and we're the only family we have left now."

I thought I could see her nodding her head in agreement.

"You're right," she said. "I'd like for us to have a better relationship."

Was it this easy to clear the air? Could years of turmoil have been avoided with one honest conversation? I'd never said these things to my mother and regretted it. My grandmother was sick, but perhaps we could live out whatever remaining time we had together bonded by our longing for my mother and unburdened by the mistakes of our past.

When she was released, my grandmother sent me a blank Snoopy birthday card. Inside was a short, eviscerating note about how "rotten and ungrateful a grandson" I was to have had such a terrible conversation with a dying woman. I don't remember the note's wording except the last line: "You could have at least waited until I was dead to bad-mouth me."

I didn't save that letter. In its place, what I've chosen to keep and read from when I need to hear my grandmother's voice is a dedication she signed in an Agatha Christie book and gave me as a gift the spring before I moved to New York:

"May the roads rise up to meet you, May the winds always be at your back, May the sun shine warm upon your face, The rains fall soft upon your self, and until we meet again, May God hold you in the hollow of his hand.

"With love always, Grandmother June. OOXX"

We'd meet again two months later in October. I hadn't seen her since I left for New York. Frank called and said, "I stopped by to check in on Grandma. The doctors say she'll last a few weeks, but man, I don't think she'll last more than a few days. You should get out here."

I didn't come home for my mother's funeral out of fear I'd become my grandmother's keeper. That I'd take my mother's place in the house. That I'd *become* my mother. Now the fear of losing my other mother without saying good-bye pushed me back to California. I flew home three days after Frank's phone call to find a boarder living in my mother's room. By request or design, he'd kept it almost ghoulishly intact from the way she'd left it when she died eighteen months earlier. I was also greeted by a woman I'd never met before nor would ever see or hear from again.

"I'm one of your mother's close friends," she said, offering a name I didn't recognize. Throughout my mother's nearly twenty years working from home, she mentioned just one close friend. It wasn't this woman.

"Your mother asked me to look out for you," she continued. "So I looked at your grandmother's trust. She was very angry with you, so I helped her change it."

Years before, my grandmother had set up a living trust that left her house to me and my mother. She gave my uncle one dollar for what she told me was "a lifetime of neglect and being a wicked son." When my mother died, Oscar visited my grandmother on occasion, offering for both of them what I'd hoped was some solace or companionship. With the help of my mother's friend, the trust had been amended six weeks before I came back home to give my uncle half the house. My grandmother's signature was unrecognizable, but then so was she.

I hadn't seen my grandmother since the night she set me free from her front porch. She was unconscious in her bed, a glucose bag by her side, unable to speak and jaundiced from cheek to leg. Her arms and body were flattened out across the bed, her periwinkle caftan riding up past her varicose thighs. Her mouth was slack open, her hands clumped into fists, a fighter on her deathbed.

I asked the boarder, "Shouldn't we close her window? It's freezing in here."

"I don't think that'll help anything," he said.

There was no movement in her hands, no response in her body, just the sound of my grandmother's heavy breathing, catching in a soupy sputter, stalling out, and then breath again.

I found a *Peanuts* collection of strips in a stack of old books preserved in my room that I'd read to my grandmother aloud as a child. Next to her clock radio, one of the many "crappy" gifts she said I'd given her over the years, was a cassette sleeve for an Ella Fitzgerald greatest-hits album. I played the tape, unballed one of her hands to hold it, and read to her from the *Peanuts* book.

You're a good man, Charlie Brown, she said to me when I was a child.

"I'm trying to be a good man," I said now. "I'm trying."

There was nothing in that darkness but her breathing. I was a toddler when my grandmother's warm breath blew across my neck. It's my first memory. Now I was hearing the last of her breath that she had fought so hard to preserve for me.

Her breath said, *I waited for you to come home. Now take my breath and be free.*

I thought about sleeping in the chair next to her but couldn't handle spending the night by her side like I had as a child. Around midnight, I turned off the light in her bedroom.

My grandmother died sometime before I woke. Her death certificate says five thirty in the morning, but this was a guess.

If my grandmother dying mere hours after my arrival sounds too coincidental, that's because we've been conditioned by liars to believe that extraordinary strength is always bullshit. My grandmother was pure strength. No bullshit.

In the morning, two of my grandmother's friends, an elderly couple bearing get-well flowers, became her first mourners. They collapsed by her bed with an inconsolable wail of pure grief. Why couldn't I join them? Their pain seemed too overwhelming, too messy, too mobile to include a safe place for me. My mother's death stunned me stiff. Her death came clean, by message, the way it does in Shakespeare. Here, death arrived the same night I did, breathing the same air I did, taking the soul from my grandmother's body and leaving her mouth agape and her eyes half lidded while I slept. From the front porch, my grandmother's favorite place to watch life come and go, I saw her body carried out of her house and down the complicated staircase the same way that my grandfather Emilio had been. My grandmother watched me walk to school on a thousand mornings from this porch. When I went to New York, she'd set me free from this porch. I clutched the railings, watched her body loaded into a wagon, and waited for the parade of mourners to pay their respects to the mayor of Echo Park. My grandmother had made so many friends in the neighborhood. I wanted more people around so I could cry and mourn her. My grandmother was a public person. She *was* Echo Park. I didn't want my grief to be private like it was for my mother. Would I have enough time to run to the supermarket and fill up the house with food and drink?

I welcomed just one next-door neighbor that first day, and nobody else on the days that followed. Her friends had passed on, moved away, or been exiled in petty arguments.

"Your grandma was something else," this neighbor said. "I remember my kid was out in front of your house playing, and she said, 'Why don't you get the fuck away from my house and play in your asshole father's yard?' I was just out of sight and said, 'June, it's all right.' She said, 'Fuck you, too!' Man, she was something."

To that, my grandmother would have said, "You're going to complain about a dead old woman hours after she's been carried out of her house? I always knew you were an asshole."

What I said was, "Yeah, she was a handful."

Four people—my grandmother June, my mother, Maria, my grandfather Emilio, and my grandmother's lover Tata—died in the house I grew up in. I didn't want to be the fifth. Every memory would become some kind of ghost trapped in its walls whose impression would leak back out over time if I'd stayed. Oscar and I agreed to sell the house.

On my last day there, I walked through its hollowed-out rooms in a sleep-deprived daze as if visiting the empty set of a sitcom that had gone on too long. The rooms were dark, the floors warped and creaky. I paused before I closed the front door, waiting for a shout from my mother's room—"Don't get kidnapped!"—or my grandmother's jangling keys signaling she was ready to hand hold me down to the bus stop. There was just quiet.

At last, quiet.

Every day since I was ten or so, my grandmother had said, "Don't give me a funeral. And please don't bury me in the ground. Just cremate me and throw my ashes in the sea." My uncle disagreed.

"We should bury her," Oscar said. "Because of the resurrection. So she can have a chance to come back."

"Do you have money to pay for a burial?" I asked coldly.

"Oh, Brando, man, you know I don't."

"Do you have any money to contribute for a service?"

"No."

"Then we should do what she wanted us to do," I said.

I charged her cremation to a credit card, picking up her ashes in a gold box that resembled a mantelpiece clock. They handed my grandmother over in a white gift bag with a pleasant air, as if I were picking up a package I'd dropped off to be gift wrapped. I wanted to scatter the ashes before I left Los Angeles, but Oscar said he'd hold on to them for a while because he wasn't ready to let her go. When I returned to New York, in one of our last conversations, he said he'd buried her ashes in a cemetery plot but didn't reveal where. He left some voice mails and sent a card asking me to call him sometime, but I never did. We were each other's last known relative, but I wanted to be free from my family. I wanted the right to choose my own.

Nowadays I get messages from aggressive collection agencies about once a year, like Christmas cards, looking for Oscar.

"I don't know who he is," I say.

I had dinner with Frank and Stephanie the night before I left Los Angeles. She asked me, "So how does it feel to have Frank in your life after all these years?"

I smiled and said, "I really think we can have a better relationship now." It sounded promising, us no longer having to hide from my mother our being in contact, as if she had been the sole obstacle between us having a father-son relationship all along. Of course, she wasn't, but I didn't want to see that what was coming for us looked just like what had gone before. A desert of long absences—punctuated by a birthday phone call or a Father's Day card—that we'd still had to march through together, and alone, still in search of the perfect name for each other.

• • •

My family was gone. Over the next ten years, I dealt with that loss by searching for mother and father surrogates (in my stepfathers' case, substitutes for substitutes) in temporary people: Kitt's mother, whom I lost when Kitt and I broke up; a boss I endowed with a nonexistent paternal streak. I searched for family everywhere in everyone, too, holding on to friendships for years, turning coworkers into friends into brothers and sisters.

I learned, slowly, how to acknowledge and embrace being a Mexican who happened to be raised as my mother's kind of Indian. This was just as difficult as inventing a new family. My upbringing was cobbled together from so many different parents, I identified with almost no culture except "pop." Who was I, really? My name itself seemed like a celebrity construct borne from a hallucinogenic orgy in a field: "Were your parents hippies?" I spent a third of my life as an Indian, a third denying I was Mexican, and this current third asking, What kind of Mexican am I? (Don't put the emphasis on *kind*. Put it on *I*.) Yet a truth that once felt too complicated to explain in an easy, pat way isn't anymore. There's a fluency that comes with sincerity and repetition.

You could say—and four of my five stepfathers might agree—the same about running a con. A Latino professor from Texas confronted me at a booth at a Modern Language Association conference when he saw my name badge.

"Your mother had to be Latino," he said. "There's no way you're a 'Skyhorse.'" He badgered me to confess my background. I felt like a fraud, but he was both more right, and wrong, than he knew. While on a book tour for my first novel, I was approached at a reading by a woman related to Paul Skyhorse Durant, who would pass away later that same year. She confronted me as some kind of imposter who had stolen the Skyhorse name. I told her my story. She'd never heard of Paul Skyhorse Johnson but believed that while he might have been an

Indian, he certainly had no claim to the Skyhorse name. We continued talking. She didn't buy a book, but she heard what I had to say.

Just before she left, she said, "We Skyhorses have to stick together."

I'm intact, but the scars are there. Some, from a losing battle with acne that gave me pimples on my fortieth birthday, are easy to see. Others aren't. I'm irresistibly drawn to people from my past in spite of the challenges in reestablishing contact and the inevitable pain when they drift out of my life again. I'm prone to hurting people, and being hurt by people who hurt people. I can disappear from contact with friends for weeks or months at a time. I have severe chronic and undiagnosed stomach problems. There are "intimacy concerns" and "abandonment issues."

On alcohol, which I avoided for years, I have the personality of a loose tire, driving smooth and reliable for hundreds of miles and then flying off and careening into a group of friends like a cannonball shot with belligerence and self-pity. I'd get blinding drunk at parties or out with friends and then be dry as a bone at home. I could hear my mother say, "You're not even an interesting alcoholic," and she was right. I had none of the harrowing tales of an addict I'm convinced my mother would have encouraged me to mine, just assorted acts of jackassery: too much loud mouthiness and puke.

Several years of therapy and Wellbutrin kept depression a restraining order's distance away but has left me mindful of its existence, somewhere around the corner, in the dark. One time I had a panic attack that I was drinking too much water and checked myself into a New York City emergency room with a self-diagnosis of hyponatremia. When the interns performed their evening rounds, I heard the litany of urban horrors—blocked arteries, septic shock, broken limbs—before they reached my bed, which had been discreetly curtained. "This is a case of someone who believed he had poisoned himself by drinking too much water," the gentle voice said, "so we're going to skip this one."

Sometimes there are night terrors. I'm in a maze where my mother and grandmother are at opposite ends, brandishing weapons and trying to kill me. Some nights I confront my mother. I say, "I'm glad you're dead." Here in a place somewhere between a dream and a nightmare, my mother listens and, I think, understands.

In 2010, right after I mailed my letter to Candido Ulloa, I traveled alone to Istanbul, Turkey. There I followed a great parade of gypsies and revelers through cobblestone alleys to a traditional spring gypsy festival by the shores of the Bosphorus Strait. In its center was a fifty-foot-high maypole with tendrils of many-colored scrap paper that fluttered and rattled, a giant *shhhhhhh* in the breeze. For a few dollars, you bought scraps of paper and wrote messages to loved ones, living or departed, pinned them to a cord, and then let the wind blow these sheets out to the water.

Under a sunset like flecked gold leaf, I wrote messages to my mother and grandmother. I was seven thousand miles away from Echo Park, California, but I had carried them with me—their voices, their prejudices, their ribald humor, their unpredictable cruelty, their astonishing capacity for kindness, their torrential fears—and I knew this was where I could let them go. If a single sheet of paper found its way to my father after thirty-three years, these scraps could be carried aloft to a place where pain and sorrow have passed away and all spirits are welcomed with love and forgiveness.

On those papers was a simple message: I will give something back to you, every day, wherever you are.

Mother, take the first words you gave me to speak.

Grandma, take my first breath you gave me to breathe.

I want to believe your souls are free.

11

My father was calling. My father *Candido* was calling. It had been a week since I'd sent my letter. His first message, left on my relic of an answering machine, was the sound of a *telenovela* in the background and a man speaking to someone in another room before the receiver was fumbled and hung up. I knew it was Candido, but I didn't pick up. I wasn't ready to talk to him yet. He didn't say anything on the message. Maybe he wasn't ready either.

The second message, a day or two later, was the same as the first. On his third call, I picked up. He asked for me by name and then spoke in Spanish.

"I'm sorry," I said, and stopped him. "I don't understand Spanish as well as you're speaking it."

"Oh, your letter was so good in Spanish."

"I had a friend write it."

"I am the man you are looking for," Candido said. He didn't use the word *father*. He wouldn't use it in our conversation. I wanted him to—*once*. Just once.

"I have been waiting for this day for a long time," he said.

"Well . . . good!" I said, half laughing. "Um," I said, and paused. *What should I say?* I hadn't prepared a list of questions, rants, insults— nothing. I had a sudden urge to hang up. Did I just need to know he'd call me back and hear his voice?

"You live on the East Coast now?" he asked.

"Yes, near New York City. I left Los Angeles when my grandmother died years ago."

"Oh, I am very sorry to hear that," he said. His tone was patient and kind. "She was a beautiful woman. I loved her very much."

"My mother is dead, too," I said.

Candido said nothing. I didn't know silence could sound angry.

"Do you remember my mother?" I asked.

"Yes, but I don't want you to be mad if I say something bad about someone that is dead."

"It's okay," I said. "I've said many bad things about my mother."

"She is why I left," he said.

How many times had my mother told me *I* was the reason my father—or any of my fathers—had left? I couldn't believe what I heard. I had to hear it again.

"You left because of her?" I asked.

"Yes," he said. "She told me if I ever came back, she'd call immigration and get me deported." Then he told me his story, about how impossible his and my mother's marriage was and about the last day he lived in our house. He chose his words the way an old man climbs a flight of stairs. His memory was exact and bitter, reciting events as if they'd happened last week, not over thirty years ago. How much could I trust his version of things, I wondered. Then he said, "The last time I tried to leave, your mother attacked me with a knife."

"I believe you," I said. I had no more doubts. I was listening to *my* story. "She pulled a knife on me too."

"Oh," he said. He seemed unfazed, so I volunteered another piece of my past.

"My mother remarried after you left," I said.

"Oh, did she like him?"

"Well, she married four more times, so . . ."

"Four more?" he said and laughed. "That is a lot!"

"Yeah, it's a lot," I said. It *was* a lot, and, really, what more was there to say about my other fathers to my father? How could I explain to him what at the time I barely understood myself?

"Where did you go when you left?" I asked.

"I lived with some friends in an apartment in East Los Angeles for a while," he said. "Sometimes when I wasn't working, I'd go to Dodger Stadium with friends to see Fernando Valenzuela pitch."

"Would you ever drive by the house?" I asked. Our street intersected with a major thoroughfare to the stadium, a five-minute drive away.

"Mmm, maybe sometimes. I don't remember." Had he thought about me when he drove to the baseball game? Did he sit in the stands holding a beer and think, *My only son lives just a short ways from here?* Or had I not crossed his mind at all? The same impulse that keeps you from jumping off an edge when you look over it kept me from asking these questions.

"Living in East Los Angeles, I met my wife, Aurora," he said, "and we moved down to Whittier. It's close to Echo Park, you know? Only thirty minutes away by car, very close."

Yes, I thought. *Very close.*

"This whole time, all these years, we have been working, me and Aurora," he said. "Work, work, work. There is always more work to do."

There it was. The answer I wanted for thirty-three years. What had happened to my father? He went away, he stayed away, and then his real life began.

"How about you?" he asked. "Are you married? Do you have children?"

Here was the chance to tell my father what happened. This was the opening I'd waited years for, to flood him with all the details of my life. The path it took *because* he left me. I'd wring out on top of him every drop of pain, anger, dysfunction, and chaos his abandonment caused, introduce him to the secondhand fathers I had to learn to love in his absence, hand him, piece by jagged piece, memories of the broken

family I assembled over a lifetime and lost for good when my grandmother died. I wanted the father I knew from pictures, that beautiful
young man in his twenties, to open a door for me, so I could rush him.
But that man—that *father*—was gone. In his place was a simple, happy
man in his early sixties, weary from the toll of a full, ordinary life spent
providing for, caring for, loving, and being loved by others. I'd brought
the bullets to destroy him, but the gun dissolved right in my hands.

"I never married," I said. "And I don't have kids. Not yet. Someday, I hope."

"Mmm, I thought I might have more grandchildren. I have one
already."

"What is your grandchild's name?"

"Your nephew's name is Dillan. He is your oldest sister's child."

"*Oldest* sister?" I asked.

"Yes. You have three sisters."

Candido's wife read my letter first. Her formal name is Maria Ulloa,
the same as my mother's first married name, but she goes by her middle name, Aurora. After a thirteen-hour workday, it's her responsibility
to start dinner and open the mail.

Aurora knew who I was—had known before she and Candy started
a family of their own. She'd ask why he hadn't reached out to me.
"You have a son," she said. "Why don't you try to get in touch with
him? Send him a letter or a card for his birthday?"

"You don't understand," Candido said. "If my old wife knew where
I was, she would have me sent back to Mexico. She would make our
lives hell."

When Candido came home from his work as a groundskeeper for
an apartment complex, Aurora handed him my letter and said, "Your
son is looking for you. Now will you contact him?"

Candido read the Spanish version and was impressed by my (nonexistent) command of the language. My last name explained why a

Google search he'd done the year before for Brando Ulloa came up blank. He knew he'd call me, but there was something more important to do first. He gathered his daughters Adriana, then twenty-nine, Kereny, twenty-four, and Natalie, twelve, in the living room of his compact two-bedroom house and, rubbing his sweaty palms together, blurted out, "Our family just got bigger."

The girls were confused. Adriana thought, *Mom's pregnant again? Isn't she too old for that?*

"You have an older brother," my father said.

Candido gave his daughters my email address to contact me if they chose. To Natalie, the youngest, the idea of a much older brother on another coast was an abstraction, something that didn't mean much amid a teenager's burgeoning desire for independence, privacy, and her own cell phone. For Kereny, a behavior therapist for autistic children, the situation was perhaps the most complicated. A self-described tomboy who grew up watching soccer with her father, she'd considered herself the son he'd never had.

"God gave you three daughters," Kereny joked with Candido, "because you always wanted a son." He doesn't remember, but I wonder what crossed Candido's mind when she said this. Did he flinch? Smile weakly? Excuse himself to the kitchen? I'm sure his appearance betrayed nothing, but I'd like to think he sat uncomfortably in his chair and felt just a little sick to his stomach, the way men with secrets in movies squirm and perspire as proof that they have a conscience.

Adriana, a schoolteacher with both a bachelor's degree and a master's degree from UCLA, maintained the greatest composure because this revelation was not a total surprise. When she was nine (around when I started high school), she was told at a cousin's birthday party, "I know something about your father. He has a son he ran away from. You have an older brother. Go and ask your father. Go and ask him about the son he never sees." Adriana was sure it had to be one of those horrendous lies that kids say to one another to be cruel, yet she never forgot it. When Candido told her about me, she thought, *Of course*. She wondered what would have happened if she had asked her father about me when she was a little girl. *Maybe*, she thought, *if I'd said something, we would have been reunited sooner. Maybe I wouldn't have had to go my whole life not knowing that I had an older brother. Was this thing somehow my fault?*

"I wanted to say thank you for searching for my dad," Adriana wrote me. "By the way, the 'my' is just a Mexican thing. People always ask me why I say 'my' even when speaking to my own sisters. I think it's a direct translation from Spanish, since we say 'mi mama o mi papa.' I know Candido is truly happy to have finally reunited with you. I am very happy to know about you and have you become part of the family. I always wanted an older brother. I am sorry this did not occur sooner in our lives, but it's never too late, and we need to think of the now and the future."

When I picked up Candido's phone call, I was the last son in a dead-end family. When I hung up, I had a resurrected father and three new sisters. Their emails revealed them to be open, loving, generous, and willing to adopt me as a family member sight unseen. They were so unlike the women I grew up with. Their openness with a complete stranger was startling, like the way a cold, clear morning can leave you breathless. I had sisters who *wanted* a brother. They wanted *me*. When I last dreamed of siblings, I was playing in my magical stuffed animal forest, wishing for total strangers to give me a family I'd never thought I'd get a second chance to have. Here they were at last. I began imagining futures with Adriana, Kereny, and Natalie. Candido almost was an afterthought. He was *their* father, but these women were *my* sisters. I tried to keep my heart tethered to the ground. It didn't do any good. I knew I was falling in love.

• • •

"Be careful," Frank warned. He and I had been in sporadic contact over the past ten years, as each of us took turns not returning the other's phone calls, but my "real" father's reappearance seemed to rouse in him a dormant responsibility. It was May 2010, three months after my first letter to Candido. I had just flown into Los Angeles and was talking to Frank in a hotel room the night before I would finally meet Candido's new family. Frank would then pick me up outside Candido's house when the meeting was over.

"So where has he been this whole time?" Frank asked.

"Whittier," I said.

"Huh," he said. "So he could have sent you money for years or stopped by whenever he wanted. He was just over in Whittier."

"That's right."

"Huh," Frank grunted again. "So I guess you have a father now," he said.

"Frank, this changes nothing between us. But I don't even know what to call you. You're so bound by rules that whenever I call you 'Dad,' you flinch, since you never married my mother."

"How could I have married her?" he asked. "I never saw a way to make it work."

"I know," I said. "She wishes you had."

"I know that," he said.

"No," I said. "That was one of her last wishes."

"What do you mean?" he asked.

My mother's will was a typed letter addressed to me. It was in a box of papers I'd taken back to New York but hadn't sorted through until several years later. She'd written her will like a suicide note, itemizing in specific detail which of her few possessions were to be left to whom. This was the first time I'd seen Frank in person since I'd read the will. She left Frank a handful of books, a framed Emmett Kelly clown print, a water-damaged Native American poster of a squaw riding on a horse, and some compact discs. These items were Frank's only if I didn't want them first, but there was one thing in her will that belonged to him and him alone.

"In my mother's will," I said, "she wrote in pen, 'Frank, you should have married me.'"

"Huh," he said. "I've thought about that a lot. I'm really happy with Stephanie. Things are great. It would have never worked out with your mother and me. But you know something? She was probably right," he said, and started to cry.

Kereny picked me up at the hotel with her boyfriend Pedro, who'd come along to calm her nerves. Our first hug was more of an enthusiastic nudge. On the drive to Candido's house, we struggled for small talk like picking up pennies wearing oven mitts.

"Are you hungry?" Kereny asked. "We can stop for breakfast at a Denny's if you like."

"No thanks," I said.

A few minutes passed. "Do you want to get some coffee or something?"

"No, that's all right," I said.

Minutes later, Kereny said, "There's a park near here. Do you want to drive there for a bit, maybe walk around?"

"I want to go to your house," I said. "Everything's going to be fine."

She drove down a long gravel driveway and then opened their backdoor security gate. Candido rose from his couch with an unguarded laugh. Seeing him, I felt a tinny electric charge of recognition, like meeting a celebrity: both my father and famous people were familiar only in pictures.

I hugged Candido tight. He clasped me like a work acquaintance showing me out of his office. We sat down in the living room, where we talked about the weather and soccer in a halting first-date back and forth.

My father wore church clothes: a fine rayon short-sleeve shirt, white narrow-toe lizard-skin boots, with rings on a couple fingers and a gold chain. His hair and mustache were inkwell black. I listened to how

he spoke. I couldn't hear my voice in his, and there was a brief palpi-
tation of panic. What if my mother had told Candido I was his but I
was, in fact, another man's? What if my mother had exaggerated one
last story and had executed her greatest lie from beyond the grave?

"I'm better than Houdini!" I could hear her say. "At least it's never
boring."

"Can we look at some pictures?" I asked.

In a stack of albums were pictures of Candy in fine dress clothes,
his hair looking more or less now as it did in the seventies and eighties. His daughters morphed from happy babies into beautiful women.
Their eyes—lucid and wide like a puppy's, like my eyes—are what
convinced me my search was over. Here was all of Candido's history:
the Christmases, the birthdays, the Disneyland trips, the graduations:
the alternate life I could have had with him, and the lives that never
would have existed had Candido stayed where he was. I spotted a picture of me as maybe a two-year-old on a pony, a duplicate of a photo
in my mother's own collection.

"That picture's always been there," Kereny said and laughed. "We
thought it was just a cousin or something." He hadn't forgotten me.
He'd hidden me in plain sight.

When all the baby and holiday photographs had been exclaimed
over and explained, Candido and I were left alone at the kitchen table
to "talk." I'd imagined that his family believed we had a lot to discuss.
I thought we would too, but as I sat across from my father, I wondered what could I legitimately say to a sixtysomething man who ran
away from a collapsing marriage and abandoned his kid when he was
little more than a kid himself? I knew why he'd left and where he was
now. He'd lived a quiet, decent life with no other broken families in
his wake. Candido's family was proof that he was capable of being the
dedicated day-to-day father I had tried to turn at least five other men
into. His one crime was that he couldn't be that father to me. But
who was left to pay for that crime? I knew what had happened, but
knowing the past doesn't *fix* it. It won't even let you mourn for what

might have happened instead. You cannot change the past. The past has already happened.

I recognized, sitting across from Candido, that in the years it took me to find him, my hurt had aged and grown old. My anger wasn't the vigorous youth it once was, able to topple a man with just one screed. My rage couldn't take the stairs two at a time anymore. My pain couldn't howl with a blood-on-the-fangs viciousness. My hurt had shriveled into something smaller, a sliver of glass embedded in my soul. I couldn't see it or feel it most of the time, though I'd have to work hard to forget it was there. My heart knew the past couldn't hurt me anymore—but, from long experience, it knew that what came next could. I wanted to broker a treaty for the future.

"I don't care what happened before," I said in words part rehearsed and part spontaneous. "I'm glad I found you," I said, "but I've been hurt too many times. So you have to stay in contact if you want to be a part of my life. You have to call and write and stay in touch. You have to do the work now. Okay?" I asked.

"Yes, I understand," Candido said. "And you should feel free to come here whenever you want. We are your family. This is your home." It didn't occur to me until much later that he'd never said, "I want to be a part of your life." I had said it for him. Was I making demands of my father based on consequences he hadn't demonstrated he cared about? He'd abandoned me over thirty years ago, and, aside from returning my phone call, hadn't done anything about it until this very moment. I felt I was going much too easy and much too hard on Candido.

It was a warm day, so we moved under an outdoor garden canopy in the backyard. Candido was on one end of the table, while I was on the other. Aurora and Natalie sat near Candido. Kereny and Adriana sat by their respective significant others, Pedro, and Adriana's husband, John, on opposite sides of the table.

"So why did it take you so long to find us?" Adriana asked.

I was surprised, but I shouldn't have been. I'd focused for so long on whether or not I could forgive my father that I'd ignored what my acceptance into his family would mean for his daughters. There was a hurt in her voice that I misread as resentment and suspicion. She was guarding herself the same way I'd been guarding me.

"Part of me felt that I shouldn't have been the one to do the looking," I said. "Then a part of me felt that if I found my father now, he'd have nothing left for me that I wanted."

With those words, Candy started to cry, dabbing at tears in silence with a tissue.

"Do you believe that now?" Adriana asked.

"I don't know," I said. "But I'm really happy to be here."

"Well, we're really happy that you're here too," Adriana said. Then she started to cry too, a rain of gentle sobs. Pedro and John looked uncomfortable.

"Bet you guys wished you stayed home watching the game, huh?" I joked.

"This is where we need to be," Pedro said. "We're part of the family, and now you're part of the family."

For over ten years, I thought I had no family. Here was a group of strangers calling me "brother." I cried then, too, though whatever sound I made was lost amid the wind chimes that billowed in the breeze.

When I left, I hugged Candy with a strength he couldn't or didn't feel comfortable returning. I noticed on my father's left bicep a faded tattoo of the Virgin Mary. The Mexican I used to deny being thought that people were delusional if they claimed a sighting of the Virgin Mary accompanied something miraculous. The Mexican I was in that moment said: not anymore.

That night, Frank drove me to his friend's house for dinner.

"Did he ask you what you'd been up to?" Frank asked. "All the things you've accomplished and done? Who you've dated? Where you've traveled to? What kind of things you want to do with your life?"

"Not really," I said.

"He didn't ask one thing about you?"

"He already knew I hadn't made any grandkids for him," I said. "But it's fine."

"Really? *Why?* Why is it *fine?*" Frank asked.

"He missed that time to get to know me," I said. "That's punishment enough."

"No, that's not enough," Frank said. "That's not any kind of punishment for someone who abandons you for over thirty years. He doesn't deserve to get away with it."

"Get away with what?" I asked Frank. "He's an old man. It's not like he's a criminal."

"Oh, I disagree, Brando," Frank said in *his* best paternal voice. "I think you'd find a court of law would say that a father not supporting his son for years when he knew exactly where he was is a *very* criminal act."

"Why are you making such a big deal out of this?" Frank's friend asked. "Brando's okay with it, so you should be okay with it."

"Because it's not fair!" Frank said. "He doesn't have the right to get away with it!"

"Do you want me to say you're a better man than he is?" I asked. "There's nothing I can do now. He couldn't live with my mother, and I understand that."

"I couldn't live with her, either!" Frank said. "She tried to drive me away for years, and I still came back. I'm a man that believes in taking care of his responsibilities. I *stayed*. I could've—" he said, and then stopped.

He stayed, I thought, *because he could leave whenever he wanted.*

"Could have what?" I asked. "Could have abandoned me too? Go ahead. Don't be afraid to say it."

"I didn't say that," Frank said. "I never, *ever* said that."

• • •

A month later, I was back in Los Angeles, on my book tour at a reading in Pico Rivera, a city adjacent to Whittier. I arrived to the bookstore manager telling me, "Your father is already here."

My father? I wondered.

Inside, sitting two chairs apart and staring straight ahead, were Candido and Frank. Candy had come straight from work. I called Frank away from his seat. Candido was my biological match, but I needed to talk to the father who knew me best.

"Did you speak to the bookstore owner?" I asked.

"Yes," he said. "Was that okay?"

"Well, he said my father was here. I assumed he meant you, but Candy's sitting over there next to you. Did you know that?"

"No," Frank said. "Do you want me to go?"

"No, no, don't go," I said. "I just didn't know who had said what. You're going to be nice?"

"Hey, you know me, right?" Frank said.

My sisters arrived and seated themselves around Candy. After the reading, Frank chatted with them while Candy stood in line to buy a book I knew he couldn't read without great difficulty and presented it at the autograph table. What name should I sign with? Signing it with "Skyhorse," as it was on the jacket, seemed rude, but signing it Ulloa would be a lie.

I signed his copy, "Brando." Frank got a book signed too, but he and Candido didn't meet each other.

Candido drove Adriana's baby, Dillan, home while Frank and I invited my three sisters out to a family-style dinner amid an archipelago of strip mall restaurants. I was leery of mixing Frank with my new unknown family, but he made the combination seamless. He told jokes about me as a child, asked engaging questions, volleyed conversation like a beach ball, and offered laughs at his own expense.

"Your dad's really funny," Kereny said.

He *was* my father that night. And for all of our awkward, introductory choreography, Candido's daughters felt like full—and not half or abbreviated—sisters. Why?

Frank told me, "Maybe you found your father to find them. Those girls are ready for a brother. And you're ready for a family. Maybe you don't need to overthink this. Sometimes love happens that fast."

I was about six or seven when my mother took me to a psychic friend who told me I'd lived past lives. She said I'd once been a Scottish prince who was trampled to death by horses in his thirties and, in a more recent life, a soldier who died in the Vietnam War from stepping on a land mine. Not long after, I had vivid dreams of falling off a carriage in what my seven-year-old mind dreamed Scotland looked like—everything was made from marbles—and of my legs being blown off in a faraway delta I'm sure I remembered from a Hollywood movie. The explosion would snap my legs on my mattress and wake me up.

In both of these dreams, I was a father. I never saw my child's face or heard its voice, but I knew I had left a child—a son, I think—behind somewhere.

I'd spent most of my twenties in a relationship with someone in her thirties, unable to commit to fatherhood even as I knew that her chances at a baby dwindled with each passing year. I told her, "I'm too young." Then I told her, "I'm too poor." When I got to my thirties and told her, "I'm too crazy," she said, "You're right," and had a child with someone else. I never had any doubt she'd become the great mother she is today, but I wonder, still: Could *I* be a good father?

It's presumptuous to assume I'll be a father at all. I'm forty years old and childless. Part of me waited this long because I knew I was an unstable man who'd make an unstable father. I didn't want to pass on my depression to my children genetically or by example. And how could I take care of a child when I had no model for what a good father was? Remembering my fathers, individually, they lied, drank, cheated, stole, and abandoned their loved ones. I know I can claim no moral high ground with them: these are the people who taught me. I've cheated on lovers, stolen people's time, and abandoned friends. I lied for years about who I was and made up stories in college about a thuggish life in an inner-city jungle that was never really that rough. My own brief sojourn into "storytelling"—inventing a life as a Sunset Strip club kid; seeing someone shot in the head at point-blank range—always rang out like the bullshit it was.

Succumbing to my mother's mythmaking made me realize that every storyteller needs more than good stories. He needs to understand *why* he's telling the stories he tells. Narrative is breath. My mother lied in her stories for the same reason I've told the truth in this one. From the breath my grandmother gave me to the breath it takes for you to read this sentence, stories sustain us. They carry us through the lives we convince ourselves we can't escape to get to the lives we ought or *need* to live instead. They create out of endless chaos a beginning, a middle, and an *end*.

It took the writing of this book, which I've been thinking about for almost twenty years, to understand what made my mother tell such incredible tales. Stories can help you survive. They can transform your life—they can transform *you*—from where you are into wherever you want to be. My mother turned her cage of a bedroom into a castle. Her prison became a launch pad for escape into a whole new identity. Perhaps that's why my mother was such a fan of killing herself off in her stories. She'd reveal that her brain tumor had taken one last fatal turn for the worst and, with time so short, revel in the temporary attention I gave her, over and over again. Whenever I hear that someone "dying" of an incurable disease has tricked an always disbelieving public through a fake Facebook profile, I sigh and think, *Mom?* But I understand.

Strangely, so do others. I talk about my mother often when I give class talks about my first novel, *The Madonnas of Echo Park*, which is set in the largely Mexican-American neighborhood (pending gentrification) of Echo Park. How is it that someone with the most American Indian of names came to write a story set among Mexicans? It's impossible to talk about that book without telling my and my mother's stories.

In Idaho, I met an American Indian college student named Effie Hernandez. I'd never told my story to an Indian before. Here at last, I thought, was my reckoning. I'd have to pay for all the attention and special treatment my name had given me. It was my turn to stay silent and absorb someone's rightful anger for appropriating a name, a culture, a people. After a thorough grilling during the class, Effie approached me afterward.

"I was prepared not to like you," she said, "but I understand now why you lived the life you did. Of all the things your mother could have wanted to be, she wanted to be an American Indian. That's pretty amazing."

The great American Indian writer Sherman Alexie once joked, "Indians have to be so careful around non-Indians. We just make stuff up." I'm almost as good a storyteller as my mother is, but I'm a terrible liar. My mother wasn't an Indian, but by Sherman's metric, she was the perfect Indian storyteller.

I'm not an Indian either but feel I'm still somewhere between two names and two cultures. It's difficult because I can't even occupy the gray space mixed children try to claim for themselves. I get emails from Stanford's American Indian alum network that say, "Dear Native Alum," while I struggle to learn Spanish beyond a second-grade level. In New York, where I live, I'm less Mexican or American Indian and more some kind of ethnic superhero—*Passing Man!* Capable of passing for whatever any member of another ethnicity wants me to be! In their Indian or Pakistani or Latino eyes, they scan me over and ask, *Are you like me?* Yes, I nod, but who *is* that? Who *am* I? I've been mistaken for Turkish, Pakistani, Indian American, Sri Lankan, Persian, Afghani, Egyptian, and a dozen other ethnicities. Each man—for it is usually a man who mistakes me as one of his own—says, "Oh, you'd be right at home in my country!" The feeling of another man claiming me as a member of his own people and his own homeland is irresistible to someone who feels he truly has neither.

I'm also somewhere between two fathers. The father who left me, and Frank, the father who stayed. He tried to raise me in between all the men my mother married. I'm no longer a boy who needs to wait under a gauzy streetlight on a curb outside a bar or hide in the backseat of a car for a father to take me home. Two fathers are already there waiting for me. One has something I want; the other has something I need. I can't decide which father is which.

When I dream of my own children, there's a fiery rosy-cheeked daughter named Nova. Or a son, who's still nameless because it took so long for me to find my own name. In my dreams, I sing to my children in a golden lullaby, "I am your father." I will teach you, every day, what every father I was lucky enough to have taught me. I will put your needs first, above my fear, anxiety, and depression, and you will help me appreciate chaos more than I did when I was a child. I will strive to be perfect and fall far short. I will fail you. I will embarrass you. I will be frustrated with you for petty reasons that will later make me ashamed. I will expose you to—I hope—limited levels of familial insanity. I will be there for you every day of my whole life.

(I hear my mother saying, like at the end of a movie when the credits begin to roll, "Do you think Brando makes it?")

Of all the things the men I call my fathers taught me, the lesson that matters most is spoken together in six different voices: sometimes it is enough to survive. And when I am a father at last, I want to gather the men who fathered me over a large family-style dinner that is a physical impossibility except in my dreams. After a few drinks, our memories would recede like the tide and the day-to-day lives we lead would spill out in all their banal glory, and we'd laugh at how ordinary our days have become, and aren't we grateful for that type of steadiness in our lives now? A chorus of six men calling me Son might sound ludicrous to you, but to me it's the sound of survival; voices that have the power, by the very noise they make, to turn madness into song.

Closure

You might as well know that I'm not looking at my mistakes, and I'm sorry about that. No one wants to hear anything bad about one's own family.

I've sinned. Who hasn't? I did a lot of foolish things to be loved; I'm surprised I wasn't killed. I used to pick up all kinds of men because I was bored at home. Or maybe I was lonely. I wonder why I never focused on the people close to me. Why did I go looking for people who were so far away?

I don't know why I can't be honest with anybody. For a very long time in life, I wanted to give up. I'm not feeling sorry for myself. If anything, I'm feeling mad. No more rages, though. Well . . . I can't say that, but I can say love looks a lot different as you grow older.

Brando, I did a lot of things for you and because of you. I could have left you many times, but I didn't. You're all I've ever wanted in a child. I know you don't think I did enough as a mother, but as you can see now, I had no choice but to share you with others and the rest of this fucking world. There's too much to do, too much to see. Make a lot of noise.

I haven't really gone anywhere in such a long time because I wanted to feel safe. If anyone takes anything away from this book, it's this: don't waste your life hiding away like I did.

—Excerpted from my mother's
unpublished memoirs, circa 1997

Closure isn't happiness, but it's a certain kind of peace. When I found Candido, I wanted to know where my other fathers—Robert, Paul Skyhorse Johnson, Pat, and Rudy—were. Each was so different as a father in how he taught me manhood, yet every man had vanished in the same way, under a murky cloud of his own making. Would their paths resemble each other's, too, when they stopped being my father?

A late night Google search revealed Paul Skyhorse Johnson's death (brain cancer) in a northeastern city in 2002 and a funeral service paid for by a loving octogenarian female companion. His biological son, Dustin, was the only living relative the coroner's office could track down and signed the paperwork authorizing Paul's cremation.

Dustin had no contact with Paul before high school and, in a weird inverse of how I discovered I wasn't Indian, didn't know his own Indian name until he was sixteen. Dustin made peace with Paul in his last years, and though he knew who I was, he harbored no animosity or anger that his own father had spent Dustin's childhood with an imaginary son instead of him.

I never met Dustin, but I'd like to think we could have been friends, maybe even brothers. After all, we shared the same father. I lost that chance when Dustin passed away at thirty-one from a pulmonary embolism in November 2010.

• • •

I was in high school when Robert made an unannounced visit to Echo Park. He got as far as the front porch. My grandmother made him a can of corned beef hash—"And that's *all* I'm gonna do for the bum"—while he tossed me a *Playboy* as some kind of reconciliation gift. He sat with my mother and asked for a loan, maybe a place to stay for a few nights. His trademark laugh and charm were intact, but time had swollen both his and my mother's bodies. The dynamic sexual chemistry he shared with my mother was gone. He finished his corned beef on the front stairs and was gone before his dish hit the kitchen sink.

"It's been good seeing you, Son," he said.

Years later, in spring 2007, Robert sent me a one line email—"hope everything is well with you!"—then in a longer follow-up caught me up on everything that had happened after he left us in the eighties. It was a life that included, he said, a "two-hundred-mile high-speed chase down Interstate 70" that ended with a collision of police cars and his tires shot out. In a *One Flew over the Cuckoo's Nest* plea deal, he was sent to a seven-year stay in a mental facility to avoid prison. He was using a pseudonym: "My name was Timothy O'Dell. Now, do I look Irish?" Upon his parole, he settled in Topeka, Kansas, where he made an unsuccessful bid before the city council to run for mayor on a platform to legalize marijuana.

"At least I tried, I always try!" he wrote. "It's nice hearing from you, my son."

"My son." Was I his son? Wasn't this just another broken man claiming a piece of a son that wasn't his? I sent several follow-up emails over the next three years, first to establish some kind of guarded relationship and then to try to interview him for this book, but the bounceback said his AOL account had been deactivated. For a while, he had a MySpace page, where I noted with wry satisfaction that he'd subtracted about twenty years from his given age. This was another disappearing act, but by this time I should have known that Robert would reappear, on his own accord, when he was ready.

Robert's death, like my mother's, came by telephone. A friendly woman named Sharon with the Office of Forensic Pathology at the Law Enforcement Center in Topeka said that Robert's tribe in Alaska needed my permission to proceed with handling my "father's final needs." He'd been in the Shawnee County Coroner's Office a week, and time for his decaying body was short.

"I'm not really his son," I said, sounding uncertain. "I mean, he was married to my mother and was my stepfather for a while."

"You don't need to be biologically related to make this decision," she said. "Perhaps you should contact Robert's friend and work it out with her."

Sharon put me in touch with Eva, whose first details about Robert's life in Kansas were promising. He'd moved in with Eva's mother, Lois, paying his share of the rent, helping out with chores, carrying the chainsaw around when wood needed cutting. He took lithium every day to keep his manic episodes in check. He graduated from MySpace to Twitter, where he collected over five hundred followers, and tweeted messages regularly to his favorite celebrity, Kim Kardashian. During the holidays, he was a paragon of paternal virtue to any neighborhood children that stopped by the house. This was important to him, he told Eva, as he had been adopted, mistreated, and possibly a victim of incest.

There were problems, sure. Using Lois's bathroom one afternoon, Eva's sister found small piles of wood shavings on a counter. Bursting into Robert's bedroom, Eva found him crouched against a series of peepholes drilled into the wall with his pants down, masturbating. Then money and credit cards went missing. *Why didn't you kick him out?* my inner voice asked, but having lived with Robert, I already had the answer. He helped out less and spoke in wistful tones, circling around a grand plan to hop in Lois's car one day and drive out to Los Angeles so he could visit his son, Brando—but not before a brief Vegas stopover to put his formidable gambling skills to use.

One afternoon in February 2012, Robert told Lois he was going to the local casino and borrowed her car with twenty or thirty dollars in his pocket. He didn't come home that night. He hated to drive in the dark because of his failing eyesight, so Lois assumed he'd stopped off somewhere so that he wouldn't crash. Robert didn't come back the next day, either. Before she could call the police, two detectives came to Robert's residence to inform Lois that her car had been found and, by the way, was she aware that her .357 Magnum was missing?

Robert committed suicide in that car, parked in a back casino lot, on the thirteenth of February, 2012. No personal identification of any kind could be found, nor were there any provisions for how to deal with his body.

"There's no money to pay to clean the car," Eva said, annoyed. "His body left it a mess." It sounded cold, but I understood how much work there is left for the living when someone dies.

I then got an email from the St. George Tanaq Corporation, a company that administers stewardship over oil rights for Aleutian Indians. Robert was a member and had named me as his son. Its email began "If Robert was your father . . ."

If. How many other men could that word *if* apply to? I wrote back with dread—and prurient interest. Had Robert made amends by naming me as the heir or beneficiary to any of his oil shares? No. Had he bequeathed to me some kind of formal tribal membership? Not exactly. He "named me as a son" once, in 1993, when he was trying to obtain for me a college scholarship through its foundation.

What an incredible gesture of kindness. How moving for him, I thought, to cling to the dream of me as a son in the same way that I clung to the dream of him being some kind of father. Then I thought some more. If this was the one time he'd named me as a son—to collect scholarship money—when did he become aware that I was in college and how had he intended to give me the cash? Was that scholarship for me or was it yet another con to defraud money for him? The answer in Robert's mind, I'm sure, was probably both.

At the last moment, someone from Robert's actual family stepped forward and took his ashes back to Alaska. I imagined them being scattered and carried aloft by his sixteen thunderous "Mighty Grandfathers," conjured by a heart that, with that gunshot, at last found a way to be sincere. His head may have been torn to pieces in that car, but his soul is intact, sprinting away from that parking lot, dashing shirtless across a cold moonlit prairie, whooping it up as he heads west to see his son, with a quick detour to Vegas to hit his lucky streak. I'm watching him go, for miles and miles, rooting for him to outrun those police sirens and that hard cask of big sky daylight that's closing in.

Here, Robert, on this page, I'll be your son if you'll be my dad. Keep running. Nobody's gonna catch you this time.

Pat has, as of this writing, neither been found nor established contact. Most of the time, I'm happy to keep it that way. But if he showed up again, I'd probably let him back in my life. I'm a forty-year-old whose nostalgia for his high school years is arriving right on time. I also know he'd break my heart again. I am sometimes still too much my mother's son.

It's been fifteen years since I spoke to Rudy, the last man I was forced to call Dad; the father my mother entrusted to watch over me should anything happen to her.

I heard nothing about or from him until June 2012, when my ex-girl-friend Kitt received a series of angry phone messages from a regional collection agency saying that Rudy or his lawyer needed to contact it immediately. Kitt's phone number, unchanged from the days I lived with her, had been attached to Rudy's Social Security number, meaning that all collection agencies would be sent to my—now her—front door.

I found Rudy on a social media site in the summer of 2013 but declined to contact him for this book, leery of reestablishing a connection. His ability to stay out of my life, if I am honest, is the only gift of his that has ever satisfied me. I don't think he needs me, anyway. A quick perusal of his page shows that he has remarried and appears to be raising a young boy. He's maybe ten or eleven and smiling. Perhaps Rudy can be the father to him that I'd never let him be to me.

As for my sisters, there's not a middle or an ending to a story that's just begun. The novelty of discovering a long-lost relative—on both my end and theirs—has in the past three years given way to the realities of day-to-day life, with so many ways to stay in touch but seemingly so few opportunities to do so. Adriana is a schoolteacher with two sons of her own, now five-year-old Dillan and newborn Marco. Kereny works full-time as a behavior therapist and is trying to find her way through her twenties. Natalie, just turned fifteen, wants an iPad and a bedroom door with a lock, not a long-lost brother who didn't have enough money to fly to Los Angeles and attend her *quinceañera*. Not only was I too late for most of the important moments in these girls' lives, I'm missing new ones.

One year my birthday gift from my sisters was their version of a memoir—a greatest-hits photo album collecting pictures from each of their life's important moments appended with bouncy captions in pink ink and a dedication from Adriana:

Here are a few memories for you to look at maybe begin to get to know our history a little bit better. The rest of the album is for you to continue to add more photos of our memories together. ☺ The front of the album is reserved for a complete family photo of us including *you*!

We've taken a few pictures together since, but there are many more spaces in the album to fill, including that one in the front. With so much of my childhood framed by pictures with fraudulent captions and fake relatives, I'm impatient for a photograph with my real sisters. I want more conversation, more in-person visits, more family time watching movies and dumb TV shows, more laughter and hugs and tears. Underneath our stacks of to-do lists and errands are the courage to connect and the patience to let us discover who we can be to one another when we're ready.

I'm learning that surviving a family is different from living with one. During a trip to Los Angeles over Christmas in 2010, Kereny, Adriana, and I were in a car driving home from the supermarket. Kereny told me she'd read something online I said about Candido.

"You said that my father abandoned you. That isn't true. He was driven away."

She was hurt and disappointed. I was angry too. Was this about to devolve into the kind of endless, vicious fighting I knew so well? How could anyone—especially a blood relative—deny that I was abandoned? My mother repelled Candido as surely as she drew him into her magnetic field, but he could have kept in touch with my grandmother. He could have made gestures that didn't require great risk on his part. He could have sent money anonymously. Or he could have taken the risk—I was his only son, after all—and tried to be in my life regardless of what my mother threatened. So much of what my mother told Candy he knew to be untrustworthy; why would her threats be any different?

Adriana strived for a middle ground in our conversation. "We don't know everything that happened," she said. What I thought was, *We do know what happened: I was left behind, and someone else got my father and my dream of a stable family life.* Would I have to prepare myself for having to learn how to defend myself in a family all over again?

"You know what you sound like?" a friend said to me. "Someone who has siblings."

Turns out, our "conflict" was an "after-school special" disagreement resolved gently with a simple conversation, not apoplectic rage. Kereny and I text often, while Adriana dashes off exhausted emails when the boys will let her. It's a happy life beyond what I dreamed possible. I just want more of it.

Becoming part of a new family means that as one layer of secrets is unpeeled, the feelings underneath them are exposed to the light. Kereny mentioned that Candido's mother was never close to them. Once, on a trip to Mexico, they saw a picture of me with other grandkids but no pictures of her, Adriana, or Natalie. Candido had seen that picture too. Every time he visited his mother Felicitas's house in Yahualica, he saw the pictures I'd sent her in junior high framed on her wall. She told Candido that his legitimate child was studying to be a lawyer.

Here's his picture, she said.

Candido saw my glasses and chubby cheeks and thought, *He's fatter than I imagined.* He said nothing, though, just stared in wonder at his almost unknown son.

Kereny had no idea who I was or why I was hanging on the grandkids wall, but she realizes that in her grandmother's conservative Catholic mind, my mother was Candido's first and only wife, since there'd never been an official divorce. She considered Candido's daughters "not good enough," or illegitimate offspring. So sad for Kereny, I thought, but so ironic for my mother. An illegitimate wife who married illegally so many times that her aliases were the length of a forearm, my mother was, in *a Mexican's home*, a legitimate wife at last.

I have a good relationship with my father Frank. We talk on the phone three or four times a year, and after nearly thirty-seven years, we're almost comfortable with calling each other Father and Son, though I slip up sometimes and call him Frank. He slips up too and sometimes calls me Tiger, which he's never stopped using since I was four. He's retired now from the "temporary" job he applied for in 1977 and spends his days going to book readings, gallery openings, and curating his own personal museum of signed memorabilia that takes up two storage sheds. Frank shows up to every Los Angeles book event I do, camera in hand, and still covers lunch or dinner when we meet up. Among his most valuable items, if you ask him, are out-of-print hardcover editions of my first book, which he was able to buy in bulk for pennies a copy.

"I don't want to make you feel bad by telling you how little I paid for them," he says, "but I *know* these are going to be worth something someday."

We reminisce about our old days together. My mother and grandmother come to life so vividly when we talk it's like they're there in the room with us—well, just the parts we loved about them. We chat more over Facebook, where he's friends with my sister Kereny, two big-hearted family members intersecting in a way I'd never imagined. My sister, and my father, and me, friends.

I've retired all air quotes around my family members, reserving them for things they've said or written. This past June, I texted Frank a single message that was for him and him alone: "Happy Father's Day."

Frank, my father, said, "Thank you so much, Son."

I lived with my birth father, Candido, for the first three years of my life. I've been in contact with him for the past three years of my life. Since we've gotten back in touch, we speak about once a year on my birthday. He knows I am busy, he says, which absolves us both, since I've called him just three or four times in return. I'm grateful he stays in touch and have no right to expect more, because he is giving me everything he has left. I am disappointed because I am thirty-five years late, and there is nothing more for us to offer each other. On the days I am cruel, I tell myself my father has failed me twice. On the days I am honest, I tell myself that had he stayed, we could have failed each other every day.

Whenever conversation drifts to Candido's disappearance, as it does sometimes, not one of his family members used the word *abandon*. Was there an inability to reconcile the kindly, present father they knew with the absentee one I didn't? Both Adriana and Kereny are fiercely antiwelfare, ignoring how welfare stepped in to do the job our father didn't, compensating for thousands of dollars in missing child support. Had I been looking at this in too one-sided a way? Was I in part the prodigal son? Over drinks and cigars, Adriana's husband, John, expressed his initial concerns about my intentions.

"We didn't know who you were at first. I'm protective of this family," he said. "Candido is like a father to me."

It was strange to hear him say that. How many men had *I* chased to be "like a father" to me? Was I doing the same with my own father?

During the one Christmas I've spent with Candido's family, I was welcomed and embraced in the midst of a large togetherness I hadn't felt when I *did* have a family to share it with. Yet the part of me that remembered Christmases with my mother and grandmother felt alone, alien, an outsider capable of understanding intimate gestures only by using a stolen dictionary. Then I saw Candido playing with Adriana's son Dillan—my nephew—and heard him call Dillan "Pappas."

"Pappas," my grandmother said, "means 'potatoes' in Spanish."

Do you remember, Father, when you called me Pappas?

Sometimes the gap between Candido and me feels too great, like an aside to the family I want with my sisters. It's as if my mother ripped out the pages of my story with Candido as she read them, let them fall to her feet like plucked feathers, and then left Candido and me to reassemble our book without the benefit of page numbers. Maybe there wasn't enough time to bond when we were father and son, and we've forgotten too much. Or maybe, if he'd stayed, we would have reached the same place in each other's lives we are today: two men leery of our past bound to stay connected by something more than obligation but not quite yet love.

A few months ago in May 2013, my father showed up one auburn afternoon at my sister Adriana's house where I was staying for a few days and invited me out to dinner. He drove me to a Mexican restaurant in a nondescript strip mall where we shared *carnitas* and a beer. He explained in his slow, proud English that, through his job, at sixty-three years old, he'd opened his first email account and was asked to pick a password.

You'll have to check it every day, he was told. Choose something you won't forget.

Candido, my father, says, "I chose Brando."

Thank You

For changing my life, twice, and your unwavering support
—Kitt Allan

For the gift of a real father—Frank Zamora

For doing the best you could—Paul Skyhorse Johnson,
Robert, Pat, and Rudy

To the brothers I wish I'd met—Dustin Paul SkyHorse Johnson
and Josh Palmer (222)

For writing and manhood lessons—Geoffrey Wolff
and George Feifer

To the freshest Life Saver in the roll—Susan "Big Red" Golomb

For embracing *Madonnas*—Amber Qureshi, Kelly Marcel,
Julia Cho,
Julie Goler (juliesbookgroups.com),
booksellers indie and major, friends old and new

Thank You

For the golden opportunity—Jonathan Karp, Martha Levin,
Peter Matthiessen, Joy Williams, Philip Levine,
Edward P. Jones, Will Schwalbe, Bob Shacochis,
Allegra Goodman, Jayne Anne Phillips,
The Hemingway Foundation, PEN/New England,
American Academy of Arts and Letters

To the best road crew in the business—
Millicent Bennett, Chloe Perkins, Ed Winstead
and everyone at Simon & Schuster

For the time and space to find my way in—Can Serrat,
El Bruc, Spain (canserrat.org/canserratart.com)
with special thanks to Elizabeth Sher

For light through a dark period—Brendon Small's *Home Movies*

For help closing the door—Dawn Trook, Chris Hokanson,
Jeff Lytle, Sophoat Lim, Daniel Maurer,
Jason Wishnow, John Reed, Amy Hundley,
The Ucross Foundation (ucrossfoundation.org),
Sharon Dynak, Ruthie Salvatore

To my Wonder Girl, who amazes me anew every day:
you're my Neon Pegasus—Erin Kelley

For the chance to be a family—John Madrid, Pedro Gonzalez,
and
Aurora, Adriana, Kereny, Natalie, Dillan, Marco,
and Candido Ulloa

"Another element of my memoir—the stupendous importance of love, friendship and solidarity—has been made immensely more vivid to me by recent experience. I can't hope to convey the full effect of the embraces and avowals, but I can perhaps offer a crumb of counsel. If there is anybody known to you who might benefit from a letter or a visit, do not *on any account* postpone the writing or the making of it. The difference made will almost certainly be more than you have calculated."

—CHRISTOPHER HITCHENS

About the Author

Born and raised in Echo Park, California, Brando Skyhorse is a graduate of Stanford University and the Master of Fine Arts Writers Workshop program at the University of California at Irvine. His first book, *The Madonnas of Echo Park*, received the 2011 PEN/Hemingway Award and the Sue Kaufman Prize for First Fiction from the American Academy of Arts and Letters. For speaking engagements and First Year Experience inquiries, please contact the author at brandoskyhorse.com.